Jobs and homes

David Renton is a barrister in the housing and employment teams at Garden Court Chambers. His previous books include *Struck out: Why employment tribunals fail workers and what can be done* (Pluto, 2012).

The Legal Action Group is a national, independent charity which campaigns for equal access to justice for all members of society.

Legal Action Group:

- provides support to the practice of lawyers and advisers
- inspires developments in that practice
- campaigns for improvements in the law and the administration of justice
- stimulates debate on how services should be delivered.

Jobs and homes

Stories of the law in lockdown

David Renton

Legal Action Group
2021

This edition published in Great Britain 2021
by LAG Education and Service Trust Limited
c/o Oliver Fisher Solicitors, Royalty Studios
105–109 Lancaster Road
London W11 1QF
www.lag.org.uk

British Library Cataloguing in Publication Data

a CIP catalogue record for this book is available from the British Library.

Crown copyright material is produced with the permission of the Controller of
HMSO and the Queen's Printer for Scotland.

This book has been produced using Forest Stewardship
Council (FSC) certified paper. The wood used to produce
FSC certified products with a 'Mixed Sources' label comes
from FSC certified well-managed forests, controlled sources
and/or recycled material.

print ISBN 978 1 913648 19 0
ebook ISBN 978 1 913648 20 6

Typeset by Refinecatch Ltd, Bungay, Suffolk
Printed in Great Britain by Hobbs the Printers, Totton, Hampshire

Preface

This book is a memoir of a year spent representing tenants and workers in the county court and the employment tribunal. It describes how housing and employment law worked before the pandemic and then during the various lockdowns of 2020.

Some stories are composites of two or more cases. To respect confidentiality, I have changed the names and other personal characteristics of those involved.

My thanks to the friends who read drafts of this manuscript: Nick Bano, Kate Bradley, Stephen Cottle, Sonia Harris, Adrian Marshall Williams, Simon Mullings and Declan Owens, and to my colleagues in the housing and employment law teams at Garden Court Chambers without whose support and encouragement this book could never have been finished. My thanks also to the editors of the *London Review of Books* for giving me permission to reuse material which originally appeared in their newspaper (D Renton, 'Becoming homeless is easily done,' *LRB*, 7 May 2020) in chapter 4 of this book. I am especially grateful to Sue James and Esther Pilger at LAG, for believing in this book, and for making its final stages as pleasant as any book I've written.

David Renton
March 2021

Preface

Contents

CHAPTER 1

Opening submissions

'There's been a misunderstanding', my client Brody said. 'I'm the opposite guy to how they've made me look.' Brody was a retired decorator and a Christian. 'I don't wear this for nothing', he told me, pointing at the cross which hung down in front of his shirt. 'The man upstairs – he's got his eye on me.' It was the first week of January 2020, and I was meeting Brody at court. He lived in a home which provided supported accommodation to the disabled and the elderly. His landlord, a housing association, had applied to court for a possession order, which is the most important step it could take towards evicting him. The landlord said that Brody's behaviour made it impossible for him to stay. Many of the allegations against him were trivial. One was that he had placed a vase with dried flowers on a communal table without asking for permission. When the housing officers asked him to remove the vase, he did.

There were other complaints too. Months before, the housing officers had decided to close the building's communal lounge. They said it needed treatment for bed bugs. The lounge was kept closed for three months while the housing officers arranged for it to be fumigated. While they delayed, the residents complained. Many were lonely; the lounge was the only place where they could meet. Brody and another tenant went downstairs, covered the home's closed-circuit TV cameras in plastic bags, and cut the bolts in front of the lounge door. For a week, they were heroes. Other tenants wrote letters thanking them for the stand they had taken. Then Brody's housing officer served him with a notice seeking possession.

Brody, a man in his late 60s who had been in and out of hospital with heart and bladder problems, preceded his mission to liberate the lounge by wrapping a pair of black Tommy Hilfiger boxer shorts around his head so that the footage couldn't be used to identify him. He told me the shorts were, 'Hopeless. Couldn't see a thing.'

Brody's solicitor wanted him to agree to the landlord's offer of a suspended possession order. This would have meant that the landlord had the right to evict him, and that it would have to refrain provided there were no further acts of anti-social behaviour. But if Brody was made subject to a suspended order, it was likely that his housing officers would say he had breached it. Given some of the grounds on which they had issued proceedings, there was a real risk we would be back in court a few months later and a judge would have to decide whether Brody had breached the order. If they decided that he had, outright possession was almost certain.

For this reason, Brody refused to accept a suspended order. 'You've seen my file. You know my housing officers and what they say about me.' His solicitor told him that if he refused a suspended order, the most likely result would be that the judge would order outright possession at the next hearing, and that would be even worse.

Brody had secured legal aid. He was entitled to it because he owned less than £8,000 in capital and had a disposable income of not more than £733 a month.[1] 'I've got three hundred in the bank, that's all.' His only income was his state pension. Brody had two adult children, but neither had a spare room to house him. I told him what happens when people apply to their local council for homeless accommodation. If the council decided that he had made himself homeless intentionally it would not house him. Where a court orders possession because of anti-social behaviour, the council almost never helps. I asked Brody what he would do if the landlord evicted him. 'Then I'll be homeless', Brody said. There was no anger in his voice or pride, just the stubbornness of someone who had been wronged. 'I'll sleep rough', he said. 'I'll kill myself. I'm not scared – I haven't had a good life.'

The subject of this book is cases like Brody's and what happened to them in 2020. It describes how employment and housing law worked before and during a period of lockdowns. Under the impact of COVID-19, our legal system was brought to the verge of collapse.

1 'Controlled work: Guide to determining financial eligibility for controlled work and family mediation', April 2019; https://assets.publishing.service.gov.uk/government/uploads/system/uploads/attachment_data/file/793459/Guide_to_determining_controlled_work_.pdf available from www.gov.uk/guidance/civil-legal-aid-means-testing.

For all the experience of our judges and the authority of our legal system, the law proved almost incapable of dealing with human need on a new scale.

Every day of the week our civil courts hear cases like Brody's – arguments between two parties to a contract, or complaints that one person has suffered a loss because of someone else's negligence. Our images of the courts are dominated by what happens in criminal trials: oak-panelled Victorian courtroom, barristers in wigs and a judge pounding a gavel. Civil law lacks these visual props. It is a world of business suits and low ceilings. But civil law is still the law. I am a barrister; most of what is needed to bring a case to court – issuing a claim, collecting the evidence to support a case, taking the client's witness statement – is done by a solicitor. It is only in the final stages, when the case is before a judge, that the solicitor instructs me. Thirty years ago, most barristers in Britain were criminal specialists, while today, most barristers are civil barristers. We appear in the county courts, the High Court, and various tribunals.

In my typical housing case, a landlord seeks possession from a tenant, and it is my task to persuade a judge that the landlord's request should be denied. Sometimes, the landlord is refusing to do the repairs that my client's home needs, and the property is unsafe. Occasionally, I represent a tenant who has been evicted unlawfully from their home; the tenant asks the court to make a declaration that they were removed unlawfully, and to make an injunction ordering the landlord to permit them to return. I also act for people who have been made homeless and are asking the local authority to house them. If the council declines, I represent them in appealing to a judge.

Employment law is different from housing law. Employment law focuses much more narrowly on whether a worker should be paid compensation. It is about money, principally, rather than declarations or injunctions. But this narrowing is not the choice of the workers who bring the cases. Listen to them carefully and they tell you that what they want is acknowledgment. Perhaps they have worked for an employer for years and a new manager has been appointed with a brief to drive out a generation of older workers. Or some new manager has used sexist or racist language about them. Workers want the court to recognise the injustice they have suffered. Yet the law struggles to satisfy this demand: the employment tribunal will not compel a discriminator to apologise. Even where a tribunal agrees that an employee was unfairly dismissed and orders compensation, a tribunal will almost never order their reinstatement.

By January 2020, I had represented workers and tenants in the employment tribunal and in the civil courts for more than a decade. I had sat in the tribunal and listened while judges told my clients that their case was hopeless. I had heard a judge determine that homophobic words were mere 'banter' and that my client should have tolerated them in silence. But I had also sat beside clients and seen the tears of relief streaming down as a judge agreed with them. I had seen judges smile with satisfaction, knowing they had made the right decision.

I trained as a barrister late – in my 30s. As a teenager I spent my holidays working on an assembly line, building motherboards in the Elonex factory in Hammersmith, west London. What I wanted to be, more than anything else, was a historian. My great-aunt Dona Torr had completed her studies at University College London at the start of the 20th century and joined the *Daily Herald* as a journalist. She championed the paper's pacifist line during the First World War. In middle age, she was a mentor to a generation of young left-wing historians, the likes of Christopher Hill and E P Thompson. I studied labour history as an undergraduate and would have made a career of it – if only there was a living to be had.

The problem with my intended career was that in the Britain of the late 1990s and early 2000s, there were few resources for history. We had a New Labour government, for whom even to speak of the past was to lapse into embarrassment. It was better to think of the future, of new technologies of communication, of the ways in which all the old social divisions were about to be swept away in favour of . . . *something*. History was no help in channelling this future, and especially not the sorts of history that interested me. These were not only the values of our politicians. These ideas seeped down deep into the public sector and into the universities. It was everywhere accepted that the universities had a glut of labour historians. People with my skills were the subject of redundancy processes, not recruitment panels.

I spent my days working in the libraries, studying the 1934 strike at Pressed Steel in Oxford after which the magnates who dominated the British car industry were compelled to recognise trade unions, and the protests the following year against the construction of a private estate at Cutteslowe. Its walls barred the residents of the neighbouring Oxford streets from access to the main road. Only the intervention of the police prevented a crowd of protesters from tearing the walls down. I returned home each night, my nose clogged with the dry, peppery, smell of the archives.

I worked for half a year at a book publisher with offices in Hackney Wick, east London; Dona Torr had been one of their authors. When the days were slow, which they often were, I would descend from our offices – an eyrie perched on top of several floors of warehouse space – and wander the tiled corridors in which the books were stacked. The firm had the rights to the *Collected Works* of Marx and Engels, 50 white hardback volumes, their spines printed in black and red type. Each book was stored in its own leather shipping pouch, to protect against the damp of a sea-crossing from Leningrad. I read the letters the friends exchanged, the news of the exiled revolutionaries of 1848, their quarrels and reconciliations.

Deep into my 20s, I secured my first full-time teaching post. The position was, however, only a fixed-term one. In my first few weeks, I saw a poster for a meeting of the lecturers' union. Thirty minutes in, it became clear that the main purpose of the meeting was to select a volunteer to become the union's next branch secretary. The seven older, wiser, heads in the room knew that this would be a tiring and demanding role, that the employer had the intention of reducing the payroll, and that whoever became the branch secretary would spend rather more of their time representing their fellow workers than they would doing their own job. With all the confidence of youth, I thought, 'Why not?' Nine years followed before I became a barrister, but no decision in all that time was as important as that first step.

If there was no housing or employment law, the chances are that employers and landlords would impose contracts on workers and tenants which would make their lives unbearable. We know this because we have court records from the 18th and early 19th centuries, before most people had the vote, and we can see how the law was used. Contracts were read strictly and literally, and the law existed only to help employers (in the language of the day, 'masters') when they imposed these terms on their recalcitrant workers ('servants').

An employment law textbook written in 1820 would tell you that a typical contract was for a year, and that an employee could not leave before then except by giving three months' written notice. Payment was most often in food and lodging, the only money being a 'wage' payable at the end of the year's work and standing as a bond for faithful service (not altogether different from the deposit in a modern-day tenancy agreement). The few cases which came before the courts tended to end badly for the workers. A master was permitted to order a servant to work at any hour of the day or night. The farm servant who refused to travel without first eating his meal,[2] or the maid who fled her workplace to comfort her dying mother,[3] were guilty of gross insubordination entitling their employer to beat them or to summarily dismiss them without payment. The servant was treated as the property of the master.

Since then, society has tried to reset the balance. In principle, both sides gain. Employees and tenants benefit from a certain moderation of the terms of their contracts, while employers and landlords acquire certainty. If the case for possession is made out, then a judge will grant a possession order and bailiffs will attend to ensure the tenant leaves. The law mediates between two sides, preventing what might otherwise be such disturbances as workers going out on unofficial strikes, or neighbours gathering in the street to prevent an eviction.

The former historian in me grasps that the reason politicians have been willing to write minimum standards into employment and housing contracts, or that judges have been willing to enforce them, is because of great social movements which have put such pressure on the system that the state has imposed itself as a regulator above housing and employment relationships. Without the factory reform movement of the 19th century, without the 1915 rent strike in Glasgow or the trade union struggles of the 1970s – there would be no housing or employment law, no legal aid in civil law, no employment tribunal.

The balance of employment and housing law has altered, but old habits persist. I think of the north London pub-owner I encountered in the mid-2000s whose policy was to take on workers for as long as they would remain in his employment, making excuses for repeated delays in paying their salaries, until the unfortunate workers realised that he had no intention of ever paying. He glued his letterbox shut and if letters were delivered while the pub was open, they came back marked 'recipient unknown'. I would not have believed such things were still possible had it not been for the workers who I met: the student who had begun working in the pub, and the backpacker who replaced her the following month, both of them unpaid.

Then there was the TV chef my client sued, whose restaurant senior manager had abused her junior employees and her customers

2 *Spain v Arnott* [1817] 171 ER 638.
3 *Turner v Mason* (1845) 14 Meeson And Welsby 112.

in racist terms. When we issued a claim, the chef applied to the tribunal to have the case against him dismissed. A star-struck judge agreed, finding that it was impossible that a man as busy as the chef could be expected to supervise the workplaces he owned. Even this victory was not enough protection for the chef. He shut the restaurant, left it closed for a month before opening again on the same premises and with the same menu, only as a new legal entity – sabotaging the employee's appeal before it could be heard.

By the second week of January 2020, I was due to represent another tenant, Ronald. The last time I represented him, Ronald told me how he had sailed to England in the 1960s from Johannesburg to help his friend Sid James, and through him found work as a cameraman on the Michael Caine film, *Zulu*. His first circle of London acquaintances included the actress Hattie Jacques with whom Ronald fell briefly, gloriously, and unrequitedly, in love.

After that, he had worked as a lorry driver. 'I'm 62, I need to get back to it', he said, and I did not have the heart to tell him that he was actually ten years older than that. Ronald had been an alcoholic for 20 years, ever since his son died in an accident while visiting his mother. For the last seven years, Ronald had given all his love to a Staffordshire Bull Terrier, named Guinness. Ronald was not able to walk his dog as much as he needed, and Guinness barked all through the night. The other tenants demanded Ronald's eviction. Before I was instructed, a judge had ordered possession against him but suspended it on terms that Ronald re-house Guinness.

I was asked to represent Ronald for the first time at an eviction hearing. The landlord complained that my client had breached the order suspending possession. But he would not, or could not, give up on his dog. 'I love him', Ronald said. 'If you take Guinness, it will be like taking me out in a body bag.'

Two friends were at court with him, Anthony and James. Ronald's solicitor, Sue, offered the court an undertaking to remove the dog herself and take it to his friend Anthony's home. This was an extraordinary piece of bravery on her part. For if the undertaking was breached (for example, if Ronald refused to let her move Guinness from his home), the landlord could have brought Sue back to court. A judge might even have jailed her.

Sue spent the next few hours hunting for the dog, beginning at the flat where Guinness was supposed to be, searching through Ronald's friends' homes until she found the dog. Once Guinness was located, it turned out that the occupant of the flat had lost his keys and locked himself out. Ronald's friend James found a stepladder, but the ladder was too short. The 5pm deadline was minutes from being breached.

For months, I had been telling people Ronald's story. It ended with a victory: Guinness was moved. He was placed in Anthony's care, where Ronald could visit him. Sue and I had saved Ronald's home. His case was not supposed to come back to court.

In January, however, the landlord had again applied for eviction. Despite all of Sue and Anthony's best efforts, Guinness was back living with Ronald.

As for Ronald, he was barely able to turn his face and speak to me. His clothes were dishevelled, his face shrunken. His hair hung wildly down.

I asked him whether it was true that Guinness had returned.

'Why does he have to go?' Ronald said. 'I've had him since he was a pup.'

I told the judge the story of Ronald's life – how vulnerable he was.

The problem was that we were before the same judge who had ordered possession. He had heard it all before. 'This is a difficult case', he said, before rattling through a two-minute judgment ordering Ronald's eviction.

Afterwards, Sue tried her hardest to keep up with Ronald. He was an old man; in principle the local authority should have re-housed him, but it refused – blaming Ronald's loss of his home on the complaints about Guinness. While the council made its excuses, it became harder and harder to take any instructions from Ronald. He barely talked. He spent his days sleeping on a sofa in his friend James's flat.

Ronald complained of stomach cramps and was admitted to hospital. James tried to look after Guinness, but one night the dog ran off and a new home had to be found for him. Ronald was worn down by grief and misery – he did not leave the hospital alive.

The employment and housing courts shape the ways in which all of us live. If you are a landlord or a tenant, then you will know the rules for the registration of tenants' deposits, and the risks to the landlord if the deposit is left unprotected. If you are either an employee or a manager, then you can hardly be unaware that millions of people's lives are shaped by laws providing for a national minimum wage, prohibiting unlawful discrimination or unfair dismissal.

While very few disputes between workers and employers, or landlords and tenants, make their way to court, the decisions of judges make their way into public consciousness and in that way shape how millions of people live.

Around three per cent of all government spending each year goes on the costs of accommodation, subsidising the rent of people whose salaries are so low that they cannot afford to remain in their homes without help. Such welfare benefits are not kept by tenants – it is retained by their landlords. The housing element of universal credit (or, as it used to be known, housing benefit) enables the tenant to sleep in a home and not on the streets. It is better that it exists than if it was withdrawn. But if you have sat at court, as I have, and read a universal credit payment note saying that the recipient will be paid £409.89 every month, to cover their food, bills and every other expense, while their landlord would be paid £2,595.68 for rent in the same period, it's clear that the purpose of that benefit is no longer to protect the tenant but rather to subsidise the landlord and to sustain house prices generally.

Since 1979, the cost of housing has repeatedly increased, outstripping the price of labour – especially in the last ten years. This imbalance gives tenants threatened with losing their home every incentive to resist. There are millions of people living in forms of social housing (local authority and housing association homes) who would be unable to rent anywhere else should they be compelled to leave their present home. To keep themselves in their homes, they challenge their eviction using every opportunity the law allows them. For their part, landlords are astonished to discover just how slow and difficult it can be to evict a tenant.

Between 2002 and 2015, the average wages of renters increased by two per cent, while their rents rose by 16 per cent. The average mortgaged household in Britain presently spends less than one-eighth of its income on housing; the average renting household spends more than a third.[4] Many of my clients pay more than half.

In a time where rent is rising faster than people can afford it, you can divide rented accommodation into two categories. In the better camp are local authority and housing association tenancies, housing co-operatives and the few private sector tenancies with a generous landlord who is willing to turn a blind eye if the tenant has a difficulty paying the rent. In the worse camp are the larger number of private

---

4 G Monbiot, 'Poor tenants pay for landlords to live like kings. It doesn't have to be this way', *Guardian*, 17 July 2019.

tenancies where the landlord is less forgiving, and any disputes end in eviction.

I once represented a worker who had been dismissed after her employer said she was incapable of doing her job. A mobility impairment made it hard for her to walk, while other conditions sent pain through her elbows and wrists. The worker half-agreed with her boss that the work was too physically demanding for her. But it would not have been, had the company considered adjustments for her as a disabled person: for example, technology that actually worked, regular breaks and working from home. Her managers held numerous meetings before dismissing her, and because of their delay her compensation was likely to be modest. The managers saw my client as opinionated and difficult. The judge, I suspected, agreed with them. During one of the breaks, the employer's barrister said to me, 'Why are you fighting so hard – for *her*?'

I wanted to reply, but there are some questions you cannot answer. My client's condition was deteriorating. This was the last job she was ever likely to have. The positive findings the judge made in his final judgment were a chance for my client to stand tall and look back on her working life with her pride restored.

Indeed, sometimes, even more is at stake than mere dignity. For a minority of tenants, losing your home means absolute poverty, street homelessness or worse. A few small pieces of bad luck and anyone can find themselves in that situation: especially the sick or the old, especially people who are quite incapable of finding a new home. That was why, as the lockdown began, I was fighting so hard for them.

In the pages of this book, you will meet some of the people who play a part in our present system: the landlords, the bosses, the tenants and the workers. I hope that by the end of it you will view the law – and our society – differently.

CHAPTER 2

January: Possession lists

It was mid-January 2020 and, as I walked through Holborn in central London, the wind grasped at my face, working apart the gap between my scarf and collar, its fingers thick, clammy and unwelcome. Today I was going to be in the county court at Clerkenwell and Shoreditch in central London's Gee Street. It is one of my favourite courts. The building is new, with many windows and high ceilings. Compare Croydon in south London, where civil hearings take place in a building which also houses a Crown Court – windows are small and do not open, ceilings are low, the walls thick and oppressive. It feels as if the Croydon County Court building was designed with the aim of intimidating anyone going before the judges and to prevent them from escaping.

There is another reason why I like Gee Street: the judges there understand tenants' circumstances. When I began as a barrister, there were county courts in Lambeth in south London and Stratford in east London, but both have closed, with the result that Gee Street covers many of the poorest areas of London's zones 2 and 3. The rents which the tenants have to pay are among the highest rents in the country, and their wages among the lowest. This reality acts as a moderating influence. No matter how bad a tenant's case seems, how high their arrears or how reprehensible their behaviour, you can be certain that the judge has encountered worse. In other courts, you are more likely to hear a judge say, 'I understand it's hard for your client on benefits. But surely she knew she needed to prioritise the rent.' As if for tens of thousands of people, overwhelmed by the struggle to put food on the table, it is only weakness that prevents them from putting on a smart suit and finding a better-paid job. In Gee Street, by contrast, a judge might give your client credit for the effort they have made and say, 'Well, at least the arrears are stable.'

That January morning, my cases were a series of first hearings in a possession list. These are claims by landlords who want the court to make a possession order – in other words, a declaration that the tenant is required to leave their home. Landlords need to obtain these orders since under the Protection from Eviction Act 1977, it is a crime for almost all landlords to evict a tenant except after applying to the court for a possession order.

A typical pre COVID-19 possession list was made up of short proceedings, with between 30 and 50 cases before a single judge and each of them needing to be heard in a morning. One reason so many cases were heard at once is that over the last decade more than a third of all county courts have closed.[1] The effect of the closures has been to pile ever greater pressure on the district judges in each remaining county court. The demand on the system was the same, only the number of judges available to hear the cases had shrunk.

The hearings were listed together at 10am. There were not enough steel benches for everyone to sit, and tenants waited, leaning against the walls. The lucky few had already spoken to a lawyer before they came to court, and had a solicitor or barrister waiting for them. Many more arrived without a representative and gave quick instructions to a duty solicitor. They watched the landlord's lawyers nervously.

The theory is that first hearings are a chance for landlords to make a case for possession. The landlord is given a chance to set out the claim in just a few words: 'The tenant is two months in arrears', or 'The tenant's behaviour has been so bad – they're scaring the other residents'. If a tenant can in a few short sentences formulate a defence, saying 'I've paid the rent now', or 'It's not true, I didn't do what the others are saying', the case will almost certainly be sent off for a longer hearing with a proper time allocation. Sometimes the judges get these hearings wrong by deciding a case prematurely and wrongly against the tenant. This happens less often in courts such as Gee Street, where the judges have real experience of housing law. It is rarer still when the tenant is professionally represented. But it does happen.

I met my first client of the day, Mr Rosselson, half an hour before his hearing was due to start. He had been a teacher for many years. Unfortunately, Mr Rosselson had dislocated his shoulder playing

---

1   G Cowie and G Sturge, 'Court closures and access to justice', House of Commons Library, Debate Pack Number CDP-0156, 18 June 2019, p4; https://commonslibrary.parliament.uk/research-briefings/cdp-2019-0156/.

football. The injury left him feeling sore and wretched. He was signed off from work and did not return; eventually he was sacked. His old employer blamed him for his departure and would not give him a reference. A year passed without work, and he was behind with his rent. There were many things he might have done: setting up a standing order to cover the shortfall between his benefit and the rent, or applying to the council for a top-up discretionary housing payment (DHP). The reason Mr Rosselson had not taken either of these steps, his solicitor had told me, was that he had suffered from depression ever since losing his job. Sending letters and liaising with the benefits authorities were beyond him.

The solicitor had written to Mr Rosselson's landlord (a housing association) inviting them to accept that the case was unsuitable for immediate possession. They had declined to answer. As Mr Rosselson waited at court, circling his hand around his sore shoulder, I wondered how he would cope if the landlord did ask for possession.

My opponent, Mr Tuck, arrived at court late. He was young; he stood bouncing on his toes. He was alive with the thought of doing his job as well as he could and showing the landlord what a persuasive advocate he was.

'I'll just be a moment', Tuck said. The association had sent its housing officers to court, and he needed to take instructions from them.

Forty-five minutes passed, during which I waited with Mr Rosselson, my guts falling with each tick of the clock on the wall. When Tuck and I spoke again, I realised that Tuck had not brought a rent schedule with him, so the judge would not know what the current arrears were. Nor did he have any proposals for how much our client should pay if possession was not ordered and the matter adjourned to another day.

What Tuck had done was bring to court the best-polished black brogues I had ever seen. We stood outside court and he looked down them, smiled, and looked up at me. With the shoes, he looked fantastic. He was a champion. As the hero of his own life, he knew it would suit his housing officers very nicely thank you if a judge ordered possession.

I asked him, 'You have seen the medical evidence, haven't you?'

'I have', he answered, uncertainly.

'And the other documents?'

He turned up his well-bred nose and twisted away from me.

'Do you really think it would be fair on my client if you applied for possession today? Just coming to court – he's finding it almost unbearable. I'd understand if the arrears were getting worse, but they're coming down.'

'Don't worry', Tuck said. 'I'll make my case. The judge will knock it out in two minutes flat. Your client will go home happy, mine won't – but at least they'll have seen a proper fight. We'll both leave here winners.'

I sighed. 'I can't stop you from saying anything you want.'

The usher outside District Judge Tanar's court had gone missing. The judge walked into the corridor and waved us in, a woman in her 70s, five-foot tall, the absolute copy of the Maureen Lipman of the BT ads, with her familiar grey hair, a matching blue dress, even the same ultra-wide glasses frames. 'A first hearing?' the judge asked.

'Yes, madam', Tuck answered.

'And no application for immediate possession?'

'No', he told her. Then, 'Actually, madam, if I may . . .' Eventually, Tuck settled on his best point, namely that although my client's arrears were low, he had been in arrears for ten years. There is a ground for possession ('ground 11')[2] which landlords can rely on where the tenant has 'persistently delayed paying rent which has become lawfully due'. Tuck insisted that it applied to this case. He said there had been previous claims for possession (this was the first I had heard of them) and previous hearings. The landlord had brought those cases because Mr Rosselson had been repeatedly behind with his rent.

As advocates, it is drilled into us that we try to win within the rules. In his address to the judge, Tuck breached several of them: he ignored the convention that barristers are not there to give evidence. It is not for us to tell judges new facts, rather we are supposed to limit ourselves to setting out what is already in the parties' pleaded case, and in their witness statements. He was also arguing a point in court without having warned me that he intended to rely on it. I bent down to my client, and whispered, 'This isn't the first case?'

Rosselson nodded. He had his hands clasped together, wrapped in front of his body. His face was twisted in pain.

The judge said, 'Mr Renton?'

I admitted that my client had been in arrears before. But he had a history of depression. Improvising, I said that none of those previous cases ended in possession. Logically, it must follow that the landlord

---

2   Housing Act 1988 Sch 2 ground 11.

withdrew them in return for my client promising to reduce his arrears. I showed the judge how you could see in the rent statement where my client had indeed paid large sums all in one go, which might be consistent with what Tuck had just told her. I explained that if my client had paid off his arrears, because the landlord had promised to discontinue previous cases against him, then he must have done so for some reason. Each time the landlord must presumably have given him its word that in return for him making a substantial payment he could remain in his home. It could not go back on its promises now.

District Judge Tanar gave judgment. Her words filled a page of my blue counsel's notepad. She quoted the points I had made, emphasising the best of them. She said I must be right: if there had been four previous proceedings, and each was withdrawn by the landlord then the housing association must have given my client some sort of promise. 'I don't know why those previous claims were compromised but compromised they must have been.'

The judge spoke calmly, quietly, but with evident enthusiasm for her task. She refused to grant the landlord possession. She set the case down for a full hearing in the autumn.

I smiled back gratefully at her.

At the end, Mr Rosselson unbent, just a little. But for nearly an hour he had had to sit there, not knowing whether his home of 25 years was about to be taken away from him. His jaw was gripped tight, his hand still draped over his shoulder.

I turned to my opponent and he was bright. He had fought hard, and that was a good thing. But months would have to pass, years maybe, before he grasped the unnecessary distress that he had just put my client through, if he ever would.

In the years when I worked as a university lecturer, I found out how to organise a picket line and to get the details of our protests into the local press. I learned that when the chief executive sent his secretary to the picket line offering us each a cup of coffee, this was not the magnanimous gesture it seemed. The task of the secretary was to wander up and the line, noting our faces, the prelude to deducting that day's pay from our wages.

I began representing fellow lecturers in internal grievance and appeal hearings. The employer wanted to make redundancies, and the branch responded with protests, including a teach-in on an open day for prospective students. Pride of place was given to the music lecturers whose jobs were at risk. The union declared a collective grievance which management reluctantly agreed to hear at a joint meeting. We were given half an hour to make a presentation. My role was to set out the ways in which college management had ignored its own policies. I prepared the talk and a bundle of documents. When we had finished, the chief executive banged his fist on the table and denounced us for daring to criticise him. At the end of the meeting, the two independent staff governors indicated that they would vote with him.

One of the governors was a full-time official of the public sector union UNISON, whose members had received a guarantee that they would be protected from dismissal. He did not seem pleased about the role he had been given of supporting the termination of lecturers' contracts as the price of protecting his own members. But I remember what he said in the meeting: 'I've often sat with my members in tribunals, and, in my experience, judges aren't that bothered by procedure, what they're interested in is substance. If all you do is complain about process, you'll lose.' Twenty years later and having done several hundred cases of my own, he was right. You won't win a finding of unfair dismissal on procedural flaws alone.

By the time of my 30th birthday, I had had more encounters with the law. In 1998 on the fifth anniversary of the murder of Stephen Lawrence, a friend and I were caught flyposting Hackney, London with signs calling the police institutionally racist. We were arrested by a police officer – our own age and more bored than hostile. We were booked into police cells, and the house keys taken from our pockets. Without being asked, and without a warrant, the police used the keys to raid our flat. Our solicitor Zehra was shocked on our behalf, but told us that the value of any complaint, should we make it, would be so low that we were without remedy.

The same flat proved troublesome again, when its ceiling collapsed. My flatmate knew the council's environmental health officer, who cast a despairing eye over the shimmering brown dust which now covered our possessions. It contained asbestos, he warned. We were already at the end of our six-month tenancy agreement. We left, demanding no greater compensation than the return of our deposit. A solicitor I had met in an anti-racist campaign wrote a letter on our behalf, and one to me directly: 'They may pay up but then again they may think sod you, you can take us to the small claims court.'

I was looking for a new career – but as what? My father had been for many years head of research at a stockbroking firm. After that, he founded one of the stock exchange's first ethical investment trusts. If everyone was going to have a private pension fund in future, he reasoned, there should be one which did not fund wars or pollute the planet. He was still hoping I would settle down into a 'normal' job – something in the City.

The only family member who had a good word for the law was my aunt Susie, who had studied the subject in Melbourne, Australia. Even her admiration for the law's rigour was tempered by the divorce hearing she'd endured, at the end of which her husband Brian had, to my aunt's disgust, secured sole ownership of their home. Brian, my aunt explained, was a lawyer, and a clubbable one. He was the secretary of Whitefriars Club dining society, a club which had counted several judges among its members. No wonder, she explained, the judge had agreed with him.

My second client that morning, Ms Jamal, was in her mid-40s and an addict recovering from heroin addiction. A year before, she had let two men in their 20s into her flat where they injected themselves with cocaine and heroin. The police raided the property. Ms Jamal was convicted of permitting her flat to be used for taking drugs. One of the tenants in the block had written to his MP demanding the landlord evict her. Our defence was based on the vulnerability of Ms Jamal, who was diagnosed as suffering from manic depression, as well as the lack of any drug incidents since her conviction. We waited for the hearing to start. Ms Jamal had inky black hair and an addict's pale skin. But she was wearing a smart grey scarf and she had brought a book to court, Paula Hawkins' *The Girl on the Train*.

I asked if it was any good.

'They made a film of it, didn't they?' said Ms Jamal, grinning at her own joke.

Ms Jamal lived on various benefits. Her effective income – the amount she kept for herself – was less than £3,000 a year. I asked what she would do if she lost. Her father lived in Middlesbrough; she had not seen him in years. Her brother in Bristol did not have time to help her. 'They've just had a baby', she said wearily.

I asked her if she had any savings.

'Nothing.'

'What will you do if the landlord gets possession?'

She stared back at me, her nostrils flaring. What could she do?

We were due on at 11am, and on the other side was a familiar adversary, Wystan. He was dressed shabbily compared to some of the other landlords' representatives, with their Bond Street suits and Chelsea boots. If you knew no better, you might think he spent less on clothes than the housing officers who instructed him. But those brown shoes, needing a daily shine, were brogues. The suit had been tailored for Wystan on Jermyn Street.

Just as I have almost always represented tenants, Wystan has predominantly acted for landlords. We had been against each other in dozens of cases before, so many times that we greeted each with a wry smile.

We found an unoccupied corner of the busy waiting room.

Sniffling with a cold, Wystan told me the housing association had instructed him to demand immediate possession.

'You can't', I said. 'My client is bipolar.'

'Then she shouldn't have let her flat be used for drugs.'

'You'd have her sleep rough – in this weather?'

He winced. 'It has been perky, hasn't it?'

In the hearing, Wystan said, 'I am instructed to seek immediate possession . . .' He pitched his case high: 'The tenant admits anti-social behaviour.' He then lowered it. 'Now, the court may have noticed that in our claim for possession, we predicted that the defendant would be sentenced to a custodial sentence. But she only received a community order . . .'

Wystan finished, 'If there's anything, M'um, I can assist you with–'

District Judge Tanar looked at me. 'Mr Renton.'

Ms Jamal closed her eyes, sucked in her cheeks.

'This is a fully defended case', I said, and I was just about to launch into the facts and the law, when the judge stopped me.

'Your client's problem, as I see it', District Judge Tanar said, 'is that there's no connection between the anti-social behaviour and her disability. I get cases where there's shouting and screaming, and the tenant is a schizophrenic and it's easy to see how their illness prevents them from controlling their behaviour. A disability defence makes sense then. Or where there's rent arrears. But you say the defence applies even when there's no link.'

'That's the whole point of a reasonable adjustment', I answered. 'If you're going to have equal treatment, you have to take account of the disabled person's impairment whether it caused her difficulties or not. Now, in this case, if my client is evicted – she won't get a home any time soon. The council won't rehouse her, she can't afford anything in the private sector either. She's going to sleep rough. And she's disabled.'

The judge turned her head to one side, twisted it to the other.

I showed her the order made in the criminal proceedings. Under it, Ms Jamal was required to attend a course which would last for 13 weeks, and she would be tested. If she did not comply with that order, she would be sent to prison. A criminal court was not permitted to make an order of that kind, unless they made a finding that Ms Jamal's drug addiction might respond to treatment. Another court had found that hers was not a hopeless case.

'That's what the defence is about', I told the judge. 'The criminal courts have already decided she deserves an opportunity to turn her life around. If she loses her home now, you'll be sabotaging that order.'

Ms Jamal was holding her head in her hands as the judge recited. 'On reflection, this is not the type of case where it would be appropriate for immediate possession to be ordered. There will be a full trial, probably in the autumn . . .'

I beamed a smile of gratitude at the judge. All morning, she had been so kind to me.

Wystan has had to tell landlords many times that they will get possession in due course but that the case will not be decided at a first hearing. 'The judges take their time', he said, 'but they get it right in the end'. Outside court, we reminisced about some of the cases we have been in. The tenant I had who was driven to court from prison with four plainclothes officers clustered around him. The landlord who had changed his name by deed poll (the man insisted) 'in order to sound more professional'. But neither Wystan nor I could understand why renaming yourself Mr Knight Frank Rutley would make your tenants pay their rent.

Wystan told me about the training his chambers gives to junior barristers. 'We tell our pupils, the hardest thing is when you're against an unrepresented tenant. You're offered an open door. You might think it's best to push through, and you'll get possession. But if the other side gets a lawyer then a case which you could have won in a couple of months, if you'd just been patient, will drag out for a year or even longer. It's awful when they appeal. The tenant asks the court for the transcript of the hearing. And if you've said something rum to the district judge then, when the circuit judge sees it on appeal, they'll crucify you.'

Waiting for me on my desk in chambers when I returned that afternoon were the papers in the case of Mrs Hafeez. The landlord, a local authority, wanted to evict her. They said she had never moved in to the flat. They served a notice to quit to end the tenancy. Mrs Hafeez insisted that she had indeed moved in, and that she had not left the flat, she was only away for a few days while waiting for repairing works to begin. On her version of what had happened, the case began with her complaining that the flat was damp and full of mould; the landlord took against her; it instructed its housing officers to investigate Mrs Hafeez, looking for anything to justify eviction. That was the context to the allegation that she had abandoned the flat. She said the landlord was wrong to think she had not moved in. Mrs Hafeez had photographs of her in her flat, surrounded by her furniture. All this should have been a complete defence to the proceedings.

One week before the papers came to me, Mrs Hafeez was due to attend a first hearing in the county court. Her case was listed for 10am, and that morning District Judge Tanar was the judge on duty. She called the case on at three minutes past 10. Gee Street is on a narrow side street at some distance from the nearest tube station. It had never occurred to Mrs Hafeez that it might take her longer than five minutes to walk from the Barbican to the building in which her case was due to be heard.

I found myself thinking of Mrs Hafeez, full of hope as she walked unknowingly late through the busy London streets.

The landlord's barrister was at court on time, and the hearing began with her in attendance but without Mrs Hafeez.

District Judge Tanar started by congratulating the landlord on the care with which it had prepared its evidence.

The barrister, to her credit, warned the judge against deciding the case in the absence of the other side: 'I ought to perhaps make you aware that there is a fairly substantial background to this matter.'

District Judge Tanar turned to her clerk and asked for a form ordering possession.

The barrister tried to warn the judge a second time, explaining that until now the defendant had always resisted its claim for possession.

The judge ordered immediate possession.

District Judge Tanar then invited the local authority to demand that the tenant pay, in the period from the hearing until her eviction, more in rent than the landlord was already charging. She said that Mrs Hafeez had lost her security of tenure. She said the market rent for the property must be several times greater than what the landlord normally demanded. Why not double the rent, or triple it, until the bailiffs attended, and Mrs Hafeez was evicted?

The barrister was flustered. Awkwardly, she tried to explain that local authorities set their rent according to policies which are signed off by the councillors. The amount charged goes up with inflation every year. The rent rise is a lengthy and complex process. As a social landlord, you cannot double the rent just because you dislike one of your tenants.

With a last 'Thank you' from the judge, the first hearing ended. Its outcome was an order giving possession to the landlord.

At 10.10am Mrs Hafeez made it to the court. She asked for the duty solicitor but he was busy, and the hearing resumed.

While the judge had taken exemplary care to speak to the landlord's barrister as politely as she could, her approach to Mrs Hafeez was different. 'Who are you?' she demanded.

Stammering, Mrs Hafeez did her best to explain.

'Why are you late?'

Mrs Hafeez said she had booked an appointment with a solicitor. They could meet her later in the week. She said, 'I'm just asking for some time to prove that I live there.'

Tanar replied, 'I can't understand what you're asking.'

Mrs Hafeez tried to speak again but was not allowed to finish.

'Silence', the judge ordered.

The judge turned to the landlord's barrister and allowed her to speak for five minutes without interruption. Mrs Hafeez tried one last time to speak. The judge said, 'I've heard enough' – and, for a second time that morning, ordered possession.

I remembered the courtesy with which District Judge Tanar addressed me in court and the charm with which she spoke to the other barristers who appeared before her. Then I found myself thinking of the way she had treated Mrs Hafeez.

CHAPTER 3

February: The visionary

My working week begins and ends in my chambers. It is where my computer waits and where I receive the papers for each new case. Often, at the start of the year, my diary is empty. It is not unusual for me to come into chambers at 10am on the first working day after Christmas to find that I have not a single case listed. That does not mean I can relax. What it means, rather, is that as that day and week continue, solicitors will be ringing my clerks to see if someone is free and put cases in my diary, then cancelling them without warning. By mid-afternoon, my diary might say Tuesday in Edmonton, Wednesday in central London, and Thursday in Slough. Any of these bookings could come in or out, and others replace them without me seeing the papers. In a week like that, it is only at 4.30pm on the afternoon before the first hearing that I will know for sure which of the cases is going ahead. It is wise to prepare all the cases a little. It is foolish to prepare any of them too carefully until I am on the train.

In that way, a barrister – any barrister – is always beginning anew, opening the emails with our instructions, encountering the client in our imagination before we meet them in person.

As I pick up each case and familiarise myself with it, I fill my memory with hundreds, perhaps thousands, of small facts. The number of times in which my opponent has previously agreed to adjourn an anti-social behaviour case; the location in the bundle of the consultant's report where the nature of the client's condition is recorded, and the diagnosis of the client's capacity to understand the proceedings and give instructions to their lawyers. At the start of the case, I cannot know which of these details is essential – but by the time we are in court, I will need to know all of them. I will have to be prepared against any judicial inquiry ('Which page number in the bundle, Mr Renton?'), and any possible attack by my opponent. At the end of the case, I will remove all this information from my memory. You could ask me on the Monday, 'How's the case going?' and I would know. You could ask me again on Friday and I'd have to say – 'That case? It's over now. I can't recall . . .' There is another reason that barristers let our cases go, and it is that there is never anyone to share the details with, not even our clients. The tenants who win do not want to be reminded of how close they came to losing their homes. The workers who lose are even less willing to share the memories of their setback.

In the first week of February 2020, I travelled to Birmingham for a half-day case. The *Guardian* economics website was running a live blog on events in China, where millions of people had been locked in their homes to prevent the spread of a new virus. The worst affected area of the country was Hubei, in which nine-tenths of Chinese car production took place. Economists reduced their predictions of growth in the Chinese economy from a booming six per cent this year to a more cautious five-and-a-half percent. Health experts warned that the disease might spread to other regions.

Our health secretary, Matt Hancock, told journalists that the government was taking no chances. The British response to the outbreak would be science-led.

As a teenager, I worked as an industrial cleaner. That introduced me to a world of pub toilets, abandoned homes, and the spaces above the ceilings of department stores. But if I had to make a list of the worst jobs in which I have ever worked, I would not include my time there. The worst jobs I have done were ones in which a manager was determined to force me out. I have described already my first full-time teaching post. Once I had been there a year, the finance director was keeping tabs on my emails. The head of personnel made me attend weekly meetings with her. Collective consultations about redundancy were followed by individual consultations whose only subject was the business's irreversible decision to get rid of me.

Over the next decade, I spent five years teaching in fixed-term lecturing posts, and three years as an equality official of the lecturers' union (National Association of Teachers in Further and Higher Education (NATFHE), today the University and College Union (UCU)). I completed a law conversion course and was near the start of my Bar Vocational Course, the penultimate stage of a barrister's training.

Next, I worked as an editor of an annual guide to employment law. That, too, proved no more than a short-term position. We were the

British offshoot of a multinational company, and the parent business had very particular ideas about the use of italics and emphasis, the structuring of a book chapter, even about the law itself. Every chapter had to begin by setting out what the law permitted, as if UK law was a constitutional system which began with statements of first principle and only later qualified them. But English common law does not work like that – our law is not that orderly. Rather, it is an overlay of statute and judicial decision-making. It is like comparing the neat grid-shape of Manhattan, each corner of which has its own grid reference, with the organic layering of Roman, medieval and modern streets in London.

Every piece of work I submitted came back with a list of corrections. The rules of the book permitted the authors to record where we believed a judicial decision had been wrongly made and was susceptible to appeal. My recurring fault was to overuse this discretion. I wrote that decisions of the appellate courts to permit non-payment of wages to workers without immigration status were incoherent. I insisted that decisions taking away unfair dismissal rights from agency workers were unsustainable. I was trying to correct the law, make it what I thought it should be, when there is only one place to challenge regressive case-law – in court.

With my first pieces of writing, my manager restricted her comments to no more than one per paragraph. Then, it became one per line. After three months in post, every word I wrote was a site of conflict. Our conversations, likewise, deteriorated. I found myself hiding in parts of the building where she would not find me. I remember the misery I felt with each email cheerily inviting me to another 'catch up' – the greasy-grey feeling in my stomach.

At one meeting, I asked my manager, 'Are you putting me on capability procedures?'

I counted the seconds as I waited for her answer: one, two, three, four, five – until, at last, the answer came, 'No, I'm not.' *Not this time,* she meant.

In the second week of February 2020, I represented another worker in a tribunal hearing. Dorian Falk had worked for a decade as a museum curator. His solicitors arranged for me to meet him in my chambers before the hearing began. We sat around the long oak table downstairs, in the largest of chambers' meeting rooms, and I thought of all the battles I had fought there. I was interviewed for pupillage (the final stage of a barrister's training) in that room. The first time, we were invited to criticise the most recent Supreme Court case on the legacy of the Iraq war. I struggled to explain the case, watching the disappointment in the faces of those interviewing me. The second time was a year later, when a more general question was asked: should radical lawyers represent men accused of domestic violence against their partners? I'd spent three years working as a trade union equality official, learning from strong political women. If I'd messed that question up, they would never have forgiven me.

Mr Falk was tall and thin. He wore a purple sweater, matching glasses and tie. He left an asthma pump just beyond his right hand. After we met, I revisited the bundle and read deeper into the papers. I liked Mr Falk, and I wanted him to win. He reminded me of a type I have met many times, people who have worked in public service and seen managers come in and shred the organisations beneath them. Mr Falk wanted vindication, the approval of someone with greater authority than his employer. He wanted to end his career with dignity.

As I read the papers, I lurched between optimism and despair. I found myself thinking: the case was fantastic; the client was sure to win; everything Mr Falk told me was backed up by documents; his case was impeccable. A moment passed – and I found myself thinking: his case was terrible; he did not stand a chance. In the documents of the case, Mr Falk came over as a decent person, who worked hard, far beyond his normal contractual hours. That was the bit I liked. The part which troubled me is that he and his colleague had made a series of bad decisions. They put on an exhibition, 'Do Not Touch', which had to be cancelled. They did not secure funding, and the number of visitors was less than it should have been.

Mr Falk's case was that as the scale of the losses became clear, he was dragged to a meeting with the museum's newly appointed director, who raged at him for the loss, shouted and swore. The director said he had no confidence in him. Falk had no choice but to resign. But the way many judges would see it is that any worker who causes his employer loss can expect rough treatment from their managers. And if a few harsh words caused him to resign, then probably half the employment judges in Britain would think the employer acted reasonably and the resignation justified.

When I was growing up, there was nothing my father enjoyed better than bringing friends round a table for dinner. Some of his stories were shocking, others were rude. He had a talent for sustaining friendships with artistic people, friends returning from years living in Goan communes, the children of exiled Spanish Communists. People, in other words, like Mr Falk. As I read into the papers, I felt my head giddying with hope, I feel my guts lurch with despair. The feeling was not unfamiliar. There is a filtering process which takes place through litigation. When two people begin an argument, the lawyers on both sides work out if their case is hopeless. The cases which are, settle. The ones which make it to a hearing are the hardest to call, with neither side certain of victory.

The employment tribunal has evolved far from the system its planners envisaged. It is the consequence of the Industrial Relations Act 1971 which provides that workers should be entitled to bring complaints of unfair dismissal to an outside body (the 'industrial tribunal' as it was originally known) which would decide if the dismissal had been fair or not. The tribunal was set up at a time when unofficial strikes were prevalent, to reduce their frequency. This would be achieved by recognising the injustices which lay beneath so many disputes; and diverting this anger from the chaotic and unruly practice of striking into the calmer, more manageable path of litigation. The architect of the scheme was Professor Otto Kahn-Freund. A few laws protected the employee, he said, 'But not against arbitrary or unfair dismissal . . . Even if the manner in which he is dismissed constitutes an imputation upon his honour . . . he cannot, except through an action for defamation, obtain any redress.'[1]

The employment tribunal was meant to be free to access and informal. Most workers and employers were expected to attend without a lawyer. The plan was that it would consist of a panel of three equal members, one with experience of employee relations from a worker's perspective (usually a trade union rep); a second member with the same experience from an employer's perspective (probably a personnel manager); and a lawyer to sit between them.

The panel was supposed to be an 'industrial jury', with the two wing members more than capable, should they wish, of outvoting the judge. But one of the injustices of the system is that in its crucial formative years the tribunal adopted all the formalities of the country's then civil law system. In the intervening 40 years, the county courts have become more permissive, but the tribunal has remained unchanged. So, for example, should a claimant before the tribunal fail to raise in their initial court papers (the 'ET1' form), an important part of their case, the claimant will be required to make an application to amend their claim form. These applications are rarely granted. Conversely, should a claimant in a county court claim make the same mistake, a district judge would be far more likely to permit amendment.

---

1   D Renton, *Struck out: Why employment tribunals fail workers and what can be done*, Pluto Press, 2012, pp27–28.

Problems of this sort pervade the tribunal system. In one conversation with me, Mr Falk's solicitor remarked simply, as if stating a plain fact, 'Of course, constructive dismissals are very hard to prove'. What she meant is that to win his case, Mr Falk would have to persuade the judge that his employer breached his contract; that the breach was sufficiently serious to justify Mr Falk's resignation; that the breach actually caused him to resign; and that the breach was not waived either expressly or impliedly, for example if Mr Falk had delayed for months before resigning. To succeed, he was required to satisfy each separate step – while the employer only needed to succeed at any one of those stages to defeat the claim. Having got that far, Mr Falk also needed to show that the dismissal was unfair on the 'range of reasonable responses' test.[2] In other words, the employer would successfully defend the case unless my client could show that the dismissal was so bad that no reasonable employer would have done it.

None of these rules, it should be noted, can be traced back to politicians or to the plain language of the Act of parliament in which the prohibition on unfair dismissal was originally contained.[3] They are rather the product of judicial decision-making, done by a caste of judges 40 years ago for whom employees were still 'servants' and the very concept of unfair dismissal was a new and unwelcome development. Each on its own is capable of justification, it is only when you fit them together that you have our present system, loaded slightly but consistently in favour of employers.

Mr Falk's solicitor Jane and I had known each other for 20 years. When we met, I was working for the TUC, on a scheme to promote adult education in the workplace; she was a further education tutor teaching employment law to workplace reps. The room in which she worked was cluttered with the ephemera from workers' protests: mugs from the Tolpuddle martyrs' festival, magazines for UNISON and the airline pilots' union BALPA, posters for the Workers Beer Company and the Simon Jones Memorial Campaign.

When she visited my chambers for the first time, Jane teased me for the plainness of our interiors. 'You're lefty lawyers, I thought you'd have a poster on every wall.'

---

2   *Iceland Frozen Foods Ltd v Jones* [1983] ICR 17.

3   Employment Rights Act 1996 s98(4).

I carried on reading the bundle for Mr Falk's case. I highlighted the passages in the bundle where I would need to ask questions of the other side's witness. As I studied the papers, an email arrived. It was from the barrister who was representing the employer: Bowls.

We agreed to speak. He was hoping to test the confidence with which I would argue the case and to see what my client's best points were. These rituals are part of the normal, competitive, nature of advocacy. Bowls began by telling me about the time he had been given to prepare the case. It is just a practical fact that in any case where one side is representing the employer and the other a trade union (as I was), the former will be better-resourced. He told me he had met the managers three times already with a fourth conference due the next day.

On the worker's side, I had met my client only once.

It is not just that barristers who act for employers get more time to prepare. They are also better paid – usually between three and six times what a union would pay. Over the years, I have had to listen as opponents complained that they wanted to represent workers, they really did – such, though, were trade union rates that my opponents wouldn't have been able to afford to keep their children in private schools. It is just easier, they told me, on the employer's side.

I was still mulling the conversation as I set off one Friday in February, feeling the lurch of the train as it escaped the platform. Central London felt bleak. The post vans were still parked from the evening before, black caps and black hoods ringed the heads of the commuters. It was a world of sullen expressions, of bodies hunched in their seats.

The *Guardian* had moved its coverage of coronavirus from its economics to its news page. Professor Yvonne Doyle, medical director and director for health protection of Public Health England, insisted that the UK was one of the first countries to have purchased sufficient tests.

I walked along St Mary Street, Cardiff's busiest shopping district, and I saw men and women in their 20s emerging from the tents in which they slept.

At 10am, the two sides were in our respective waiting rooms: one for the claimant (the worker), one for the respondent (the employer). There were too many of us for the room: Mr Falk; his union official; a colleague from the council; Frances, the solicitor from the union. Mr Falk wanted to know about the judge. 'Is she *awful?*'

I asked the same question of Mr Bowls. It turned out that earlier this week Bowls had been in a different case before the same judge, Employment Judge Geisler. He told me that she had worked all her career as a solicitor, at a law centre representing workers. I knew not to make too much of this background: the courts are full of judges who spend their working lives on one side of an argument only to 'change sides' when they are promoted to the bench.

'She's marvellous', Bowls said. 'She'll have read all the papers in an hour, and then she'll know the case better than you or me.' The bundle was over 900 pages – carrying it strained my arms: reading it in an hour would be quite a feat.

While we talked, Bowls handed me a written note he had prepared to summarise his client's case. I was surprised to see it so soon, but I did not complain – it would help me to know how he was planning to run the case.

'How about you, chum, can I see yours?' asks Bowls.

'I'm so sorry', I told him, 'mine's not finished yet'.

It was a white lie. I did have a skeleton, and if anyone was to read it then it would have seemed finished. It was the written form of the final speech that I would give at the end of the hearing. But I would be updating mine as the case went on. I was planning to hand mine in, as barristers usually do, at the conclusion of the case and not before.

While barristers are not allowed to coach our witnesses, there was no rule to stop me from taking my opponent's note and handing it to Mr Falk.

He took out his pencil, a much-loved Faber-Castell in a battered silver case. He set to work covering my opponent's document with notes of his own. He read the respondent's summary of what happened in his workplace. He told me, 'It wasn't like that.'

The usher called us to the door. I had that feeling, that last burst of adrenaline. I always feel it, whether I am trying to mitigate a defeat or pressing for victory.

We went in. As the claimant's representative, I sat on the right, Bowls to my left. Every witness in civil proceedings, as in crime, must swear to tell the truth. Mr Falk stood tall as he gave his oath in Welsh. From the rhythm of his sentence, I recognised one or two words: *gwir* for truth.

Bowls' theory was that Mr Falk did not need to resign when he did, but was over-sensitive to any minor slight. After the costly exhibition, the museum took a decision to move my client sideways – from Digital and Exhibitions to Estates. Bowls' case was that my client was upset at being moved within the organisation and it was that anxiety, not any angry words used by his managers, which caused him to resign. For the next three hours, Bowls returned to this theme. Again, and again, Mr Falk found a new way of explaining firmly and politely that no, he had not only worked in Exhibitions. That in two decades of gallery work he had often been asked to work in different areas. He had been placed in Furniture and Textiles just a few years before and enjoyed his responsibilities. Plainly, Bowls was not expecting those answers, and as the day went on, he failed to keep eye contact with my client. Rather than asking closed questions capable of only a yes or no answer ('It's right that . . .', 'It's true that . . .'), he asked open questions, 'Well, are you saying . . .?' He was losing control of the witness.

On the second day of the hearing, Mr Falk was still giving evidence. Invited to criticise his team, he refused. One colleague 'had fantastic analytical skills – it was a real pleasure to work with him'. Is it true that he was pushing for an 'outstanding' in his performance rating? Not at all, 'I've never suggested what rating I should be given'. He even praised the managers who later bullied him. 'It was exceedingly difficult for our Director. Given the lack of time he had, and the expectation that he'd master everything, I thought he was doing well.'

As Bowls wilted, Mr Falk grew in confidence. We came to a part of the evidence where he needed to explain why he had lobbied so hard for the idea of a freer, more tactile exhibition, and why it was necessary – despite the risks.

Mr Falk said, 'Do you know how many "Do Not Touch" signs we had? I counted them myself. It was fourteen hundred and thirty-seven. What sort of message do you think that sends?' His words left Bowls floundering for a reply.

After that, it was my turn to cross-examine the respondent's witnesses. I was watching Employment Judge Geisler. She could have ruined the case for me at this stage with just a well-timed interruption. Instead, she nodded, 'Mr Renton, your turn.'

The first witness was Mr Falk's manager Charmaine Baccarat. She wore a grey suit, a silk scarf cascading from her neck. She was asked to affirm.

'I don't have to do the Welsh bit, do I?'

'You don't', the judge told her.

Mrs Baccarat had chosen to project herself as the kind and caring face of business. I took her to the various accounts we had of the final meeting, where Mr Falk said she was angry and shouted at him. She accepted she was upset but said she was restrained. 'I don't speak angrily in meetings.' But it was not just Mr Falk. Witness after witness, even the employer's witnesses, all recalled her shouting.

'I'm just not like that', she told me.

The employer's case ended with the evidence of the museum's director, Thornton Edsell. Bowls smiled at the prospect. 'It's not my job to warn you', he said, 'but what pedigree!' As Mr Edsell stood to swear his oath, even I had to acknowledge a certain ruggedness in his expression. With his diamond blonde hair and chiselled jaw, the smile he beamed at me and at the judge, he seemed just the sort of person you would want to run a museum. The profile on the museum's website described Mr Edsell as a broadcaster, a much-loved public figure. He was a public servant who within two decades of leaving university had already graced the worlds of literature, education and energy, although none of those areas for longer than two years at a time. It would be churlish to observe that in return for all the gold-dust which he sprinkled over these various worlds, he had not been poorly rewarded: his salary at the museum was more than £50k a year – in return for which he was employed just one day a week.

Mr Edsell insisted he did nothing wrong. 'I had been approached by the Welsh Government, the Minister had considerable concerns. I was asked to lead the board to oversee the recovery of the museum. After the difficulties it had been experiencing with previous exhibitions, the future of the business was a stake.'

I caught a glimpse of Bowls smiling at his own client.

Edsell continued, 'I have a lot of experience in this area and I recall expressing that this was simply an unreformed part of the public sector. If I hadn't acted, the potential for reputational damage was huge.'

The smug certainty of his speech left my skin raw.

By the time of the events that had caused my client's resignation, Mr Edsell had been in the job just seven weeks. He accepted telling the staff including Mr Falk that they were 'pitiful', 'shambles' and 'a complete shower'. He admitted he'd had only a very general sense, at the start of his appointment, of the museum's recent history. He was unaware, for example, that Mr Falk's two previous exhibitions had been commercial successes. He had no hesitation, however, in telling Mr Falk that his mistakes had been unforgiveable. This, he insisted, was a reasonable opinion. 'The costs', he said, 'the risks . . .'

As he spoke, something curious happened to the director's face. When I asked him questions, Edsell tried to flatten his features, as if to conceal any emotion. But then, when it came to the crucial meetings, his teeth bared – as if he was remembering calling his staff to attention. He became a walnut, a pink and furious walnut.

'At the meeting, you were angry.'

'I wasn't.'

'You reprimanded your staff.'

'I didn't.'

I reminded him that three people in the room were taking notes as he spoke and in every version of what they noted, he turned on Mr Falk and said that he had no confidence in him.

'I never said anything of the sort.'

'So, on your evidence, it was quite a normal meeting?'

'It was.'

'You were professional at all times?'

'I was.'

I reminded him of what one of the employer's own witnesses said earlier that day, that the meeting with Mr Edsell was the worst he had experienced in his career.

Grimly, Edsell answers, 'Then he's been lucky, hasn't he?'

'That's your evidence? Your own manager goes home and is so distressed, he's in tears, and you say he's *lucky* it never happened to him before?'

'I do.'

In that sentence, I could see the sheer contempt he had for his more junior employees. If they were upset, Mr Edsell did not care.

The last day came around and Mr Falk wanted to know, 'Am I winning?' He was ahead, I reckoned, and I was happy to tell him that. But that is the thing about civil law: your chances depend on the judge and you never know what they are thinking.

Judges are people – they get tired, they get distracted, and they change their mind. They come up with decisions you would never expect.

Bowls told the judge that Mr Falk had nothing to complain about. That after the exhibition went wrong, the losses were dreadful. 'This wasn't a case', he insisted, 'of some renegade teacher lecturing his pupils'.

When it was my turn to speak, I said, 'But that's exactly what it was.' I invited the judge to remember Mr Edsell and those last words of his ('He's been lucky') and the attitude which underpinned them. I told the judge that we saw what Mr Edsell was really like on the stand: callous, indifferent to the people who worked under him.

Employment Judge Geisler said she would reserve judgment, warning us it could be weeks before she had time to type up her decision.

I spoke to Mr Falk, thanked him for the way he gave his evidence. I asked what he would do on the weekend and he told me he would go walking. I imagined him, standing on the crest of the Black Mountains, studying the wooded valleys below.

'Enjoy yourself', I told him, 'get out of the house. Think about anything you can other than the case; it's out of our hands now.'

We received the decision in the post. I was full of hope as I began to read. The senior managers were at fault in various ways, the judge found. They worked Mr Falk hard; they failed to give him credit for the steps he had taken which had helped to rescue the business. She accepted that Mr Falk was working far beyond his contractual hours, and any plans to reduce his workload took months to work out and that by the time he resigned there was no prospect of his workload reducing soon. She pointed out, however, that he was a longstanding employee and could be expected to work hard.

My heart sank as I read on and I saw the effort the judge had taken to contextualise all that was said in the crucial meetings. Emotions were running high, she found. Such was the crisis in the organisation that the senior managers were entitled to express concerns and 'speak plainly and directly' – or, as the witnesses described: to criticise, to raise their voices, and to belittle the staff working for them.

The judge found Mr Edsell a credible witness. Sometimes, the judge wrote, when men in the public eye give evidence, they enjoy making speeches. They are uncomfortable when confronted with a question not to their liking. But Mr Edsell, she insisted, suffered none of these flaws. He was a most impressive witness, and it was hard to conclude that he could have been anything other than a fair and decent manager, in control of his behaviour and sympathetic to his employees. I tried – as hard I could – to match her account to what she and I both saw in the witness box, but the task was beyond me.

The judge concluded that senior managers did not speak to my client in a way that amounted to a breach of the implied term of mutual trust and confidence. It followed that the dismissal must have been fair.

Gracious as ever, even in a harsh and unmerited defeat, Mr Falk wrote, 'While the decision is clearly disappointing, I don't regret bringing the claim.'

I sat silently at my desk, thinking of him.

CHAPTER 4

March: Law as the virus arrives

By March 2020, the coronavirus had reached Italy. Seb, the barrister with whom I share a room in chambers, said he'd seen a sign in Boots instructing customers to purchase no more than a single bottle of hand sanitiser. I took my youngest son to his primary school and on the way there we passed half a dozen children, wiping their hands before they went in to class. The housing barristers in my chambers held our monthly meeting. 'Everything will close', one colleague predicted, 'schools, courts . . .' But nothing did.

For a brief and vertiginous moment, life continued much as normal. The streets of London were busy, and the museums full of people. I went to court, and I listened while a judge ordered, 'By the 16th of this month, the claimant will decide whether disability is still contested, and it shall write to the defendant . . .' Would they? Would there still be any solicitors in the office who could send the letter? 'By the 30th, the parties will jointly instruct a consultant to report on the issue of disability status.' I found myself thinking: *We're at the top of a precipice and the drop is so far, can't you see it?*

I did not object to the calmness. It was essential, enduring – I was in awe of it. It was the steadfastness which made life possible.

Ten years ago, when I was training to be a barrister, I spent my weekends at the College of Law. I remember the lecturer on our course. She was younger than I was and had a silver ring threaded through her nose. One morning she began, 'What's your superpower?'

The 12 of us in the room shook ourselves awake.

'Come on guys, what's your superpower?'

None of us answered.

'Your superpower is – you're *persuasive.*'

It sounds fantastic, doesn't it? But you can only be a successful barrister if the person in front of you is willing to be persuaded. And for all the gifts any barrister brings, our sense of eloquence, or the care with which we scour our case papers and find a compelling detail – there's always someone else at the other end of the table, trying with equal diligence and ingenuity to find the best point for *their* client.

Prime Minister Boris Johnson gave a press conference on 5 March. It was the same day as the country's first death from COVID-19. He said, 'The scientists have done a very good job of explaining to us what the risks are, and they are really quite small.'

The plan, the government's Chief Scientific Adviser, Sir Patrick Vallance, explained, was to accumulate infections in the younger generation while keeping older and vulnerable citizens safe. As soon as a significant proportion of the population had suffered and over-come the disease, we would acquire 'herd immunity'. If a few us – those best equipped to survive the disease – could arrange our lives so as to be infected first, then everyone else would be safe.

I waited in my chambers, preparing for a hearing in the case of Blessing Musona, a tenant who had lived in her home for 30 years. There was mould growing on the walls and a boiler which for 18 months had been decommissioned, with a sticker on its side saying, 'Do not use'. The lack of a heater explained why the damp was so bad. Ms Musona's health had suffered, she used to work in shops but now found the work exhausting. She was a single mother and her family's strong shield. But, because of the 'bedroom tax',[1] she had a shortfall between her rent and her housing benefit of £120 per month.

The idea of the tax is as follows. Where people are occupying a flat which has more bedrooms than the family use, they should swap it for a smaller home. Suppose a couple obtain a flat because they and their child are in need. Twenty years later, the child moves out. It is only right for the couple to downsize, otherwise homes are kept in tenants' hands which could be let to larger and more needy families.

However, this neutral-seeming provision contained three malign calculations.

The first was the assumption that it is appropriate to force working-class people to move when their children left home, that is, in circumstances where middle-class people would not. For one of the unacknowledged truths about Britain is that we have never been in greater housing affluence than we are now. Between 1971 and 2007, the population of Britain increased from 54.3 million

1   Housing Benefit Regulations 2006 SI No 213 reg B13, as amended.

to 59.2 million, or by around nine per cent. During the same time, the number of homes rose from 18.6 million to 24.4 million, or 31 percent. The reason why we are still 'room poor' despite this significant rise in available space, is that while the average household had three people living in it in 1971, by 2007 it was only two-and-a-half people.[2] This fact, multiplied across tens of millions of individuals, has more than offset the absolute increase in the number of homes. I am by no means suggesting that owner-occupiers with spare bedrooms should be driven from their houses. I am simply pointing out the double-standard under which the government did nothing to solve this problem of under-occupation, did nothing to encourage owners to share their homes, but took steps to evict poorer families.

The second piece of malice was in the estimation of how many rooms a family might reasonably occupy. Local authorities apply the bedroom tax narrowly, by looking at how a property is recorded on their databases, and if it has ever been designated as a two- or three-bedroom home, that is how they will treat it, even where the spare bedroom is tiny, and even where the family has given it a new use. If a married couple share a bedroom, they are allowed a single bedroom. One of the longest-running bedroom tax cases concerned a couple where the wife had spina bifida and needed a special bed with a wheelchair beside it. Doctors refused to allow the husband to share his wife's bed, and he could not sleep on the floor: there had to be enough space for him and for nurses to attend to the wife's needs. The family rented a two-bedroom house. The council deemed them to be under-occupying. The government defended the refusal to pay full housing benefit through repeated hearings – even as far as the Supreme Court (where it won).[3] The hundreds of thousands it ended up paying in legal costs was a mere drop in the ocean compared to the millions it saved in payments to impoverished families.

The third piece of cruelty was the assumption that there is somewhere else for the family to move to. The bedroom tax works by reducing a tenant's housing benefit to the point where they are compelled to move. But if moving is impossible, then all that remains is the deliberate insistence that the poor should be forced to go hungry or lose their homes.

My client Blessing was the tenant of one of Britain's largest housing associations. Her housing officer told her that if the flat

---

2   D Renton, 'Housing: as it is, and as it might be', *International Socialism*, Issue 134, 27 March 2012.

3   *R (Carmichael and Rourke and others) v Secretary of State for Work and Pensions* [2016] UKSC 58.

remained in any debt at all, the landlord would refuse to authorise a move. She asked about home swapping or mutual exchange – but both schemes were closed to her. It was simple, the landlord said – she should be evicted, and the council would house her. Except that when people like Blessing do approach the council, it refuses to house them. The council says that by failing to pay the rent she has made herself intentionally homeless. If she is evicted, she will be street homeless.

I prepared for the hearing. Blessing was asking the court to stay her eviction. The disrepair was so bad that most judges would grant an adjournment. The compensation for 18 months without a heater might be of the order of £4,000 or £5,000. If that was set against her arrears, they would be reduced to a manageable level, perhaps to nothing. She also had a second advantage – the other side were legally represented, and I was sure their lawyers would want to be in court during the pandemic as little as I did. But the only way to get the hearing adjourned was by the other side's consent. The day before she was due in court, at 10am, Blessing's solicitor phoned the other side asking for an adjournment. She called again at 11am, at 12pm, at 1pm. At 4.59pm they called her back – and agreed to stay it.

My next hearing took place in the Central London County Court within the Royal Courts of Justice. It rained as I walked to court; the water falling in thick flakes, white as snow. They hovered in the air, before melting on contact with the ground. You will probably have seen the main entrance to the Royal Courts of Justice on television, since most High Court and all Court of Appeal cases are heard here. Twin metal barricades stand at the building's front, and most days of the week some news item features a picture of protesters standing there, holding their placards and banners. But, as well as the front entrance, there is also a back way through which lawyers often walk. That is the path I followed, hiding from the rain, strolling through the quiet Victorian corridors, passing the marble statues of the judges from a century ago.

The papers for the hearing amounted to barely two dozen pages. I was due to represent Ms Silver, a woman in her mid-50s who had lived in her home for 20 years. She was an agency nurse, and her blue scrubs poked out from beneath a black waterproof coat. She told me she worked in end-of-life care, and as she explained her job, I found myself distracted, not listening to the words she said but the way she spoke them. She was calm, blissfully so. I felt warmer, happier in her presence, and I was the one who was meant to be helping her.

We had half an hour before the hearing was due to start and I asked her about her family. Her son was seven years old. Ms Silver dropped him off at breakfast club on the way to court. 'He's very quiet', she told me. 'Every day, when I wake him up, I say good morning to him, and I have to remind him to answer me back.'

We talked about her husband, who was a Muslim. Ms Silver was a Christian. He travelled round the country looking for work, sending back what money he could – it wasn't much.

The reason Ms Silver was behind with her rent was that five years ago she suffered a series of delays in renewing her registration as a nurse. The body that handles registrations needed her employers to write confirming she worked for them. But her trust managers would not, no matter how many times Ms Silver asked. They were always too busy. There was always some crisis which had to be dealt with first. Ms Silver's work situation was not important to them. Days became weeks, and in the end Ms Silver went six months without registration. During that time, she was unable to work. She tried to keep up with her rent, and the benefits advisers told her that if she declared herself self-employed and set up a part-time business she would receive as much benefits as before. She did what they suggested, but it did not work: her benefits were not paid, and she fell behind with her rent. On the days when she was not phoning her employer and chasing them for the missing letter, she tried to establish an online business selling jewellery. But that work brought hardly any money in. Eventually, the housing association took her to court and obtained a suspended possession order.

Ms Silver was ordered to pay the rent every week plus a further £10 towards her arrears. If she did, she could stay. Should she default at any time, however, the landlord could ask the court to send in bailiffs. And, unless she acted and applied to the court to suspend the eviction, the bailiffs would remove her. A suspended possession order leaves you stuck, perhaps for years, on the verge of eviction. At our hearing, the landlord was seeking to evict her.

'It isn't fair', Ms Silver said, her eyes red with worry. 'I've been paying my rent. Perhaps I missed one or two payments, but that's all. The walls are covered in mould, I've had so many leaks. But I'm the one that gets in trouble – never them.'

After 2015, Ms Silver was able to persuade the nursing bodies to accept her registration. After that she was in work, and she paid her rent every week without fail, as well as the £10 per week towards the arrears that the court had ordered her to pay. For two years, in fact, she paid her rent plus £20 every week, so that through 2016 and 2017 her arrears came down much more quickly even than the court ordered. Unfortunately, in 2018, she suffered a further setback. She showed me a letter from her GP, and it described a bursa in her left foot. Ms Silver explained that it was a cavity in a joint. She was prescribed with painkillers. In her job, she was required to work 12-hour shifts, standing up all the time. The injury prevented her from working the hours she used to. Ms Silver was signed off sick and fell behind on her rent, and by the end of 2018 the arrears were every bit as high as they had been when the previous court order had been made. By that point, Ms Silver knew her home was at risk again.

But if 2018 was a bad year, 2019 went much better. Ms Silver learned to cope with the injury. She worked 40-hour weeks and managed to sustain them. As a result, she was back on top of her rent. She received some housing benefit, although (since she was working) there was a shortfall between her benefit and her income. She paid the shortfall, and more. She set up a standing order to pay the shortfall plus £30 a week. In 2019, she reduced her arrears by £2,000 altogether. Then, at the end of the year, although Ms Silver was doing all that any judge would ask, the landlord applied for a bailiff's date and her eviction.

That was the part which confused me. Why punish a tenant when they are doing all you have asked of them? I asked, 'Did you upset your housing officer?'

'I didn't', Ms Silver said. 'I promise you, I didn't.'

Ten minutes before the hearing was due to begin, Ms Silver asked, as tenants so often do, 'Will I win?'

I told her that her landlord must have hundreds of tenants in arrears by £5,000 or more. In most of those cases, the rent situation was getting worse. Hers was a unique case. Of all the cases the judge might see in a week, there were probably only one in a hundred where the rent arrears were coming down as fast as Ms Silver was reducing hers.

As we were about to be called on, the housing officer introduced himself. He was in his 20s with a puffa jacket. He was late. He smiled awkwardly at Ms Silver. He saw me in my suit; he seemed to shrink a little. He made his face settle, and said, 'I can save you having to make a speech; we agree to suspend the eviction.'

I thought of the tears in my client's eyes, the distress it had caused her coming to court, when she had been paying her rent. The housing officer rushed on, doing his best to explain. He told Ms Silver, 'Everything in the office is computer-operated. You get a letter telling you about arrears, and it isn't like a person wrote you that letter. That's just how it is.'

There were barely seconds now before the judge would hear us, and I wanted to win some concession – to justify the morning Ms Silver had lost when she could have been at work. I asked the housing officer to agree that from then on rather than the shortfall plus £30 a week, Ms Silver could pay just £10.

The housing officer shrugged. 'Why not?' For him, it was nothing. For Ms Silver it was the difference between two meals a day and three.

I drafted an order in the hope that the judge would approve it.

In the corridor, the housing officer took the seat beside Ms Silver. Shyly, as if addressing his aunt at some family gathering, he asked her if she liked living in London. 'I do', she told him. 'I've been here long enough, haven't I?'

I told her that the standing order would work for now. But she would need to pay more if her hours at work increased (which would mean that her housing benefit would be reduced), or when the rent was put up, probably in the spring.

I told her she needed to speak to her housing officer every three months, just to make sure that the payments were going in.

The housing officer corrected me, 'Every month.'

'Every month', Ms Silver echoed.

Such an outcome is not unusual. This is how it goes, when rent arrears cases end well. After you have been a barrister for a while, you would much rather the housing officer liked your client. Most housing officers originally chose their profession because they believed it was an opportunity to do their best for vulnerable tenants. And if, in their working life, they found themselves sending tenants to court in much greater number than their younger selves would have chosen – that was the consequence of larger social processes than they control. It was because the housing associations are huge private businesses far-removed from their tenants. It was because the housing associations wanted to grow, wanted to house more people than they did, and borrowed from the banks at commercial interest rates in order to build those homes. It was because senior managers put pressure on junior managers and then on workers in the frontlines, setting targets, demanding they evict a portion of their tenants.

When you meet a housing officer and assert your greater knowledge of the law and browbeat them into conceding, that housing officer will remember you afterwards. Next time your client makes a mistake, the housing officer will be looking for an excuse to return your client's case to court. They will spend whatever money it takes to ensure they win, sending a solicitor rather than a housing officer, a barrister rather than a solicitor, or if need be the most experienced and expensive landlord barrister they can find. As good as any tenant barrister thinks they are, there is always someone else who will fight harder and nastier than them.

If you address the housing officer by their name, if you treat them as a person who is doing their best, they will remember you after the hearing has ended. If you help them to see the efforts that your client has been taking in unforgiving circumstances to prioritise the rent, they will think the better of your client afterwards. The time you spend at court is such a small part of your client's life. Any goodwill you can earn for your client will help to protect them once you have gone.

On 10 March, England's Chief Medical Officer (CMO) Professor Chris Whitty told journalists that the country was in a situation of extreme risk, 'where everybody who has even minor respiratory tract infections or a fever should be self-isolating for seven days'. That was the plan, but the laws to give it effect still remained to be written. A lockdown would start soon, but what we would do in it remained vague. I sat in court and I watched a landlord's representative demand immediate possession against a tenant in her mid-40s, who was in rent arrears by £2,000. Their barrister made several points, some good, some bad, and spoke for about 20 minutes altogether. Then, it was my turn, and all I said was, 'The tenant has chronic obstructive pulmonary disease, and you want her to be street homeless, today, with all that's going on outside?'

The judge signalled he was ready to give his judgment.

I and the claimant's counsel bent our heads down. We were staring at our blue books, with our pens ready. We were waiting to record the judge's decision, not just whether the tenant could stay or had to leave, but his reasons for the decision.

'No', the judge said.

'No?' The landlord's barrister asked.

'No', the judge told them.

It was the shortest judgment I have ever heard.

In the courtroom outside, my client asked me what had happened.

'You won', I told her.

On 12 March, the Prime Minister gave another press conference. He was less optimistic than he had been before: 'This is the worst public health crisis for a generation . . . many more families are going to lose loved ones before their time.' I was in my late 40s, and I could not have been the only middle-aged person drawing up a private list. My mother was in her early 70s, my aunt was older still, while my father was almost 90. I found myself phoning them every evening – speaking to them more often and longer than in years.

On 17 March, the Lord Chief Justice announced: 'Emergency legislation is being drafted which is likely to contain clauses that expand the powers in criminal courts to use technology in a wider range of hearings.'

The same day, the nearest thing barristers have to a trade union, the Bar Council, argued for all jury trials to be stayed: 'All those involved in court proceedings, be they barristers, witnesses, defendants, jurors or members of the public (let alone staff and judges) should not be expected to attend court, whilst the rest of the country is very strongly urged to work from home.' The Lord Chief Justice put a halt to all new Crown Court trials which were likely to last more than three days. The guidance left open whether civil hearings were to proceed.

I was due to catch a train to Leeds the next morning. I was going to represent a worker whose employer required them to speak English at all times in the workplace. The employee said the practice was discriminatory, and I was preparing for the hearing when my phone rang. I recognised the phone number. It was a familiar adversary, Mr Bowls.

'Sorry to bother you', he said. 'But my solicitor's been playing up. She wants to know how we're going to practise social distancing. She's 68, you see.' (Bowls was no younger.) 'It's not the court, it's the conference rooms . . .'

The way the Leeds Employment Tribunal has been designed is that each party has their own designated room, where they wait for the case to start. If the case went ahead, we were likely to spend most of the morning in those small, crowded rooms, with more people in each than there were chairs to accommodate them.

'My sainted employer has only called nine witnesses, hasn't he?' Bowls gave out a deep sigh and said, 'One of them's already in self-isolation. And the others, well, they're every bit as worried as the solicitor.'

'I don't know', I told him. 'It seems to me the government wants us to keep our hearings going, come what may.'

'You're right, they're buggers. But the bundle is a thousand pages. Seventeen witnesses, we'll never get through the hearing in four days.'

'Then ask the judge', I told him.

'Look', Bowls said, firmly, 'I don't like to do this. But I've had an awful cold these past few days.' He coughed at me, a shiver in his throat.

He coughed a second time. 'My doctor isn't even giving appointments.'

My resolve broke. 'I'll see what I can do.'

Stories circulated on social media, of tenants – even doctors and nurses – threatened with the loss of their home. The Labour Party called on the Conservative government to introduce a stay on evictions. On 18 March, the government announced protection for renters: no new possession claims were to be issued. But for days, the announcement remained nothing more than a press release. When a draft Coronavirus Bill was published, the original text made no mention of these supposed protections. Meanwhile, new claims were issued every day, new hearings placed in my diary. The legislation provided that where a landlord wished to serve a notice on their tenant telling them to leave, they were required to wait for an additional month before starting proceedings – but it did nothing to protect people who were already in the middle of cases which would continue unaffected.

The reason that legislation was needed was that people in part-time jobs were being dismissed, self-employed contracts were being cancelled, zero-hours staff were being given no hours to work. All these workers were faced with the immediate prospect of massive debt. Simply saying that for an extra month or longer there would be no possession claims did not address that build-up of arrears – rather it created the conditions for landlords to bring cases to court in the future, demanding that the tenants leave and were subject to court judgments, leaving them in debt. What we needed was some mechanism to write off the arrears that had accrued, both under coronavirus and under the years of austerity which preceded it.

While the government decided whether or how to introduce this stay on new proceedings, cases continued to be listed. One of my solicitors, Angus, was called in to court for the possession list at Clerkenwell and Shoreditch, where 37 cases had been listed for possession in a morning. A barrister in my chambers was stuck for a day at Central London County Court, where the toilets lacked hot water, soap or hand towels.

The Housing Law Practitioners Association (HLPA) wrote to His Honour Judge Luba QC, the Designated Circuit Judge for the London

Civil Courts, asking him what he proposed should happen to housing claims. He answered, explaining that he had written to all his county courts, asking them to stop block-listing possession cases. On 23 March, the Lord Chief Justice determined that hearings requiring the physical presence of parties should take place only if a remote hearing was impossible. The situation remained utterly vague in relation to the large number of housing tenants who were brought to court for possession hearings and had no representation. Most had never been in court before. Many were poor, or disabled, or had a very poor sense of their rights. How could they have access to the duty solicitor scheme, when it was a term of that scheme that duty advice could only be given face-to-face?

Meanwhile, the question remained unanswered of what should be done for the large number of employees who were made redundant by their employers. On 20 March, Chancellor of the Exchequer Rishi Sunak had promised to underwrite 80 per cent of the wages of any employee threatened with redundancy. At first sight, this furlough scheme seemed a breakthrough, and the Trades Union Congress (TUC) General Secretary Frances O'Grady tweeted her praise for the announcement.

On social media, the mutual aid groups which had sprung up during the coronavirus crisis were overwhelmed by questions. Was there any way, people asked, to force the employer to offer the furlough? 'No', I had to answer. Was there any way to claim the money directly? Again, 'no'. Many employers had plainly decided that the scheme was simply more trouble than it was worth and made redundancies, or simply offered no work to zero-hour contract workers.

A civil servant with an autoimmune deficiency told me her employer was refusing to allow her to work from home. I helped her to draft a grievance letter, and within minutes the employer conceded. A tenant wrote. He was due to move to a new house and was terrified that London would be reduced to lockdown with the result that he was trapped paying rent on two properties at once. I suggested he write to the landlord and bring the move forward. To the tenant's surprise, the landlord agreed.

I was approached by a teacher from a nursery school whose employer had closed its premises, but the outraged parents complained. The parents, many of whom were well-paid workers in the City, were offended by the suggestion that they would have to combine caring for their children with holding down full-time jobs. As bankers, they insisted, they were keyworkers. Hadn't the government insisted that schools should be kept open for keyworkers? The staff were ordered by the school to work, in effect, as nannies for the richest and most demanding parents, which would be demeaning enough if the employer had not added injury to insult by requiring them work in a different banker's home every day of the week, maximising their risk of infection. The teacher wanted my advice as to whether she could walk out of work and still be paid her wages? I pointed her cautiously in the direction of our laws permitting a worker to leave the workplace in response to a health and safety emergency.[4]

A new mother had been given an eviction date by her housing association. What could she do? Or, more accurately, what could the friend who had connected us do while the mother was self-isolating? I encouraged the tenant to telephone the court and obtain from them an N244 form, the document you needed to use when requesting a stay of an eviction. Miraculously, her call was answered by someone still working in the county court. The worker agreed that, while the tenant was self-isolating, she could receive the N244 form by email. They put her case before a judge, who had to decide whether to list it for a hearing. While her situation remained uncertain, the housing association announced that all its evictions were halted.

The decision was a welcome climb-down – but how many landlords in the private sector, I found myself wondering, had shown an equal generosity?

On 23 March, Prime Minister Boris Johnson spoke again to the nation to announce a national lockdown beginning on 26 March. Travelling to and from work was permitted, but only where it was 'absolutely necessary and cannot be done from home'. Lawyers were inundated with requests for clarification. When Johnson said work from an office was permitted if necessary – did he mean that the work must be necessary or that the journey was necessary? We opened our collective hands and shook our collective heads. A government press release explained that travel to work was permitted, where work 'absolutely cannot' be done from home. Next, a tweet from the Department for Business, Energy and Industrial Strategy said it was the work not the journey which must be essential: go in, only if you were a keyworker.

London in the lockdown was cold. The city had become, for the moment, a world of manual workers. Every person apart from me

---

4 Employment Rights Act 1996 s44.

was wearing a yellow or an orange bib. I cycled past the building site at King's Cross. The employers were Keir and Bam: two of the companies who were exposed 10 years ago for using a corporate blacklist to prevent trade unionists from obtaining jobs with them. Managers were everywhere, in beanie hats and suits, carrying clipboards. There was no pretence of social distancing. Workers stood inches apart as foremen delivered site instructions. The din of hammers, of pipes, was overwhelming.

If any of those workers were going to be ill in two or three weeks' time, the companies would not pay them in their absence. This was not about essential services, the capital already had a surfeit of unused office buildings. Nor would I criticise the workers for coming in. They were at work because the employers refused to give their staff paid leave during the pandemic, and the government had sided with the bosses.

On the streets, a middle-aged man spoke into his mobile phone: 'Flu's just as bad . . .' he insisted before launching an explanation of the healing powers of Earl Grey tea. The shelves of the Tesco's opposite my chambers had been stripped bare of food. Only a single packet of red and white quinoa remained. A sign instructed shoppers to keep two metres apart; but I was the only person in the store to read it.

As I cycled back to chambers, late in the afternoon, the din of the building work had subsided. An unkindness of ravens had settled in Lincoln's Inn Fields. The birds cawed, dominating the newly empty space.

One of the lessons of the pandemic crisis was the connectedness of employment and housing. Early in the lockdown, it became clear that millions of workers were employed on contracts which their employers regarded as impermanent and capable of being terminated at will. Many employers declared themselves insolvent; while others, even though they continued to trade, simply opted out of all employment protections. Among the companies to close were payday lenders such as CashOnGo Ltd and Uncle Buck, and rent-to-own providers such as BrightHouse. It was another small detail making life harder for the poorest people in Britain. Tens of thousands of people had outstanding complaints about the affordability of credit agreements – with the collapse of these businesses, any prospect of compensation disappeared.

Around two million people made universal credit claims in the first six weeks of the lockdown. (Some of those claims will have been made by people suffering from reduced hours at work, not all will have been dismissals.) For each of those dismissed, the loss of employment was a disaster: they had less money; but they were still obliged to pay all their existing debts.

Research conducted by Britain's 187 district councils estimated that before the lockdown, half a million private sector tenants were paying over half their income in rent.[5]

A survey by HouseMark found that social housing tenants were also in danger: total social housing debt, it estimated, rose by £100 million more in the first six weeks of the lockdown than in previous years, with total rental income falling by three percent in a month.[6]

The threat posed by COVID-19 was not limited to renters, whether in the private or the social housing sectors. It was hard to imagine anything that would be of greater destructive effect to the legitimacy of a modern-day British government than if millions of people who held their home by mortgages were to fall months behind with the payments and have their homes repossessed. Behind the scenes, a subtle prioritisation of support was taking place. Homeowners were awarded the greatest protection. The Chancellor announced a three-month mortgage holiday. This was backed up by guidance from the Financial Conduct Authority (FCA). The guidance said that where banks or building societies insisted on requiring mortgage payments, they were likely to suffer regulatory action, including the removal of their own right to trade.

By contrast, support for tenants was partial and grudging. No minister suggested that they should be granted rent holidays. Still less was there any proposal of regulatory action being taken against landlords using the excuse of coronavirus to make tenants homeless.

Finally, unwillingly, and only after criticisms in the press and parliament, the government grudgingly conceded a three-month stay on all possession proceedings. From 27 March, there would be no new possession orders, no eviction hearings.

I was contacted by a roofer in his 40s, Darren Phipps, who posted on social media a short clip showing 20 building workers at the start of their shift, crowded around a table without the merest pretence of social distancing. The video opened with the sight of a door on which, for less than a second, you could see the main contractor's name.

5   M Ford, 'Councils warn of "avalanche of evictions"', Localgov, 21 August 2020; www.localgov.co.uk/Councils-warn-of-avalanche-of-evictions/50968.

6   N Barker, 'Social housing rent arrears up £100m since coronavirus outbreak', *Inside Housing*, 28 May 2020.

When the company found out what he had done, Darren was dismissed. By posting the clip he was said to have brought his employer into disrepute. He was a skilled electrician and had worked at the company for over a year. The day after Darren's dismissal, the site on which he was working closed. Its normal work conditions were incompatible with the government's advice to self-isolate.

I encouraged Darren to take the first steps towards issuing a claim for unfair dismissal. That meant filling in an online 'early conciliation' form with the Advisory, Conciliation and Arbitration Service (ACAS). He was not yet a member of a union, and I urged him to join one. He needed to have someone (ideally, a union; but, if not, a solicitor) writing to his employer and insisting on his immediate reinstatement.

One of the difficulties Darren faced was that the government's advice to unemployed workers was to claim for universal credit. But the application process required workers to complete an online form to validate their identity. Darren logged on at 4pm in the afternoon. At that point, there were 44,000 applications waiting in a queue. The following morning the number had dropped to 18,000. 'As soon as I reach zero', he said, 'I'll call.'

Hours passed. I was in contact with others who had also been recently dismissed. A woman who worked in pub catering had been given notice. She asked her landlord for a rent holiday and he refused. She joined the universal credit queue the day after Darren and in that time the waiting list swelled to 138,047 people.

CHAPTER 5

April–May: At home, being watched

By the start of April 2020, all possession claims had been stayed. This was a victory for the renters' unions, the tenants' associations, for Jeremy Corbyn, Leader of the Labour Party and Leader of the Opposition, who had raised the problems with the government's response in his final Prime Minister's Questions, and for all the people who criticised the government in the press and online.

As a self-employed barrister, you might expect me to regret the change. It left me with nothing to do. In principle, no steps should or could be taken in proceedings without the court's permission: lawyers could not assemble bundles or agree witness statements or doing anything that might bring a case closer to its conclusion, except by the court's consent. If I was not working, I was not earning.

In truth, I was delighted. For my clients, the stay meant security. For me, it meant I could stay at home and relax with my family. The delay that barristers experience between work and payment by solicitors can run to several years. It is a legacy of those past times when only those with independent wealth could afford to practise at the bar, and agreements between barristers and solicitors were unenforceable. The delay shielded us through the crisis, meaning that the revenue of old work continued to come in, deferring to the future the hit to our income.

The sun burst through the slats of the windows of our spare room. Work continued, but it was a different sort of activity. Instead of representing people at court, I found myself attending remote meetings: of my chambers' housing team, of the executive of the Housing Law Practitioners Association (HLPA). The latter saw the best attended meeting we'd had in years. I joined a Facebook group, the Workforce Coronavirus Support Group. Ten thousand people signed up in its first week, and we had ambitious plans for a handbook of workers' rights under the pandemic. At its first online meeting, attended by some 150 or so people, earnest discussions took place as to whether it was possible for large numbers of workers to walk off their jobs, invoking the protection of health and safety law and in particular section 44 of the Employment Rights Act 1996 which permits such action in response to serious and imminent danger. I addressed webinars for disabled workers, discussing how the same section might assist workers who had been sent home and whose managers demanded a rapid escalation in their workload, so much so that the worker's health was endangered.

The rules of our lockdown were contained principally in the Coronavirus Act 2020 which gave constables and various other people powers to fine those suspected of being infected with the disease when they refused to comply with a direction. The Health Protection (Coronavirus, Restrictions) (England) Regulations 2020 SI No 350 prohibited people from leaving their homes, save where they had a reasonable excuse. The regulations went on to provide a list of reasonable excuses which would allow a person to leave their home: shopping for food or medicines, or to obtain money, to obtain medical assistance, and so on. These restrictions on movement applied to everyone, whether they were suspected of carrying the disease or not.

Stories began to reach the press of over-zealous enforcement of the lockdown rules. In Derbyshire, the police used drones to photograph walkers heading out into the hills. They circulated a short film shaming the miscreants, and two million people watched it. The footage began in a rural carpark: 'These vehicles should not be here.' It proceeded to show an elderly couple, stooped over, walking their dog slowly over a road. 'Not essential', the film insisted. Other walkers were also filmed: 'Going for a walk, miles from home: not essential.' County police forces boasted of issuing three dozen enforcement notices every day. Among the problems with this approach were that it had drifted beyond anything in the regulations. The Derbyshire walkers were presented to the public as people who were breaking the law when they were doing nothing of the sort. The regulations permitted people to leave their home 'to take exercise either alone or with other members of their household'. Nothing in the regulations said that such exercise must be essential; or that there was anything wrong in taking your exercise in an empty space far from your home. Mere common sense suggested that walking in the unoccupied Peak District would be rather safer for someone who lived in Manchester or Sheffield than exercising in a busy urban park. Police in Newcastle fined a woman £660 for loitering at Newcastle Central station. Days later, the conviction was rescinded after it turned out that the police, a prosecutor and a district judge had all proceeded without reading what the law said and checking whether there was any such crime.

They were not the only instances of people misunderstanding the rules. I was asked to advise a hospital administrator in Newport after her employer instructed her to come in to work. She had a disabled child who had been taken out of school when the pandemic began, and the administrator's duties could be done from home. I sent her the regulations and explained how they made it a criminal offence for anyone to travel to work, should it be possible for them to work from home. By ordering her into work, I advised, her employer was making itself complicit in a criminal offence.

A child chalked a rainbow on the pavement outside our house: 'NHS'. The residents of our estate gathered at their doors and balconies, applauding health and care workers, sharing with one another the insistence that we were going to survive the crisis.

Prime Minister Boris Johnson's spokesman was asked whether he would join in the public display of support for health and care workers. His spokesman said Johnson 'might'. Then, with his usual insistence on grabbing every opportunity for publicity that came his way, our Prime Minister became an enthusiast for these collective moments, insisting on being photographed clapping.

On 5 April, the BBC reported that Johnson had been showing symptoms of COVID-19 for 10 days and intended to stay overnight at hospital. Junior ministers insisted that the measure was an act of extreme caution. They told us he was leading the country from his bed. He was doing well, they said. He was improving. On 7 April, we were told he had been moved into intensive care and was receiving oxygen treatment.

The ban on possession proceedings did not extend to other housing cases. These included, principally, hearings where the landlord complained of anti-social behaviour by the tenant. In such cases, the landlord was not seeking to remove the tenant from their home, or not yet. But while the tenants could remain living there, the landlord sought an order from the court: an injunction restricting their behaviour. I represented tenants in a series of these cases.

Judges tend to make such orders whenever the landlords ask them to. As they see it, the landlord is entitled to require some minimum behaviour from people living near one another. It is already a term of most tenancy agreements that a tenant will not cause nuisance to their neighbours. All an injunction does is require the tenant to abide by something which is already part of the tenancy agreement. But in making the order, the court changes the relationship between the tenant and the landlord, giving the power to the latter to demand that the tenant is imprisoned if they are unwilling or incapable of complying with the court's order.

Once you have been a barrister for any length of time, you seem to ascend invisibly to a second rank. You are no longer a 'baby' barrister. You are a serious opponent to be spoken to politely outside court. The temptation is to find yourself agreeing with much that landlords ask for. Not the immediate possession of your client's home, of course, the other side's barrister would not be so crude as to expect everything all at once; but perhaps a suspended possession order. In injunction cases a tenant's barrister might be asked to accept not a broad exclusion order, prohibiting your client from returning to their home. But perhaps something narrower, maybe just an order preventing them from carrying out disturbances in their flat. Your opponent might tell you that the judge is going to order this, whether you agree or not. And the judge probably will. The unspoken message is that if you argue against the injunction, you risk losing face with a judge. But the last concern of tenant's representative should be their own pride.

   The historian and peace campaigner EP Thompson once wrote that any radical 'Must, to survive as an unassimilated socialist in this infinitely assimilative culture, put oneself into a school of awkwardness. One must make one's sensibility all knobbly – all knees and elbows of susceptibility and refusal'.[1] This is the spirit in which any lawyer should advise tenants in anti-social behaviour cases. In much of our daily practice, the risk to our clients is limited: argue a claim for repairing works badly and the tenant will still get something, just fewer works than are needed, done more slowly than they should have been. If you do wrong in an anti-social behaviour injunction, if you represent your client fearfully – they will lose their freedom.

Outside, the days were long and bright – but inside it was cramped and dark. Small moments of change became an intense pleasure: a spoon of marmalade with my breakfast porridge, the sharp lines left by planes in the clouds which I could see through my back window: razor cuts through a silk background. It felt strange to fight my cases

---

1   C Hill, 'From the awkward school', *Guardian*, 30 August 1993.

online stooped over a computer, listening by telephone or video-link to a judge's indistinct questions.

My first hearing in weeks took place by telephone in the County Court at Bromley. Six years ago, the housing association granted a tenancy to Mr and Mrs Curlew, and now they wanted an injunction to compel the parents to restrict anti-social behaviour by the Curlews' children, Jade and Geoff. Both faced multiple allegations of wrongdoing but, by the time the case came to court, the frequency of complaints had reduced to just a single theft in the last year, a pair of boxing gloves from a gym. The gym's owner had asked for no action to be taken.

I spoke to Mr Curlew and his solicitor. His solicitor had told me about the tattoo on his arm, 'Palace till I die'. I remembered a particularly grisly match between my own favourite team and his, an FA cup semi-final which Crystal Palace won. I was listening through the radio my of parents' car. Distracted, I drove it into a concrete bollard.

Geoff explained to his father the options (video on and off, mute) which were available on his phone. But how was Mr Curlew supposed to send messages to me if his only means of communication was through the same phone by which he would be listening?

Mr Curlew told me he would attend the hearing from his own car, with his mobile phone charging from its engine. At least, he would have peace and quiet there, he said.

The landlord's barrister Ms Makk was friendly enough when we spoke by Skype. She remembered me from the cases we had fought before the lockdown. 'David, isn't it? You must call me Jamila', she insisted. The lockdown had done nothing to alter her appearance. She was quite as happy, indeed as radiant, as she always was whenever she represented landlords. She repeated the little snakes of gossip that her own housing officer was no doubt using to justify the decision to bring the family to court. 'Your Mr Curlew is a serial complainer', she said. 'He's complained about us' (although he hadn't once in the more than a thousand pages of documents before the court), 'he's complained about the police. You'll be next', she warned.

She boasted about the number of tenants she had made subject to injunctions. 'Five last week', she told me, 'one every day of the week'.

'How did you get the hearings?' I asked – meaning, how was it even possible to be so busy, when the courts were on their own form of lockdown?

'It isn't difficult', she said. 'In my chambers, we know our landlords. We work hard, we win cases for them – and they look after us.'

The court sent out advice on how to conduct an online hearing. 'While a remote hearing may seem less formal than a conventional hearing', it began, before reminding participants of the need to approach the hearing in an appropriate spirit. 'All participants should ensure they are in a quiet room free from distractions and ensure that telephones are off or muted.' A sentence in bold warned us that recording a court hearing was a criminal offence.

There was an awkward moment before the hearing began when half a dozen people had joined the call but neither Ms Makk nor Mr Curlew. My opponent connected. She had been trying through her computer but could not get it to work and joined us via her mobile. The image was clear, but the sound cut in and out.

The last to join was my client. 'Hello', Mr Curlew said, 'hello, sorry I'm late, I couldn't–' before the clerk muted him. It was the last part he played in the hearing: although, of course, it was his family which was at stake, the future of his children.

The Curlews were not willing to agree to an injunction, so the case would have to go to a full hearing. The main task facing the judge was to decide how many days would be needed for the trial. His Honour Judge Pagnam asked each side's counsel for a flavour of the dispute.

The signal from Ms Makk's phone was poor: one word in four was lost, then one word in two, until Pagnam had to tell her that her audio had seized up altogether.

The judge's closing words addressed not the merits of the case but the suitability of conducting further hearings electronically. 'We've shown that it's possible', he said. 'These conditions are not ideal – but it's possible.'

The point the judge was raising is that for years, the senior judiciary, government ministers and civil servants had believed that the courts should go over from our present system of hearings in court buildings to one where most, or all, judicial decisions were made online. But this had previously been a long-term ambition. Under conditions of coronavirus, with judges and lawyers locked in our houses, the demand for this change became urgent.

One process which made online courts attractive was the greater availability of such technologies as smartphones, video conferencing software, etc. When supporters of online courts justify them, this is where they begin.

Yet the pressure driving the adoption of online courts was something else: the closure of courts and the sale of land. For roughly

30 years, governments of both left and right have been closing courts and using the capital generated by selling the land to pay for the annual costs of running a low-tax state. Between 1997 and 2009, Labour governments closed around one in five magistrates' courts and around one in ten of all county courts.

Between 2010 and 2019, this process of court closures accelerated, with 162 of 323 magistrates' courts closed, 90 out of 240 county courts, and 18 of 83 tribunal buildings. Valuable city centre land has been sold. However, the money raised by closures was relatively modest: just £224 million between 2010 and 2018.[2]

The effect of the closures has been to increase the distance between the parties and the court. When the Combined Court in Morpeth closed, for example, cases were transferred to Newcastle. Many tenants then faced a bus journey of up to an hour each way to reach the judge who would decide whether they could stay in their homes. The case for online courts was that by moving hearings online, litigants in person could get the same access to justice as before. There would still be hearings: unrepresented tenants would access them online. The benefit would be the more efficient use of a smaller number of expensive people: judges and court staff. These savings were being put before substantive justice.

During the lockdown, the Master of the Rolls, the President of the Queen's Bench Division and the Chancellor of the High Court issued a protocol to all judges: 'The current pandemic necessitates the use of remote hearings wherever possible.'

Mr Curlew's solicitor asked him what he made of the hearing. He did not complain about the way that his voice and image were switched off in order to save bandwidth. What annoyed him, rather, was that midway through the hearing Ms Makk had said that if they could not get my client's agreement to an injunction, they would switch to possession proceedings. The cold, indifferent, way in which she raised this possibility shocked Mr Curlew.

One of the loudest voices to be heard on the future of the court system was Richard Susskind, an academic at the University of Oxford, Gresham College and Strathclyde University; the Information Technology Adviser to the Lord Chief Justice; and chair of the of the Civil Justice Council's Advisory Group on Online Dispute Resolution.

2   O Bowcott, 'Court closures: sale of 126 premises raised just £34m, figures show', *Guardian*, 8 March 2018; G Cowie and G Sturge, 'Court closures and access to justice', House of Commons Library, Debate Pack Number CDP-0156, 18 June 2019, p4.

HM Courts and Tribunals Service established a website on which Susskind tracked the introduction of online courts outside the UK: in Australia, Brazil, Dubai, Holland, Kenya and many other jurisdictions. Professor Susskind argued that the use of technology was the only means to prevent coronavirus from destroying the legal system. In an opinion piece for the *Financial Times*, he wrote that 80 per cent of the country's court and tribunal caseload was now being handled remotely. In the same piece, Susskind wrote that 'most remote hearings have gone well over the past month'.[3]

Legal Twitter shared the story of a case in the Court of Protection, in which a decision had to be made about the long-term care needs of a vulnerable adult. The parties learned only the day before that the hearing would go ahead. The meeting was hosted on Skype for Business, preparations were made to ensure that the sound quality was good. Journalists were invited to attend. Despite some bandwidth difficulties, at the end of the case the barristers acting for the vulnerable adult declared it a success. In a widely read article, they wrote that 'judicial time was not wasted, nor was a sensitive and difficult case adjourned, possibly for months'. As lawyers, they argued, the process 'felt comfortable and familiar'. In the judgment itself, the judge struck a different tone, his pride in the technology mixed with a grim determination to continue: 'In the current national crisis, it must be expected that hearings will be conducted remotely in this way as a matter of routine practice.'

Less coverage was given to the experience of the man's daughter. It felt to her as if the lawyers spent such a long time congratulating themselves on their technical expertise that they lost sight of her father's needs. As Celia Kitzinger of the Transparency Project explained, the daughter became invisible to the court. Once her evidence was over, the other users closed off the video-link from her device. She could see the lawyers and hear them, but they could not see her. Lawyers constantly talked about her, not in a rude or denigrating fashion, but in the normal, insensitive way we too-often do, by putting her in the third person, referring to her father by his first name. They could not see the distress it was causing her to be the silent subject of legal proceedings. In her words, 'Skype took away from me the ability to look these people in the eyes – these people who have their opinions about my Dad and only knew him

---

3   R Susskind, 'Covid-19 shutdown shows virtual courts work better. Legal access improves and justices have not harrumphed at the change', *Financial Times*, 7 May 2020.

through third-hand notes. I wanted to look them in the eyes and make them hear the truth, but I was looking at a computer screen.'[4]

To justify our own existence, when almost everyone was locked at home, the courts had to be seen to stay open. The only way to achieve this was to hold hearings online. We had no choice but to get used to it.

As for anti-social behaviour injunctions,[5] they are a recent creation. They are successors to Anti-social Behavious Orders (ASBOs) which were pioneered by Tony Blair's New Labour government and intended to operate at the intersection of civil and criminal law. They are heard in the civil courts. The test in deciding whether an injunction should be granted is the less exacting civil test (in other words, on the balance of probabilities) rather than the criminal test (only if a judge or jury is sure). The subject matter of the injunction is also civil in another sense; it is behaviour which is not so bad that the state has outlawed it. In a typical injunction claim, the tenant is accused of slamming their door, or playing their music loudly, or walking loudly on the floor of their flat in such a way as to cause a disturbance to the tenant below. Our criminal laws do already prohibit nuisance in a public setting; but no government has ever sought to criminalise such behaviour in someone's own home.

Anti-social behaviour injunctions follow the laws of evidence of civil law. It is common for landlords to apply for an injunction without requiring a single witness who saw or heard any of this behaviour to attend court. The evidence is supplied on a hearsay basis, with tenants providing diary entries making vague and unanswerable allegations, 'On the 3rd, he played his music. On the 5th it was very loud . . .' and housing officers attend court only to say that these complaints were passed on to them. Where defendant lawyers demand an explanation for the witness's non-attendance, we are told in vague terms that the witness was distressed; and that, in those circumstances, they could not possibly be expected to attend. Some judges insist that they cannot make orders without direct evidence; others will authorise any proposed injunction, no matter how weak the evidence to support it.

These injunctions are in other ways criminal cases. Lawyers attend robed; these are almost the only hearings where I wear my wig

---

4   C. Kitzinger, 'Remote justice: a family perspective,' Transparency Project, 29 March 2020.

5   Anti-social Behaviour, Crime and Policing Act 2014 s1.

and gown. Legal aid is only available to solicitors to represent tenants if the firm has a criminal contract. If an order is breached, the tenant is imprisoned – a criminal sanction.

In my first six months as a barrister, I worked in criminal law. Several of my clients were threatened with ASBOs. (Since 2014, these orders have been renamed criminal behaviour orders (CBOs)).[6] There is not much difference between the old ASBOs and today's ASB injunctions, save that the former were heard in the magistrates' courts, and the latter are heard by a civil judge. Many ASBOs would have the effect of excluding a teenager from their own home. The police officers who sought those orders assumed that the families could house their children somewhere else, and the courts were willing to go along with them. They did not care what would happen to the teenagers after they were removed.

One case comes to mind: it was in my second week as a barrister. Five young men were accused of anti-social behaviour, the main allegations being that they had been smoking cannabis on their estate. The police repeatedly stopped and searched them, but nothing was ever found. In the absence of any charges or convictions, the police applied for ASBOs to exclude the youths from their homes. I represented three of the boys, including the skinniest and shortest of them, Atik, in a hearing on the top floor of Westminster Magistrates' Court. His bony appearance was down in part to the fact that he was barely eating. Sixteen years old, the repeated searches of his family's home had torn his mother's nerves to shreds. He was now sleeping rough and returned home only to get his clothes washed.

By about 3pm on the day of the hearing, I knew the day would end in defeat. The district judge had determined that interim ASBOs would be made. All that was left was to finalise the terms and serve them on the defendants.

During a short recess, I found myself at one end of the corridor, watching as something inexplicable happened to Atik. At first, he was standing normally talking to the other boys. Then, he appeared to be levitating in mid-air. *Don't be stupid,* I found myself thinking. *He can't fly.* Slowly the situation explained itself. As Atik had been waiting in the corridor, one of the police witnesses had attempted to grab him without warning. To which my client responded by kicking him – sending his own body upwards and out of the officer's grasp.

6   Anti-social Behaviour, Crime and Policing Act 2014 Part 2.

Atik was doing a surprisingly good job of defending himself. The officer shouted, Atik's mother screamed. While all this was going on, my first thought was to look for one of the other lawyers, to see if we could resolve this matter before things got even worse. I could not understand why the police had attacked my client, but I assumed they must have some sort of excuse. I needed someone more experienced to advise me. Yet I could hear doors closing all around me, as all the other barristers who had spent the morning in court found ways of absenting themselves from the fight.

I saw an officer lifting his truncheon, in preparation to strike Atik. Calmly, as if I knew exactly what I was doing, I lifted my client into the air. Then, before Atik could turn on me, I pushed him through the door of the nearest interview room. As the officer looked at me, his arm still hanging in the air, I motioned Atik's mother into the same room. I could see other officers approaching. Before they reached me, I forced myself into the room. I held the door with my shoulders as the officers tried to smash their way in.

After three or four more pushes from outside, everything stopped. Eventually a plainclothes officer knocked on the door. 'Mr Renton', he said, 'I don't know what happened outside, and neither do I care. But let me explain how this is going to end. Your client has failed to attend court on a previous occasion. My officers are in the process of arresting him. We shall now do that. We will hold him overnight in a police station and then tomorrow we shall release him to court, where he will have to explain his absence. Is that clear?'

'I'm sorry officer', I answered, 'but your men have no right to remove my client from a court case which is still ongoing. He's already in court. He's already before a judge. You've got no right to take him.'

We waited. If I left the room in which I had barricaded myself, I faced every prospect of being arrested for obstructing the police. I could not leave, but nor could I stay. The stand-off ended when the district judge's clerk agreed to put the dispute to the judge.

As I came back to court, the council's barrister contributed to my good mood by holding his hands in front of his face, as if he was a prisoner and they were bound in cuffs. He passed me a note with a picture of a cake, and a file being hidden inside.

The judge did her best to resolve the situation fairly. She permitted me to make a bail application for Atik and I was able to explain that he had indeed failed to attend on a previous occasion. He had been ill. His mother confirmed the fact of his illness. Documents before the court for the ASBO showed that my client had been interviewed repeatedly by the police in the intervening months, there had plenty of opportunities to do something about his failure to attend, and that there was no need to pounce on him without warning outside court.

The judge agreed, releasing my client on unconditional bail.

Up until that point, Atik's life had seen many setbacks. He had been in court before; and every hearing had been a defeat. As he left court, he was suddenly a foot taller than he had been. The officers, for their part, discernibly shrunk.

As for me, I quit the building, walking one way and back. I found an empty patch of ground, devoid of policeman, lawyers, anyone.

There, I sat, the tears burning down my face.

I could not have remained in crime. I did not have the strength to face down the solicitors who never seemed to bother, even to take instructions from their clients. I could not endure the travel, the delays in court, the days when I walked through security not knowing even my client's name. I do not regret leaving crime. But I miss the clients: the lost boys with their hopeless schemes. When I began at the bar, I represented the teenagers for whom crime was a break in the tedium. After a decade on my feet, I represent their parents.

As the lockdown continued, the papers competed to express their admiration for our leaders. 'The health of Boris Johnson', a *Daily Telegraph* journalist wrote, 'is the health of the body politic and, by extension, the health of the nation itself'. 'Boris is out', the *Sun* declared on 10 April as he left intensive care, 'Now that really is a Good Friday.'

Deputising for Boris Johnson who was still recovering from coronavirus, Home Secretary Priti Patel was given the opportunity to apologise to the families of those nurses who had died without facemasks to protect them. Patel said she was sorry, 'if people feel there have been failings'.

In my borough, more than 6,000 people had joined a Facebook mutual aid group. There were so many volunteers that when an elderly woman living on my street contacted the group, a volunteer was assigned to her within three minutes of her request. Yet even while we looked out for one another, people were reporting their neighbours for real or imagined infractions of the lockdown rules or for other acts of nuisance. The West Midlands police told journalists that it was receiving complaints of breaches of the COVID rules at the rate of 2,000 a day.

When ASBOs were introduced, many lawyers disliked the way they combined the worst elements of criminal and civil law. In the negotiations that led to the formation of the 2010 Conservative and Liberal Democrat Coalition Government, the latter party insisted on various reforms to prove that this would not be simply Conservative government as normal. One such reform was that ASBOs would be abolished. Ten years later, only the names had changed.

The bleakest cases I did in the lockdown were for tenants who had been made subject to anti-social behaviour injunctions, and breached them, and were threatened with committal proceedings (in other words, imprisonment). This was wretched work because the people accused of breaches were often vulnerable, through alcohol or drug addiction or mental impairment. They had suffered harm, and it had made them irrational and angry. Many had only a vague memory of the incidents of which they were accused.

Defending in these cases began by getting a report into the client's mental health. If a psychiatrist was willing to say that the tenant could not modify their behaviour, then the case for imprisonment might well be dropped. But the landlord would then say that a tenant like that should not remain in the property. And so, what began as a claim for an injunction would be followed by a second claim – this time for possession.

In the cases where the tenant could modify their behaviour, the court would intervene ever more firmly into their lives; first by ordering them to stop, then warning them they were on the verge of imprisonment by giving them a suspended prison sentence, next sending them to prison if the behaviour continued.

The cases became a fight to protect the authority of the court against a tenant who seemed to be ignoring its orders. The risk was that, by the end, the court would lose sight of the behaviour which it was meant to be limiting. The judges I most admired hated these sorts of hearing. There were others, I suspected, who found a grim satisfaction in them.

During the lockdown, I took up yoga; I played football with my son. I slept in the afternoon. When I woke, I did not know whether it was a Thursday or a Friday.

I took a phone call from my mother: my father had suffered a fall. I needed to cycle at my fastest if I was going to see him before the paramedics arrived. The day was hot and humid, and I struggled to breathe. As I made it to their house, he was already in the ambulance. I shouted out his name and he waved a hand in greeting.

In early May, I represented a woman in her early 20s, Yasmin. I returned to chambers to collect the papers for her case. I found that businesses in central London were actively preparing for the ending of the lockdown. Six weeks before, Lincoln's Inn Fields was quiet: the only sound was the cawing of ravens. Today, the birds had been rendered inaudible. Someone had equipped the building site (a hundred yards away) with drills and their noise dominated the park. Workers unloaded metal pipes in pairs, their hands close enough to touch. The shops were full of office workers, managers, getting their businesses ready for life after the lockdown.

A year before, Yasmin had been made subject to an injunction preventing her from 'congregating' in a group of two or more people in the borough where she lived. The case against her now was that she was found with two men in a car. The police did not think she had committed a crime, but she was stopped in an area where (they said) drug dealing was rife.

'These men with you', the officer asked, 'are they trouble?'

'Trouble?' she said, repeating the world helplessly, 'They're my friends.'

Maybe her tone annoyed him. The officer took her name. He rang it in to headquarters and that was how they found out she was already subject to an order.

Section 1 of the Anti-social Behaviour, Crime and Policing Act 2014 limits the scope of anti-social behaviour injunctions to 'preventing the respondent from engaging in anti-social behaviour'. It did not take me long to find a decision of the higher courts in which it was held that 'congregating' in a group is not a public nuisance and should not be prohibited. As the Court of Appeal found, an order banning someone from being in a group would be breached the moment a person attending a sporting or other outdoor event.[7]

Yasmin also told me that she had only been in the car to visit her grandmother, who had collapsed in the street and been taken to hospital. Yasmin did not have a car of her own or a driving license and when the news reached her she simply rang the first friend she remembered. Even in the Orwellian world of anti-social behaviour injunctions, it is a defence to breach the order with a reasonable excuse.

7   *R v Boness* [2005] EWCA Crom 2395.

The case was listed for a telephone hearing at Clerkenwell and Shoreditch County Court before District Judge Tanar once again. While I did not trust the judge, she had always been sympathetic to my clients. I told District Judge Tanar that I had had the chance to take full instructions from my client for the first time that morning and that I needed more time to draft a proper statement. I invited her to adjourn the hearing. Deep down, I knew I was relying on the judge's worst instincts: her caution, her lethargy, her desire to accommodate the wishes of the professional representatives who attend her court.

On the other side, the landlord had instructed a barrister I had faced often before, Wystan, and he opposed my application with his usual decency.

Despite his objections, the judge agreed to adjourn.

I spoke to my father by telephone. As we talked, I found myself remembering how he was in the company of friends. The way he would begin a story. At its start, his eyes would be cast down, his right hand pressed against his cheek. My father would let his hand fall away, freeing his face. You would know a smile was coming from the way his nostrils flared. He might take a sip from a glass of wine. His whole face would burst into life, his lips crease, his eyes sparkle with delight.

'I miss you,' I said.

I represented another tenant, Gaspar Vogel, in a remote hearing. He had suffered post-traumatic stress disorder (PTSD) after an incident several years before when he was attacked in his home. It was a remote hearing, with images of Mr Vogel beamed from a friend's sofa on which he had slept the night before. He held his fists tight in front of his chest and clenched his eyes shut. Mr Vogel's landlord had obtained an order banning him from his home. This exclusion order was meant to be temporary. So, Mr Vogel was obliged to pay the rent; even though he was not allowed to return to his flat. For a while, he slept rough, finding such rest as he could in night buses. But this became impractical when the country went into lockdown. Friends offered him a night sofa-surfing here, or there. After that, he would try the buses again, or the street.

One of the consequences of his PTSD was that it caused Mr Vogel to cry out in pain. The shouts were loud and happened at any time of night or day. He did not control them, nor was he fully aware of them. When confronted, he could not understand why other people were upset with him. He took medication to reduce the intensity of his panic attacks. When he was three months into the exclusion order, he allowed his medication to run out without having obtained a new prescription. He knew he had a full bottle of medicine at home. He had been told so many times to take his meds. He went home, where he was spotted by a neighbour who called the police. The officers arrested him – hence today's hearing.

The landlord was represented by a senior barrister whom I had encountered in dozens of these sorts of hearings before. Her position was that Mr Vogel had breached his order, so now the court should commit him to prison for six months. I struggled to comprehend why they were so hostile to him. It was not as if the landlord would gain anything by insisting on Mr Vogel's imprisonment. It would not even cause him to change his behaviour: the medical evidence stated that this was beyond him.

The judge addressed my client. 'Can you hear us, Mr Vogel?' My client turned to his friend, a confused expression on his face.

The problem appeared to be with the speaker in his friend's computer. For a time, it worked but then it cut out and he could not hear us.

The friend lent Mr Vogel the headphones from his own mobile.

The hearing resumed.

The judge, initially, agreed with my opponent. He said that Mr Vogel's behaviour (which in the past six months had consisted of just returning to his own home, on one occasion, while was ordered to stay away) was so serious and shocking that it would terrify anyone who shared accommodation with him.

The judge was on autopilot. He was not thinking of Mr Vogel, but of the label that had been put on his conduct: anti-social behaviour. The law stamps with a mark of disapproval the lives of people who live in cramped proximity to one another, who hear the sound of feet above them like thunder. The judge was choosing the complainant, believing the worst *always*, because that was what our system expects of him.

We were 30 minutes into our allocated hour, and I had hardly had a chance to speak. Finally, I did, and I asked the judge if he had read all the court bundle.

The hearing was going on too long, the judge complained. There were other cases in his list that morning. He could not understand why I was fighting the decision.

I begged the judge to delay his decision until he had read the medical report. He could put us back an hour and call us on again.

The judge said that Mr Vogel's behaviour had been cruel, reckless.

I said, 'There's a risk here of a real injustice. If you get this wrong, my client will have served all his sentence before he can appeal.'

At the word appeal, the judge lifted his face from the papers. 'Look', he said. I could hear the pressure in his voice, the toll of long hours in the pandemic. 'This is the way remote hearings work, you have to take the cases in list order. I can't change the timetable.'

'I'm just asking you to read the report.'

My opponent said the judge did not need to waste any more time. The report said that my client had litigation capacity; he understood what it meant to be subject to a court order. If he had capacity, and had breached the order, he should be in prison. That was the end of it.

I told the judge, as firmly as I could, to read the report.

He finally agreed to read it.

When the hearing resumed, hours later, the judge thanked me for making him read it. He told me that he saw the distinction it drew between litigation capacity, and a person's capacity to control their behaviour. He said the injunction had been breached but my client was an ill man who could not stop himself from crying out. He found that my client had breached the order but had a reasonable excuse for so doing. No enforcement action would be taken. Neither would he extend the exclusion order: my client was free to go home.

A few cases were reported where the parties, or some of them, wanted a trial to be halted but the court refused. In one care case, the mother had caught the coronavirus and was unable to attend court. Her internet access was poor, and she struggled to understand how she could properly engage with a three-week remote hearing.

A week later, another case saw a young child being taken into care after a judge refused to grant an adjournment. The case was appealed to the Court of Appeal, who were baffled that a decision of such seriousness was made following a telephone appearance, in a case where the parties had less than a day's warning of the hearing. The appeal judges blamed the decision on the exhaustion of the judge, who prioritised the need of keeping the system going over substantive justice. 'By [the time he gave judgment], the Recorder had been working, almost continuously and mainly on the telephone, for 10½ hours. Our observation is that, although we have found the decision in this case to have been unquestionably wrong, the nature of the workload faced by the Recorder, experienced as he is, was surely a contributory factor.'[8]

---

8 *Re B* [2020] EWCA Civ 584 para 20.

The Civil Justice Council commissioned a report into online hearings. Over 1,000 judges, lawyers and litigants in person contributed to the survey which underpinned it. The report described a system in which the most basic and immediate forms of legal advice were barely functioning, not just possession duty desks, but any in-person advice. Judges were adjourning hearings wherever they could. Nearly half of all hearings suffered technical problems. Six out of 10 respondents described their audio or video hearings as worse than an in-person hearing. Over half of those surveyed described online hearings as tiring.[9]

An equivalent report carried out by the Nuffield Family Justice Observatory for the President of the Family Division of the High Court described litigants trying to engage with court hearings from mobile sheds or from the side of the motorway on pay-as-you-go mobile phones, witnesses coaching each other through their evidence, a mentally ill parent who was 'screaming constantly' as the hearing went on.[10]

In my own cases, the client's contribution to the hearing amounted to them being there at the beginning and listening in silence once the hearing had started. Once the online hearing had begun, their opportunity to instruct me was reduced to zero. The longest mid-hearing dialogues with my clients came in WhatsApp chats: 'I'm the one with the glasses', 'I can see that's a lot of books you have there.' 'Yes – that's me.' If the judge or an opponent said something unexpected, they expected me to answer immediately. I had no meaningful chance to speak to my client and check their instructions before continuing.

On 10 May, Boris Johnson gave another speech to the nation. He announced his intention to start loosening the lockdown rules. His hair desperately straightened, he described the lockdown as 'restrictions on . . . your freedom – of a kind that we have never seen before . . .' The tone our Prime Minister was aiming at was the oratory of 1939–40, but he fluffed his lines, speaking the words too fast, gulping 'in peaceorwar'. The message of his speech was bleak. Instead of staying at home we should 'stay alert', but what that meant in practice was left to us. Until now, the government had taken responsibility for paying our

9   Dr N Byrom, S Beardon and Dr A Kendrick, 'Report and recommendations: The impact of COVID-19 measures on the civil justice system', Civil Justice Council and The Legal Education Foundation, May 2020, p56.

10 M Ryan, L Harker and S Rothera, 'Remote hearings in the family justice system: a rapid consultation', Nuffield Family Justice Observatory, 2020.

wages and ensuring we had the means to feed ourselves. Now it was passing on that task, each of us would be required to live in a state of alertness, keeping safe in the face of an invisible enemy. Johnson insisted that public transport (on which most people in London depend) remained too dangerous to use; he also said that manufacturing and construction workers should return to work.

Johnson went on to praise, 'The incredible bravery and hard work of our NHS staff, our care workers', and this term – bravery – was all around.

I found myself re-reading the old words of Mike Marqusee, a historian of sport and popular music, who was diagnosed with cancer. 'The stress on cancer patients' "bravery" and "courage"', Marqusee wrote, 'implies that if you can't "conquer" your cancer, there's something wrong with you, some weakness or flaw. If your cancer progresses rapidly, is it your fault? Does it reflect some failure of willpower?'[11]

A little more than a week later, on 22 May, Johnson's chief strategist Dominic Cummings was in the news. At the height of the lockdown in late March, Cummings fled from London, driving his wife (who was suffering coronavirus symptoms) and son 264 miles to his parents' farm in Durham, apparently because in the absence of his wife he could not envisage looking after the four-year-old boy himself. On 24 May, the Prime Minister insisted that his aide 'acted responsibly, legally and with integrity'. The notion that Cummings acted with integrity was almost perfectly calculated to offend the tens of thousands whose relatives were suffering but were told not to see them.

The incident was the clearest possible case of one rule for those in power, another for everyone else. As to whether Cummings' action was legal, the regulations at the time were clear: 'no person may leave the place where they are living without reasonable excuse'.[12] Thirteen possible excuses followed, not one of which was travelling to escape London, or because a family member was ill, or because you were too important to care for your own child.

On 25 May, Dominic Cummings gave a press conference in the garden of 10 Downing Street, bitterly insisting that he had done nothing wrong. The same day, my father was released from hospital into a care home. The home, unlike our government, respected the

---

11 M Marqusee, 'The politics of cancer', *Red Pepper*, 15 November 2009.
12 Health Protection (Coronavirus, Restrictions) (England) Regulations 2020 SI No 350 reg 6.

rules of the lockdown. I had not been living overnight in the same house as my father – therefore, I was not permitted to see him.

In my final injunction case of the lockdown, my client Adrian had worked as a banker. Around a decade ago he had had a dispute with his then employer which ended with Adrian in a room with his Human Resources manager, raging and screaming, until a security guard came and led him off the premises. He was homeless, and for nine months slept in his car. From that low point, he managed to return to something like his previous life. He was taken on at a different bank. Once again, he had a clash with his employer. Again, it ended catastrophically, with Adrian smashing his phone, his keyboard, throwing his monitor so hard that it broke the partition between his workspace and his neighbour's. After that, Adrian grasped that there was something he could not control, some capacity for anger that was buried deep in him. He took a decision to give up work. Fortunately, one of the homeless charities with which he had previously been in contact made a referral on his behalf.

To treat his anger, Adrian chose to medicate himself by becoming a regular cannabis user. It was never very much, he insists. But that was not the issue, as far as the court was concerned. All that mattered was whether he was still smoking.

His housing association insisted that Adrian still smoked. Several neighbours came forward to complain. They insisted that the smell of drug use was unbearable. The first time Adrian was in court, he agreed to an injunction ordering him to stop. The second time, he admitted breaching the order and received a suspended prison sentence.

The forthcoming hearing would be the third, and the same witnesses came forward to testify against him once more. The letter instructing me concluded, 'Counsel is instructed to do his best', as if Adrian's solicitor thought he was doomed.

Adrian admitted that he was drinking alcohol, but insisted he remained cannabis-free. The admission of alcohol use was likely to go against him. At previous hearings, he had promised the judge he would attend Alcoholics Anonymous religiously.

I had not worked with Adrian's solicitor before and, in the conditions of the lockdown, we had no opportunity to speak except by telephone. She was late filing the client's witness statement and I asked her why. It took three emails before she told me what she was thinking. 'I misread the order', she said glumly. I told her we still needed a witness statement, a proper one, and a pdf with all the documents attached in a single computer file. During the pandemic, judges worked from home, the same as everyone else. They were refusing to read documents if it meant clicking through dozens of unconnected computer files. And a judge had instructed our client to submit a witness statement. We could not ignore the order.

There was a catch in her throat as she answered. 'I don't have all the papers at home. Some I've got scanned but not all of them. And I'm not killing myself on that bloody tube.'

'Can you walk to your office?' I asked.

'It's too far.'

'Can you cycle?'

'I don't have a lock.'

I told her that although we had missed the deadline in the order, there was still time.

It was midday. I had been up for seven hours already, drafting documents in an appeal, an application to the Legal Aid Agency (LAA). I had not eaten breakfast, still less lunch. I had not even found time to change out of my dressing gown.

Adrian insisted that he had not smoked since the last order was made. But over the last two months, the landlord's witness had repeatedly complained against him, and of course each diary entry was backed up by a time and date. 'Where were you last month?' I asked Adrian. 'I need to know about the 5th, at 11 in the morning.'

Adrian told me he could not remember.

We could disprove six of the ten allegations, I reckoned. On those days, Adrian was at medical appointments or at a meeting with his keyworker.

If we were given a fair judge, on a good day, he had a chance.

But, on the other four occasions, the judge was likely to find the order was breached. I was asking Adrian for anything we could use, maybe his bank statements so that we could prove that he had been out shopping that morning.

'I can't get them', he said.

I was thinking about evidence – Oyster card for public transport, maybe.

'What about the Human Rights Act?' he asked.

'There's no human right to smoke.'

I thought of the last time I had represented a cannabis user. The judge refused to believe him and committed him to prison. At the end of the hearing, my client ran. He bounded through the door at the back of the court, leaving it flapping uselessly behind him. He ran up the stairs, sprinted over the road. My client was not running from the law. He escaped only to the nearest supermarket from which he emerged clutching a small bottle of whisky. The police came, took my client into prison – but not before he had drained the bottle. It broke empty on the ground.

Something about that memory gave me heart.

'Give me a moment', I told Adrian, my mind busy with schemes and – despite everything – an inexplicable sense of hope. 'I'll think of something . . .'

CHAPTER 6

June: Preparing for the lockdown to end

Save for my injunction cases, there were very few other hearings in the lockdown. In Central London Employment Tribunal, all hearings were converted to case management hearings by telephone. 'Do I have the claimant on the phone?' the judge asked. 'Bear with me, I am going to try the respondent again.' When the hearing began, she said, 'I am working from home remotely. I have some paper documents, but if you're expecting me to have the full paper file for the case, I don't.' Every lawyer I met invited judges to keep trials listed whenever they could. When it was not possible to do so, they were adjourned into the distance.

At a hearing in June, one judge at an out-of-London employment tribunal told me that my client's relatively straightforward unfair dismissal case (four witnesses, around 300 pages of documents) could not be heard until spring 2021. Between now and then, every date was already taken.

In housing, meanwhile, all claims were stayed. Only a very few housing cases, principally injunctions, trickled through the system. The County Court at Clerkenwell and Shoreditch wrote to legal aid solicitors and large landlords. 'Our staff will need to generate revised notices to accompany court papers', and these papers would need to explain 'that there will almost certainly be no "duty solicitor" scheme in operation'. Solicitors worked urgently to gather the evidence to show the difference that the duty scheme had made, and to urge the court to reconsider. In the last 12 months before the lockdown began in March 2020, duty solicitors from one Law Centre represented tenants in over 700 possession hearings at Clerkenwell and Shoreditch. In only 11 per cent of these cases was an outright possession order made.[1] Without a duty scheme, they argued, you would

---

1 *Arkin v Marshall* [2020] EWCA Civ 620, Housing Law Practitioners Association evidence.

expect that proportion to be closer to 50 percent. Without the scheme, hundreds of people who had saved their homes would have lost them.

The listings I was given were often ineffective. One Tuesday at 11am, my clerk took a call from a desperate solicitor at a law centre. A case had been listed at 2pm, the final hearing of a possession claim – could anyone in chambers cover it? In theory I was the best person, I had spoken to the solicitor before the previous hearing, and some of the case papers had been sent to me. More documents had come in but were now lost in the Law Centre's files. The solicitor was working from home with only a desktop printer, as was I.

I had just three hours to prepare for the hearing. No one had warned the client. We had not had disclosure from the landlord – of the half-dozen procedural steps that were supposed to be taken to make us ready for a trial, none had been taken. The judge was going to be livid with the landlord and equally annoyed with us.

For two-and-a-half hours, the solicitor and I wracked our brains trying to work out why the judge thought a possession trial could go ahead when all such cases were stayed. I remembered an email from the landlord saying they were planning to sell the house: was that the explanation? We had heard from the judge's administrator who said she had seen an order but could not remember what it said. 'I'll email it to you', she promised, 'I'll do it now.'

Trying our hardest to keep calm, the solicitor and I made a written application to adjourn the hearing. At last, the solicitor received an answer. The judge had not meant to say the hearing should go ahead. Quite the opposite, they had vacated the hearing. The administrator misspoke, she had not read the order properly before telling us about it.

The final stage of qualification to become a barrister – 'pupillage' – lasts for roughly a year. Twenty or 30 years ago, the near-universal model was that all chambers would begin the year with five or six pupils. At the end of the year, one and one only would be recruited as a 'tenant', that is, an ordinary member of chambers. Since that time, the number of pupils has remained constant – at about 500 people per year across the UK, or, roughly speaking, one place for every 30 applications. Pupillage is much the same as it was three decades ago: a year-long job interview, with security for those taken on and nothing for the rest.

I remember what it was like to be living in central London and to be paying for a mortgage when my children were aged five and one.

I recall that awful uncertainty as to whether or where I would be working in a year's time.

That powerlessness made me dependent on the people above me, the hundred or so members of my chambers who might be involved in the recruitment decision. I looked at them in awe, as if they were gods of my future working life – when they were people from similar backgrounds to me, with similar working lives and similar opinions. I was desperate to be taken on. Even after the simplest interactions I would find myself asking, did I speak too loudly to one barrister, or too softly? Did I come over as informed or needy?

I remember the feeling when, thank goodness, the meeting of chambers took place and voted to accept me as a tenant. A dear friend from the Haldane Society of Socialist Lawyers rang and gave me the news. I was swimming with my partner and our children at the Holloway swimming pool, with its sloping beach and water slides.

I wept to hear I had been taken on. I was 36 years old, and for the first time in my life I had both a career that I wanted and a permanent contract.

In June 2020, I was asked to represent a tenant, Ashwin, at a telephone hearing. Ashwin's private landlord had evicted him from his home without a court order (in other words, unlawfully) and since then he had been living in a hostel for 16 months, in a dirtier, smaller single room, rather than the tolerable one-bed flat he used to occupy.

Ashwin was evicted without warning; a letter was shoved through the letterbox on the same day his locks were changed. The landlord lost my client's bed and his TV set. He broke the door of Ashwin's fridge, bagged his suits up and dumped them in a garage where snails crawled over them. The letting agent even demanded a £320 fee for keeping the few of Ashwin's things they managed to put into storage.

The difficulty Ashwin faced and the reason for the hearing was that the landlord had brought his own counterclaim for damages, £10,000 for scuff marks on the floor, and my client's solicitor had failed to put in a defence to the landlord's claim, with a result that there was an order ('default judgment') that Ashwin had to pay the £10,000 sum in full.

Our hearing was due to start at 10am, but the hearing could not begin on time. The defendant's solicitor's phone was not answering. Then the court was unwilling to add the claimant to the call. Wasn't it enough that I was there – his barrister?

'It's not enough', I insisted.

Finally, the hearing was ready to start. I asked the judge, 'Do you have the case papers?' He did not. I emailed the papers, and the parties hung up while he read them.

The defendant's solicitor was missing when we tried again, while his answerphone was playing some sub-Dire Straits guitar solo.

The usher asked, 'Do I have the district judge on the line?'

No answer.

We began the hearing over an hour late. I told the judge that the order for default judgment had been wrongly made. After that, we had one of those arguments you often get in the county court, with my opponent (a solicitor, who qualified in the same year I was called to the bar) dredging up the name of High Court cases which no one else had read and the rest of us having to search online for them.

I took the judge to a few more recent cases; I showed him that my opponent's memory of the Civil Procedure Rules was several years out of date.

The judge started saying, 'I agree with Mr Renton', and then with more force, 'I'm sure he's right about this. Really.'

My opponent conceded the point, saying, 'I can see what Mr Renton is saying now – now he's explained it to me. If I knew, I am not sure I would have fought. I feel like I've a brought a peashooter to a gunfight.' This was gratifying, as far as it went. But my client was still in temporary accommodation. Even with the order for default judgment set aside, he was still having to argue for the court to bring forward the hearing – the *next* hearing – which would decide whether he could get back into his home.

The judge told us that the delays caused by the lockdown were so bad, that if we asked for a one-day hearing, the case would not be listed before autumn 2021.

I spoke to my client afterwards.

'The judge wasn't serious, was he?' asked Ashwin.

'I'm sorry – he was.'

'Another year?' he groaned.

There was light enough to play football with my son after supper. Whenever we left the house, whether to shop or to exercise, we washed our hands: once, as we left, and a second time when we returned. The skin cracked beneath my son's fingers.

The days were hot – painfully so. The air thickened as cars slowly returned to the roads. When I did my shopping, I kept to the shade.

I talked to friends by Skype – doubtfully, disbelievingly, we plotted what we would do when 'normal life' returned.

I telephoned my father. He told me that he and I had spoken already that morning (we hadn't). Was he remembering a dream?

'Come and visit', he said – but the rules of the care home were perfectly clear. I was not a member of his household – I was still not permitted to see him.

In my first hearing in June, I represented a chef, Andrew, who had worked in the London Mayor's office where he became ill. He was diagnosed at first with depression and later with chronic fatigue syndrome. His employer's Health and Wellbeing Service recommended that he be redeployed to a desk-based, administrative role. His managers refused to accept this advice and insisted that any redeployment must take place through interview. Andrew attended a dozen such interviews without being offered a post. In the week leading up to the telephone hearing, a week in which casualties from coronavirus increased faster than at any other time in the crisis, the employer wrote to the tribunal insisting that the hearing went ahead.

The employer told the tribunal that Andrew was unrepresented, explained that his case raised a complex issue of law (namely: what was the provision, criterion or practice (PCP) that the employer had breached by dismissing him?) and suggested that Andrew would be incapable of resolving that question unaided. Since he did not have a lawyer, they asked the tribunal to have his case struck out. In truth, he did have a solicitor, and an experienced one, but she was the head of her firm, and had been inundated with work. She was also covering for several colleagues working from home. The first thing she did was to come on record, in other words tell the tribunal (and the respondent) that Andrew had a lawyer. The respondent then withdrew their application to have Andrew's claim dismissed, and our telephone hearing became a very straightforward event in which the judge asked us to confirm whether we thought the final hearing of the claim could go ahead. Both sides told him it should.

At the end of the call, the judge explained that if the country was still on lockdown in the autumn, we should anticipate that our hearing would take place online. 'The software will be ready by then', he promised.

The outbreak of coronavirus encouraged utopian thinking. In Italy, former Prime Minister Matteo Renzi called for a commission into the future. Centre-right politicians in France set up an interactive website 'Le Jour d'Après' (The Day After) with detailed proposals including a significant increase in inheritance tax: 'The surplus wealth should firstly be used to finance education, particularly but not uniquely, so as to allow the poor to access the same quality of education as the rich.'

For some time, the *Financial Times* had been predicting that coronavirus would legitimise state intervention: 'Radical reforms – reversing the prevailing policy direction of the last four decades – will need to be put on the table. Governments will have to accept a more active role in the economy.'[2] From the other end of the political spectrum, the *New Statesman* insisted that there was already a consensus for greater state intervention: 'Debates around economic policy in Britain had already been turning away from growth as a goal, with arguments over Brexit far more likely to centre on questions of sovereignty or democracy. That tendency looks likely to continue, post-Covid, with the issues of economic resilience, individual security, and social justice coming to the fore, and the state occupying a far bigger place in the economy.'[3]

Something else had changed during the lockdown. Over the past few decades, for most people in Britain the lives of the poorest had become almost as unimaginably distant as the lives of the super-rich. This gap was filled by the stories that appear in the tabloids, in lurid Channel 4 documentaries. We told ourselves that the poor were lazy, unjustly privileged, that it was not fair how hard people had to work to pay their mortgages when someone else enjoyed almost as fine a life without needing to lift a finger. COVID-19 dispelled that ignorance, the smugness and security of those who were doing alright. Suddenly half the British population was living on state benefits of one sort or another, mortgage holidays, a furlough scheme that provided for everyone from the night-time cleaner to the company director. Even people with steady incomes started to see that there really was not much at all that separated their lives from those others who they had previously been taught to despise.

If it was correct that the state was going to be playing a larger part in our lives in future, and that there would be greater empathy for the recipients of welfare benefits, I found myself asking how housing and employment law should change?

We regard the typical form of employment as a permanent full-time job. Yet its prevalence has been eroded by the rise of self-employment, and of part-time, impermanent and zero-hours contracts. Even the

---

2 'Virus lays bare the frailty of the social contract', *Financial Times*, 3 April, 2020.
3 J Meadway, 'Why the coronavirus crisis will force the UK to adopt a transformed economic model, *New Statesman*, 6 April 2020.

seeming security of a full-time permanent contract is less than it was. This, after all, was the experience of the coronavirus epidemic: that even people on secure-seeming contracts were in danger of dismissal.

As for housing, here too we have an expectation which fewer and fewer people meet. We assume that the typical person lives in a family home, possibly held on a mortgage or even that (with luck) the mortgage is fully paid.

Between 1945 and 1979, the largest number of homes built in the UK were built by local authorities. In December 1979, there were 21 million homes in the UK, of which the largest number (12 million) were owned by the family who occupied them. The next largest group were local authority homes (seven million); then around two million homes were privately rented. Because family sizes in local authority homes were larger than in owner-occupied properties, just under half of the population of Britain lived in council housing. The next two decades saw a dramatic transfer of homes from council housing to owner-occupation. By December 2004, the number of owner-occupied properties had increased to 17 million, while the number of council homes had collapsed to three million.[4] This was almost all down to just a single government policy, that council tenants should be granted a 'right to buy' their own homes. I will return to the effects of that policy in a moment.

In the last 20 years, owner occupation rates have remained steady at around 17 million. Meanwhile the number of households renting privately has increased from three million to five million. The total number of renters, including all social housing tenants, stands at nine million households.[5] Tenure is polarised by age. People who own their own home or occupy a council home tend to stay in it; younger people rent. Older people do not just live in more secure homes, they also inhabit larger houses, and they are more likely to have gardens. During the COVID-19 lockdown, they lived in more space.

As housing has become more expensive, more and more people have become stuck in conditions where if they lose their home, they cannot afford to find a new one. This is especially a problem for people who rely on social housing – many of whom took up their tenancy 20 or 30 years ago when there was much more social housing, and it was easier to access. Should they find themselves applying for

4 D Renton, 'Housing: as it is, and as it might be', *International Socialism*, Issue 134, 27 March 2012.

5 'English Housing Survey: Headline Report, 2018–19', Ministry of Housing, Communities and Local Government, 23 January 2020, pp1–2; www.gov.uk /government/statistics/english-housing-survey-2018-to-2019-headline-report.

social housing now, they would be refused. Meanwhile, they simply do not have the money to rent privately.

My solution to the crisis is a simple one: make it harder to dismiss and harder to evict, give workers and tenants greater security in both halves of their lives.

While the lockdown continued, I was asked to advise in a case where the landlord had complained in his claim for possession that a tenant's late payment of the rent was jeopardising his mortgage. I checked through the details. The property was originally a six-bedroom house; the landlord had changed the cupboards and the lounge into separate rooms, and split the largest bedroom in two, converting the property as a whole into 13 flats. In each, he charged the tenants £1,300 per month or £15,600 a year. The total rental income he generated was £202,800 a year. His salary – from renting out just one house – was more than the Prime Minister's. And the property was, a surveyor had found, in no fit condition to occupy, with ten of the 13 flats showing evidence of rat droppings. The stay of possession cases meant that I never did get to ask him how on that sort of rental he was having trouble paying his mortgage.

Landlords like him have been a feature of my practice. Before the lockdown, I found myself acting in a case against a landlord, Mr Xavier. Eighteen months before, Xavier had accepted my client, Mrs Potter, as his tenant. A few days later, he learned that my client was proposing to pay her rent by universal credit. 'That's simple', Mr Xavier said, 'you've got to leave'. He changed the locks and put the tenant's belongings in the street. His action was not merely a civil wrong it was also a crime, an illegal eviction.

After much perseverance, the tenant sought an injunction to return to the home. Mr Xavier delayed the hearing. Being advised by his own lawyer that he might have no alternative but to allow the tenant to return to the flat, the landlord settled on informal remedies. He made allegations to children's social services. He approached the housing benefit authorities. He told them that the tenant could not be allowed to return, since she had no written tenancy agreement, or since her landlord (Mr Xavier himself) had converted his building into two separate flats in breach of planning permission and the property was no longer licensed for rental. Obstacle after obstacle was strewn in Mrs Potter's path and one by one, she overcame them all. My previous involvement ended with the landlord agreeing to settle by promising to pay Mrs Potter a five-figure sum for the eviction and to write off 18 months of rent arrears.

Mrs Potter had a new haircut for the hearing – it sculpted upwards from her head. There was something defiant about her, a rebuke to the sadness all around.

I sat on the steel chairs on the second floor at the county court in Gee Street, and I listened to Mr Xavier's complaints about the world. 'I don't understand your client', he told me, 'I'm trying my hardest, but I don't'. In everything that had happened, he said, he was the victim. He should never have agreed to settle the case, and he would not have if his barrister had been any good. At the end of the last hearing, it had been written in the consent order that Mrs Potter would apply for housing benefit, but no benefits were being paid. Because of that, he said, he did not have to pay her the money that he had agreed. Politely, even deferentially, I observed that the agreement did not say anything of the sort. What it said was that Mr Xavier would contact the benefit authorities and revoke his previous denial that there had ever been a tenancy agreement. Which he had done, but only in the last two days before the hearing.

Mr Xavier said he should not have to pay my client compensation for her unlawful eviction. He could not afford to pay, he told me.

So, I asked, would he be willing to allow me to see the details of his current and savings accounts? If I could see them, I would be able to see how little he truly owned.

'Of course not', he answered.

I pointed out that if I could not see the accounts Ms Potter would have no good reason to let him off with paying less.

Mr Xavier again refused to pay. He was polite, if obdurate. He gave me a little, practised smile and for a moment I thought I saw him how he had been as a child: highly-strung, needy, the apple of his doting mother's eye.

He said it was unfair to make him accommodate my client. 'She . . . she . . .' and he was looking for a word that conveyed the unfairness of life – that the courts had compelled him to house a tenant when he was a rich man and she was nothing, she was less than nothing. She was a single mother, she lived on benefits. She was dirt. He said, 'She drives a BMW', as if by doing so she had exposed herself to the scorn and ridicule of the entire world.

'Do you?' I asked her later.

Ms Potter looked pityingly at me, as if I had fallen for the lies the landlord likes to tell. 'I drive a Toyota Prius – a second-hand one.'

The case was called on. Before either I or Mr Xavier could speak, the judge observed that the application he had made was not to change a court order but to change the terms of a settlement agreement between him and Mrs Potter. That was the thing about settlement agreements: a judge could not rewrite one simply because it would suit one party or another to change the terms of their agreement. Barely five minutes after the case began, it ended with an order dismissing Mr Xavier's application and awarding the costs of the hearing to Mrs Potter.

Eighteen months after Xavier evicted her, he still owed her more than £10,000. With each court appearance, that debt was growing.

In another case, I represented a tenant in his 50s. He worked as a security guard in a warehouse and he lived in a basement flat and the landlord had been ordered to fix the damp proof course ten years ago and the work was never done. So far, it was an utterly normal case. The thing that struck me most about the case was the Sex Pistols poster on the wall. An original, from the 1970s, my client insisted. I asked the tenant if he wanted to stay there and he said he did not. He had tried to move, he had looked at a dozen flats in the local area. But they were as expensive and as badly maintained as the one he had already.

Every time a court made an order against the landlord, he changed the ownership of the property. He created company after company and moved the house from one to another, so that whenever he was sued, he would close the company subject to the judgment and start a new one. No debts, no obligations, no laws applied to him. A decade before, when the tenant sued for disrepair, the landlord insisted he was the owner. Over the next ten years, he changed the ownership four times, with each company having a different legal relationship to him.

The landlord sued to obtain possession, using his own name. His lawyers wrote a dozen different letters to the court, a statement of case, a reply, various chasing letters, all signed, all insisting the property was his. When the landlord issued proceedings, the property was still owned by one of his companies, not by him. The company had the right to sue – but the landlord had no such right. He tried to amend the claim. He was given a deadline – he missed it.

My opponent, in her reply, said that our defence was 'ill-conceived and misconstrued'. But the longer we spent in court, the worse it became for her. The judge asked, 'Who owned the property when the case was issued?' and my opponent was incapable of giving the question the same answer twice. The case was so poorly presented that the judge agreed with us that the landlord was obliged to disclose how many other properties he owned.

The landlord would not say, he shook his head. It was sensitive, commercial information. 'I don't know', he said, 'I've lost count.'

He told the judge, 'It's north of 500.'

Ownership, on that scale, offends against the principle that anyone's wealth ought to bear a minimum connection to what they have done with their life. The executive of a large business might justify their income by saying that they have chosen their subordinates' ideas, brought them to the market, known which to promote and which to let go. Their position has brought them rewards – but at an emotional cost. Few private landlords of multiple properties could formulate a similar justification: their skill has been to hoard ownership of a resource, taking a rent at premium rates while often refusing to fund the building's maintenance.

How is it possible for anyone to own more than 500 homes? To explain this, you must go back to the Conservative governments of the 1980s presided over by Margaret Thatcher, and their 'right to buy' scheme. The Housing Act 1980 set out to create a revolution in home ownership by giving council tenants an option to purchase the home in which they lived at a discount of up to 60 per cent compared to the market rate, depending on the length of time they had lived there. There was no guarantee in advance that enough numbers of council tenants would buy their properties to make the scheme work. Some council tenants liked the idea of owning their own home. Others found the scheme repugnant. A third group were concerned only with the practical elements; with tenants asking themselves if they could afford to replace their own boiler if its maintenance was left to them.

The key to making right to buy work or to moving people from the third of these categories into the first, the Conservatives realised, was the extent of the discount. A tenant with a 20 per cent discount could anticipate paying monthly mortgage repayments thereafter of a little less than council rents, making right to buy attractive to them but not decisively so. With a 60 per cent discount, however, the tenant could expect their mortgage payments to be half or less of their existing council rent. Tenants really were being given money for nothing.

The right to buy scheme privatised a large part of the welfare state, in the process changing a group of Labour-voting renters into Conservative-voting owners. It succeeded because the funds were found to finance it on terms so advantageous that only the positively foolish would turn down what amounted to a massive bribe.

Right to buy generated significant sums for central government: £40 billion in its first 25 years. However, it devastated the public housing sector, withdrawing properties from stock and increasing competition for those houses and flats remaining in local authority control. It fuelled the mortgage boom of the 1980s and the repossession bust of the early 1990s. It also changed the social demography of council tenancies. Until the 1980s, both of our main political parties had agreed that council housing should be available to everyone who wanted it, an approach explained by Nye Bevan, the founder of the National Health Service (NHS), who argued that 'The segregation of the different economic groups' was 'a wholly evil thing'. Right to buy transformed council housing for the worse, making it a scarce resource limited only to the non-working poor. In 1979 most council tenancies included at least one person in full-time employment. By 1995, however, 95 per cent of those newly housed by local authorities were on benefits.[6]

In the aftermath of right to buy, concerted efforts were made to stop local authorities from building new stock which might otherwise have been used to replenish the lost council homes or to prevent house prices from rising uncontrollably at the cost of those who did not own their own homes. Local authorities were prevented from borrowing to replace their stock. Some private housebuilding took place, but at levels incapable of meeting increasing demand.

Right to buy was accompanied by other housing laws which also harmed tenants. For more than 60 years, and ever since protests in Glasgow in 1915 against rent profiteering, Britain had had laws limiting the ability of landlords to increase rents (the Rent Acts). The Housing Act 1988 dismantled them, freeing private landlords to charge whatever rent they liked and also – with section 21 – granting them an expanded freedom to evict. Both private and social housing were subject to parallel processes. The government created an expanded private market, and one as unfavourable to new tenants as they could make it.

The outlines of this story are well known – politicians from all parties are willing to accept that too few homes are being built, that housing prices have been kept artificially high to the detriment of those who do not own, that the collapse of social housing has reduced our opportunities to house those in greatest need.

What is often poorly understood is how right to buy assisted a relatively small number of landlords to build up property empires. At the time, most people expected house prices to fall after an initial rise,

6   D Renton, 'Housing: as it is, and as it might be', *International Socialism*, Issue 134, 27 March 2012.

while others did not grasp that (for example) by aggressively subdividing a building and converting it to multiple occupation by tenants on housing benefit it was and remains possible to pay off the cost of buying a large building, in many cases, within just three to four years of purchase. Among the beneficiaries of right to buy were people who often had not owned much previous wealth but knew the property market and were well-placed to acquire homes at knockdown prices. In court, it is hard not to notice how many of today's landlords were, 30 years ago, a local estate agent with a small neighbourhood business employing just one or two people. Being employed to advertise these homes that were now for sale, they saw an opportunity to purchase a first home and then a second, and in no time at all they had acquired a portfolio of properties and a massive income.

One 2017 survey found that that over 40 per cent of former right to buy properties in Britain were now rented out by landlords.[7] It is worth trying to think why such a high proportion of former council homes are now owned by landlords and not lived in by their owners. Part of the answer is that it has been for some time government policy to privilege the interests of private landlords, not just over tenants, but over other homeowners. In the mid-1990s, the banks introduced 'buy-to-let' mortgages, which assessed buyers' creditworthiness on the rental yield from the property, rather than the buyers' existing income. This easy finance gave landlords a significant advantage over other people buying in the property market, including first-time buyers. Under both main political parties, buy-to-let landlords have also enjoyed tax relief: mortgage interest relief, and a wear and tear allowance. These tax breaks have been reduced since then, but the broad picture remains the same.[8] Landlords remain privileged over those purchasing to occupy. Although the UK's 2.7 million landlords are a small minority in society (roughly one in 20 of all adults), because the market has been loaded in their favour, one in six of all homes sold, and one-quarter of all new homes, are purchased by them.[9]

One of the poster-boys for the landlord class is Islington's Andrew Panayi. The owner of about 180 units dotted around Islington's Caledonian Road, he has been repeatedly in the news over the last

---

7 N Barker, 'Revealed: the scale of ex-RTB home conversions to private rent', *Inside Housing*, 7 December 2017.

8 G Monbiot et al, 'Land for the many. Changing the way our fundamental asset is used, owned and governed', Labour, 2019, p24.

9 J Partridge, 'Buy-to-let sales boom as landlords rush to benefit from stamp duty holiday', *Guardian*, 14 December 2020; E Magnus, 'A game changer for buy-to-let and tenants?', *This is Money*, 19 November 2020.

decade, including for renting out unlicensed underground properties without any access to natural light. In 2014, 19 of his properties
were found to have 'category 1' hazards, in other words to be so small
(at nine square metres) that they were unfit to occupy.[10] In 2013, when
his company Ploughcane was first in the headlines, it was reported
that its accounts showed a turnover of £2.7 million, of which £2.3
million was operating profit, from which we can infer Mr Panayi was
hardly exactly carrying out a great volume of costly repairs.[11]

To put this income in context: by 2013, Mr Panayi's one-man
rental business already paid him fractionally more money than the
Chief Executive of the Royal Bank of Scotland, or five times as much
as the Chairman of Santander. Mr Panayi was not paid this money
because he had invented some new technology which had changed
all our lives, or because he had a skill as an artist or composer. Not
one of his tenants could say that their lives had been enriched by
knowing him. Nor does anyone suggest that he would face the pressure of a chief executive having to manage a business with tens of
thousands of employees.

Mr Panayi made this money because in the 1980s and 1990s he
was an insolvency practitioner, with a shop on the Caledonian Road.
As businesses went bankrupt around him, they had premises and
land to sell. There he was, perfectly located, to acquire the freehold of
abandoned properties. In the conditions of rising house prices, he
was betting on a lottery – and he had been told the winning numbers
in advance.

Following Labour's defeat in the 2015 general election, the party leader
Ed Miliband stood down. In the resulting leadership election, the most
left-wing candidate – Jeremy Corbyn – won the support of hundreds of
thousands of younger voters by promising to help private sector
tenants. The first policy unveiled by Corbyn in his leadership campaign
was a promise akin to right to buy – but, this time, aimed at private
sector tenants. The idea was that if they paid their rent for ten or 20
years, a proportion of this money could be used as a fund to enable the
acquisition of those same homes. It was this policy, more than any
other, which made Corbyn stand out from other candidates and made
it feel like he was offering something new.

10 R Booth, 'London flats "worse than prison cells" condemned by council',
    Guardian, 5 September 2014; R Booth, 'Landlord must hand back £70,000 in
    rent for letting substandard flat', *Guardian*, 22 October 2015.
11 E Anderson, 'London landlord fined almost £90,000 for "substandard" base-
    ment let', *Telegraph*, 22 October 2015.

Other tenant-friendly policies followed, once Corbyn had become leader of the Labour Party, including an inflation cap on rent rises. In the 2017 election, these policies helped to win Labour massive support among younger voters: nearly two-thirds of the vote among under-30s. Strikingly, the swing to Labour was almost entirely restricted to private renters: among whom Labour's polling lead rose from 11 to a staggering 23 per cent between 2015 and 2017.[12]

The reason why Corbyn's policies resonated was that, while the generation who bought their homes in the 1980s had used that money to achieve some prosperity, there was no mechanism to pass the wealth on to a younger generation except through the inheritance of those homes after their owners died.

The generation who had bought their homes through right to buy did well from it. But there were no advantages for those who came after. Instead, they experienced housing shortages, house prices so high that they had no prospect of ever buying their own home, and rents in the private sector which took up a far higher proportion of their incomes than their parents had been required to pay at the same age. Alongside Corbyn's opposition to wars, support for healthcare, and identification with the oppressed, part of the reason for his success was the reality of the widening gap between house prices and incomes.

But understanding British politics through the prism of home ownership also helps to explain why Corbyn eventually lost. 'If only under-30s [voted]', wrote the historian of architecture and politics Owen Hatherley, using data from the 2019 general election, 'there would be no Conservative MPs anywhere in Britain.' But, if only the over-70s voted, 'there would be Tory MPs in every constituency apart from South Wales, Merseyside, the City of Manchester and inner London'.[13] In a political system which was increasingly polarised by age as much as anything else, older voters who owned their own homes calculated that they had little or nothing to gain from Corbynism. What he seemed to offer was potentially a fall in house prices – a diminution of their capital and security in retirement.

As spring gave way to summer 2020, London councils predicted a coming 'avalanche of evictions' and asked the government to publish plans to increase the proportion of new homes that would be built as

12 'Private renters now key to political battleground, Shelter research shows', Shelter, 2 October 2018.

13 O Hatherley, 'The government of London', *New Left Review*, Issue 122, March/April 2020.

social housing. The housing charity Shelter warned there would be an 'onslaught of people' who have been put at risk of homelessness by coronavirus. Robert Jenrick, the Secretary of State for Housing, belatedly acknowledged the problem. His solution was a new pre-action protocol. We already had a protocol – that is, a code setting out what parties should do before litigating, but this only covered social landlords. He proposed that in future, private sector landlords would be required to 'act in good faith' and investigate solutions other than the law before issuing proceedings. The problem with the idea was that under various statutory grounds a landlord was entitled to seek possession and, should the criteria in those grounds be satisfied, a court had no choice but to order possession. The proposed protocol would be an encouragement urging to landlords to 'be nice'. But why should they, in cases where the law said they were entitled to possession?

A cross-party select committee described the proposed pre-action protocol as 'toothless'. The key problem was that when landlords apply for possession, certain categories of claim are 'mandatory'. In other words, if threshold criteria are met, a judge has no choice but to grant possession. These include 'section 21',[14] when a private landlord or a housing association asks for possession and 'ground 8',[15] when a landlord seeks possession, and the tenant is in two months of arrears. A pre-action protocol would not change these rules.

The Law Centres Network called for reforms that would amend section 21 and ground 8 possession cases, making them discretionary rather than from mandatory. Under pressure, the government agreed to extend the stay on possession proceedings by a further two months, until 23 August. This move bought us all – government, the opposition, housing lawyers – a chance to set out what sort of legal system should be in place for when the lockdown ended. By the end of the stay, there would be tens of thousands of unresolved cases waiting in the system. Meanwhile, the rise in unemployment inevitably meant than tens if not hundreds of thousands of extra people were at risk of losing their home. The courts were facing a crisis: with more possession cases stacked up and waiting to be heard than ever before.

The politicians were making their decisions, and I was looking for an opportunity to address them. The opportunity arose by chance. A friend from university, Iris, worked as a journalist. Her employer

14 Housing Act 1988 s21.
15 Housing Act 1988 Sch 2 ground 8.

wrote to its several hundred employees, inviting them to consent (by 5pm the same day) to a variation of their terms under which their posts could be varied to become either 'furloughed' workers (on 80 per cent of pay) or 'laid off' workers (on a maximum salary of £145 per week). Large numbers of employees declined to agree such a variation. The next day, the company's human resources officer sent out a new letter. Those who signed it granted that the business was entitled to dismiss them at any time of its choosing with 'no right to remuneration' should the company do so. I told Iris that if she refused to sign, her existing contract would still apply as would her old terms and conditions.

The advice worked: Iris was one of just 14 employees who refused to sign either letter. She did eventually, however, receive a response from her senior managers saying they respected her position and would take no steps against her.

Iris encouraged me to jot down any suggestions I had on housing policy. She promised to send them to the new leader of the Labour Party, Keir Starmer, members of whose office she had known for many years. It occurred to me that the new leader might not be grateful for the advice. An article I wrote for the *Guardian* during the Labour leadership contest had steered a line between Starmer and his critics on the left – before siding with the latter.

'Do you really think he'll want to meet me?' I asked.

Perhaps not, Iris admitted. 'People in politics can be quite thin-skinned.' We came up with a compromise, in which the approach would come through her. We would leave my name off the first draft and see if either the new leader or anyone else wanted to talk with us.

I had my own idea of why Labour lost the general elections in 2017 and 2019. It seemed to me that Labour would have had more success if Corbyn's supporters had been clearer in grasping – and showing voters they understood – that while tenants and landlords have competing interests, the same is not true of tenants and homeowners.

It had been open to Labour to say that right to buy did not simply create two classes of people: homeowners (the older generation of former council tenants) and future tenants (the younger generation) – it also created a third group of people, namely professional landlords. It is here that a properly explained version of Labour's policies might have broken through. Take the idea of long-term renters establishing a right to purchase the home in which they lived. If this was directed at the single homeowner who split a two-storey house in half and rented out one floor of it, many other homeowners would find this objectionable. They could be expected to feel an affinity with a landlord who had little spare wealth and tell themselves that such a person should be free to do with their home whatever they liked. But if this policy was restricted, for example, to landlords owning a minimum of five or ten properties; there are enough landlords in that position so that it would still make a difference. And where someone is hoarding five homes, why shouldn't there be a limit to the profits they can make?

In London, and in all our larger cities, right to buy did not produce a class of homeowners sharing their homes with their nuclear family, generation after generation. It could not; our homes are just about large enough to house one or two generations of people (parents plus young children) but not three generations or four. Rather, it led to millions of younger people paying an unsustainable proportion of their salaries in housing, so that for all the formal increase we have had in paper wealth, millions of people are poorer and lead less secure lives than the generations which preceded them.

Many people in the older generation are aware of how hard life is for the younger generation. Hundreds of thousands of people save money in their 70s or beyond, not because they want to have an extravagant lifestyle but for the sake of the generations who come after them, and because they want to be generous in their will. If their plan is to help the younger generation to buy a house, then rising house prices are no benefit to the elderly, only a cost – it obliges them to save more, as ever more money is going to be needed to provide a deposit to the younger generation caught in the trap of high rents and low savings.

From the perspective of the kind-hearted parent or grandparent, the benefit of high house prices (the paper value of their wealth) never materialises; but the cost is only too real: it compels the members of their family to live in cramped housing, to work increasing hours, to have less money than they should, and to spend their days working excessive hours so that they have no spare time for older relatives. If only Corbyn had been able to explain all this; if only had he been able to articulate the best instincts of his own generation.

The new Labour leader was, of course, no Corbynite. So, the points I made were narrower.

First, the people on whom we depended in the crisis should be paid more. In the first days of the crisis, the Living Wage Foundation estimated that a single person on a full-time wage needs to be paid £10.75 an hour in London or £9.30 an hour outside London to pay for food, clothing and household bills. The GMB union calculated that 92 per cent of shelf-fillers, 73 per cent of pharmacy dispensing assistants and 60 per cent of nursery nurses, all of them keyworkers, did not earn enough to live.[16]

Hundreds of thousands of people were working through the epidemic, in conditions where social distancing was impossible. A chief offender was the construction industry, where sites remained open although key tasks – loading materials, fixing plasterboard, operating cherry-picker baskets, and so on – could not be done while keeping a two-metre distance. Most building workers were on casual contracts and ineligible for the furlough scheme. At the start of the coronavirus lockdown, the government promised to support self-employed people by providing them with an income equivalent to four-fifths of their earnings, but the details of the scheme were not published for several months, and many workers reasonably feared that any payments paid to them would be modest. That was why they stayed at work.

Between 1978 and 2018 the proportion of UK employees who were categorised as self-employed rose from eight to 15 per cent of the workforce.[17] In some cases, this has been due to the expansion of occupations which are genuinely self-employed: a medical consultant offering his services to a group of private sector hospitals is meaningfully a business, trading in a position of equality in relation to those who would buy his labour. The same is also true of barristers. Solicitors contact us, invite us to work for them and purchase an amount of our time.

In a fairer system, self-employment would be restricted to a tiny number of genuine self-employees, while all other workers and employees should be in a single category of 'worker' with full access to the minimum wage and unfair dismissal rights. The existence of such universal rights might well have allowed workers to feel that they could leave their workplaces, as happened during the pandemic in offices but not on construction sites. Increased rights would almost certainly have slowed the spread of the disease.

As workers lose their jobs, the risk is that their homes will become vulnerable. No criticism could be made of the support the govern-

16 A Gouk and V Castle, 'The key workers in Kent paid less than the real living wage', *KentLive*, 2 April 2020.
17 B Chiripanhura and N Wolf, 'Long-term trends in UK employment: 1861 to 2018', Office for National Statistics, 29 April 2019, Figure 8.

ment has offered to homeowners. The nine million British house-holds which rent were given weaker protection: a month was added to the gap between the serving of notices seeking possession and the start of possession proceedings, which were stayed. The government's advice was that 'tenants should continue to pay rent'.[18]

Where employees lost their jobs, this would inevitably cause rent arrears. The government delayed the tenants' loss of their homes. But it did nothing to prevent landlords from seeking possession as soon as the emergency ended.

Both private sector and housing association landlords often claim possession on ground 8 of Schedule 2 to the Housing Act 1988, where a tenant is in eight weeks' rent arrears. Where a claim is made on that ground and the tenant is that far behind, the court *must* order possession. A judge cannot defer payment even to give the tenant a chance to solve benefits difficulties or obtain a loan. The effect of the stay on proceedings was simply to delay these cases. It meant that huge numbers of them were stacking up, waiting for the lockdown to end.

The obvious reform would be to abolish ground 8 and section 21. Such a step would provide tenants with a further opportunity to get their finances back in order. But it also would strike a balance – landlords would still be able to claim possession on grounds 10 and 11 of the same legislation (grounds which potentially entitle the landlord to possess where there has been non-payment of rent) but only if it was reasonable to grant possession. The difference between ground 8 and grounds 10 and 11 is that under the latter, possession is a discretionary rather than mandatory remedy, so a judge could delay granting possession if the tenants had a good payment history but were suffering from debt because of COVID-19 and had a credible offer to reduce their arrears, or if the family had no prospect of being housed elsewhere.

The other remedy that was needed was an amnesty for tenants who have accumulated rent arrears – for example, a resetting of any arrears more than £1,000 which would be reduced to zero. Such an amnesty could only realistically apply to social housing landlords and would require support to the landlords who operated it. Otherwise, its only effect would be to push those landlords (housing associations and local authorities) into further debt.

Something along these lines was fast becoming a necessity, since there were many tenants who already suffered a shortfall between

---

18 'COVID-19 and renting: guidance for landlords, tenants and local authorities', Ministry of Housing, Communities and Local Government, www.gov.uk.

their housing benefit and their rent. They included tenants on the bedroom tax, or whose benefits were subject to the household benefits cap and tenants whose rent was more than the local housing allowance. The local housing allowance is a figure set by government in according to the size of the property, but capped at the 30th percentile of rents in any given area. So, a single person living in Leeds could not receive more housing benefit than £62.31 per week.[19] Long before coronavirus, these measures were putting tens of thousands of people in danger of eviction.

Hundreds of thousands of people were in rent arrears not because of any fault of their own, but because of policies beyond their control, and whose seeming value had been limited. If the purpose of austerity had been to reduce national debt, it failed: before the lockdown, the debt was £1.8 trillion, or around 80 per cent more than it had been a decade earlier. The longer the lockdown went on, the larger it became.[20]

Conversely, if the purpose of welfare cuts was to encourage people to leave more expensive properties for cheaper ones, and to achieve this change without stigma, on this measure too they have failed. We have not seen any obvious freeing up of social housing properties, instead people have clung to the homes they have, making social housing an ever scarcer and more precious resource. Social landlords do not own a surplus of unused, smaller, homes into which they could move willing tenants. They have not encouraged downsizing or relocation. Rather, tenants have been made to endure repeated suffering: poverty, hunger, the humiliation of court proceedings ending in possession orders or orders for money judgments.

I sent off a version of the above advice, with Iris tweaking the introduction. 'There is nothing to prevent many thousands of renters being evicted from their properties in a few months', she wrote. 'The Labour Party can call on the Government, in a spirt of national co-operation not party rivalry, to change policy to prevent this from happening.'

The shadow housing minister and I spoke by videolink. She told me about the housing system she wanted to see: one which followed

19 'Local Housing Allowance (LHA) rates applicable from April 2020 to March 2021 – amendment as instructed by the Social Security (Coronavirus) (Further Measures) Regulations 2020', Valuation Office Agency.
20 S Nagarajan, 'The UK's national debt tops £2 trillion, and passes 100% of the country's GDP for the first time in over 50 years', *Markets Insider*, 21 August 2020.

coherent rules, one which was efficient. She was outraged by the thought that people were living on benefits and could not afford their rent. She was no less horrified to think that there were people on estates who caused nuisance to their neighbours. Yes, there needed to be an eviction ban, but it need to distinguish with utter precision, she argued, between good tenants who deserved to stay and the bad who ought to leave. For my part, I struggled to see how that could be achieved without putting cases back before judges. She wondered why I had written at such length about tenants. What about homeowners? I did my best to answer. She spoke – with conviction – about the difficulty that young purchasers were having in buying new homes. Three times she said how unjust it was that half-a-million-pound homes were being trumpeted by developers as 'affordable'. She was trying hard, it seemed to me, to understand the situation of private renters. She needed to make no comparable effort to grasp the lives of homeowners.

The dominant message of the first two months of coronavirus was that governments could mitigate what might otherwise have been a catastrophic weakening of the economy. The International Monetary Fund (IMF) warned of a three per cent slump in global growth.

For weeks, the news was full of the high-profile companies who had applied to the government for financial relief: half of Britain's smaller and medium-sized companies had requested support. Spurs and Bournemouth football clubs asked for funds, as did Victoria Beckham's fashion label. After 14 years living as a tax exile, the multi-millionaire Richard Branson demanded a one-billion-pound bailout for his company Virgin Atlantic.

The historian in me knew that how any country deals with a crisis gives you a clue as to what the next decade or longer will feel like. The first moves towards a welfare state in Britain were taken in the direct aftermath of the Boer War in the early 1900s. Britain was then an empire, and one whose territorial expansion depended on the mobilisation of hundreds of thousands of soldiers. The fact that nearly half of all volunteers to the army had to be rejected on grounds of ill-health turned public health into news. It provided the impulse which led to unemployment insurance and old age pensions. Yet faced with the cheering crowds who introduced into the English language a new term 'jingoism', it would have been a bold person to predict that reforms were coming. The First and Second World Wars may have ended in domestic reform, but there was nothing inevitable about catastrophe giving way to progressive laws. Recent war-leaders in

Britain (during the Falklands War in the 1980s) and the US (during the Iraq conflicts in the 1990s and 2000s) did not promise homes fit for heroes, or anything like them. The wars' aftermath was greater inequality: in Britain, the miners' strike, the anti-union laws; in the US, falling real wages and decaying infrastructure.

Social change happens through a process of changing values, so that habits which were widespread at one moment come to seem outrageous in another. I have seen this happen repeatedly in my own lifetime – at one moment, driving under the influence of alcohol was ubiquitous, and then of all a sudden we stopped. Violence against children was at one time considered normal, and then unthinkable.

Those are simply the changes I have lived through. On a longer timescale, there are even clearer examples: the acceptance of democracy, the sweeping away of the laws which prevented women from holding property, the decline of overt sexism and homophobia. Behind all these changes were subtle, but real, shifts of public opinion which swept everyone behind them: turned liberals into social democrats, made reformers of judges. In the days that followed the outbreak of the coronavirus epidemic, I was watching all around me, wondering if our society would emerge changed from our lockdown. Much of our law, both in employment and housing, rests on subtle notions of reasonableness. I wanted to know if these notions would change in the aftermath of the virus. Would we protect jobs and homes, or would it be the same as before?

CHAPTER 7

July: Housing the homeless

At the start of the COVID-19 lockdown in March 2020, the Secretary of State for Housing, Communities and Local Government, Robert Jenrick, wrote to local authority homelessness managers and rough-sleeping co-ordinators instructing them to 'get everyone in' – in other words, to house every rough sleeper they could. The instruction was broad enough to include even those with no recourse to public funds, meaning those who did not have immigration status or a right to reside in the country. This was not a matter of charity, he insisted, but of mutual survival, to 'stop wider transmission particularly in hot spot areas'. Local authorities were told to provide rough sleepers not merely with accommodation but specifically housing in 'single room facilities', as well as providing food, medical care and assistance for anyone with drug or alcohol problems.

No new legal rights were conferred on homeless people. Rather, rights and duties which had always existed were now to be properly resourced. The government promised £3.2 million to local authorities to sustain homelessness services. Meanwhile, although hotels were prohibited from offering accommodation during the crisis as part of the general lockdown, this ban was lifted where the accommodation was for homeless people. The homelessness charity Crisis estimated that 4,200 homeless people were rehoused. Concerted action proved that rough sleeping could be significantly reduced; although any victory was incomplete. For, although some nine out of ten street homeless people were accommodated, the closure of other services – including homelessness day centres, community centres and public toilets – meant that a second generation of rough sleepers followed them onto the streets.[1] They, too, needed homes.

---

1 A Gentleman, 'Thousands of rough sleepers still unhoused in England, say charities', *Guardian*, 30 March 2020.

While the allocation of these funds was welcome, and homeless charities reported a sustained improvement in the number of people housed and the speed of their treatment, some care must be taken to explain why that action was needed. The UK is the sixth richest economy in the world. We have more than enough resources to house our homeless in normal times. Indeed, we already possessed laws whose effect was intended to be just that.

The Housing Act 1996 provides that where a person may be homeless or threatened with homelessness, a local housing authority must make inquiries to establish whether the person is eligible for assistance.[2] If someone is in apparent priority need, the local housing authority must accommodate them while they make further inquiries.[3] If the enquiries show that the person is homeless, in priority need and did not make themselves homeless intentionally, they must be housed.[4]

Part of the problem is that in ordinary times local authorities lack the resources to give effect to their legal obligations. There is not enough council housing for the people who need it. Previous chapters of this book have described the effects of the 'right to buy' scheme in reducing the stock of local authority accommodation. Forty years ago, there were seven million local authority homes. Since then, right to buy, joined with prohibitions on local authorities borrowing to build new properties, have reduced the total local authority stock to just two million homes. By 2020, nearly half of all local authorities in England (185 out of 350) no longer owned any council housing *at all*.[5] Almost all the remaining two million homes are occupied, and in many cases are likely to remain so for years to come. So as of December 2019, Tower Hamlets had 20,000 households on its waiting list; Lambeth 25,000; Newham 27,000 and so on.[6] These boroughs were Labour-voting, and Labour-run, but the councillors and officials who led them pursued active policies of reducing their housing stock: for example, between 2010/11 and 2017/18 Lambeth sold more than 300 council

2 Housing Act 1996 s184.
3 Housing Act 1996 s188.
4 Housing Act 1996 s193.
5 N Barker, 'How the social housing white paper will affect the sector', *Inside Housing*, 24 November 2020.
6 'Households on local authority waiting list', Ministry of Housing, Communities and Local Government, December 2019; www.gov.uk/government/statistical -data-sets/live-tables-on-rents-lettings-and-tenancies.

homes and between 2014 and 2018 built only nine to replace them;[7] in Newham, between 2010 and 2018 the number of council homes shrank by 1,000.[8] Some local authority homes do become free every year – whether through the death of a tenant, a voluntary move, or possession proceedings; and councils do build some new houses. A typical London authority will let around 1,000 properties each year – enough to keep its waiting list static but not to reduce it.

Although ministers, journalists and even judges often speak of 'social housing' (meaning both local authority and housing associations homes) as if this was a single sector with the same tasks and duties, it is not. Unlike a council, a housing association has no obligation to house the homeless. I sometimes negotiate with officers in the local authorities who have sold off their entire housing stock. When they are faced with a person who is eligible for homeless housing, the council officers have no option but to spend their days phoning up the housing associations in their area, begging them to take the homeless person. Sometimes, a housing association agrees, often (for example where the tenant is vulnerable with addiction or with a disability and it would be costly to house them), the association declines. The council is obliged to house eligible homeless people; housing associations have no duty to help them.

In this respect, housing associations are much more like private landlords than they are like councils: they can evict a tenant in reliance on Housing Act 1988 s21 (without needing a reason) or on Sch 2 ground 8 (the mandatory ground for two months' rent arrears). This reflects the reality that, although many housing associations have their roots in philanthropic or idealistic calls for the housing of the vulnerable, for decades they have sought to grow through house building and borrowing from the banks, who in turn expect them to produce a similar profit per housing 'unit' to what the worst of the private sector might obtain. In the larger housing associations, decisions are made by managers on six-figure salaries who would be just as happy in fully private sector positions as they are in their present semi-public roles.

Local authorities can be slow and bureaucratic, their lawyers barely accountable. There is a scandal still waiting to be told about how black and minority ethnic (BAME) people were kept out of

7 'People's Audit uncovers scale of great Lambeth housing sell-off', *Brixton Buzz*, 21 October 2019.

8 E Youle, 'Revealed: Number of council homes in Newham lost through Right to Buy', *Newham Recorder*, 2 August 2018.

council housing in the 1960s and 1970s or given access to accommodation only in the higher floors of tower blocks.[9] All that said, the security which local authority accommodation offers tenants, and the lower rents which councils charge, make council housing a much better and more secure option for tenants than housing association homes.

A homeless person who is housed by their local authority is not guaranteed to be housed in the local authority's own housing stock. There are in fact two separate processes. One is 'allocation', the name for the mechanism by which a person applies for council housing, and that housing is distributed according to need. Most councils have nomination policies which determine who can join the register for social housing and the criteria against which housing applications will be assessed and prioritised. A large family with several children, or including a disabled person, will score more highly; a single applicant will receive a lower score. The families in the top bands are given the greatest priority in bidding for council properties. Those who have the lowest priority may find themselves removed from the council register. Applicants at each point are encouraged to meet their needs in the private sector – if possible.

The other process is 'homeless accommodation', which can mean anything from a hostel or hotel through to a secure council tenancy. The mundane reality of housing the homeless, especially in London, is that even where people are in need, and eligible, homeless people are rarely housed into the nearest available local authority home but spend months or years being shuttled between hotel rooms, studio flats and nights on the street. I meet the families who live like this, the parents' eyes glazed, their children apathetic.

The dependence on hotels helps to explain why the government was so keen on hotels keeping open – albeit for homeless people only. At the start of the crisis, various hotel chains – notably Travelodge and Comfort Inn – responded by simply closing for business altogether. The doyen of housing law bloggers, the solicitor Giles Peaker who maintains the *Nearly Legal* housing law blog and website, collected the responses of council housing officers. One called the hotels' action 'devastating'; another said it was, 'the rug being pulled from under us'.[10]

Where a local authority can house a homeless person in its own accommodation, the cost to the authority is relatively modest. A typical

---

9 H Osborne, 'We know there's a housing crisis – but why is it so much worse for black families?' *Guardian*, 3 October 2017.

10 G Peaker, 'Throwing out the homeless – hotels and coronavirus', *Nearly Legal*, 24 March 2020.

local authority tenant might pay something like £6,000 or £7,000 a year in rent for a two-bedroom council flat, and on rent at that level, even once costs such as maintenance and repairs are factored in, the local authority will make a profit. For a single unit in homeless accommodation (meaning a single bedroom without a toilet or a kitchen), the landlord would typically charge the tenant (and the council, who are paying the housing benefit) at least double that amount.

Between 2010, when the austerity measures associated with the Conservative and Liberal Democrat Coalition Government began to take effect, and 2016, total council spending was reduced by 37 per cent, with further cuts already scheduled for the remainder of the decade. Between 2010/11 and 2017/18, a third of local authorities reduced their housing budget by more than half.[11]

The contradiction between protective laws which placed an onus on the local authority to house the homeless, and the cuts to local authority spending, has been resolved by local authority lawyers finding ever more ingenious ways of treating the laws as if they excluded the very people they were intended to protect.

Often this conflict has been expressed in legal arguments over the meaning of 'priority need'. A person was said to have this need if they were pregnant; a parent; threatened with homelessness as a result of flood, fire or disaster; or if they were 'vulnerable as a result of old age, mental illness or handicap or physical disability'.[12] For decades, local authorities made decisions on the basis that most homeless people were inevitably vulnerable, and the sheer act of becoming homeless put them at risk, and so the protection of homelessness provision could only be extended to a vanishingly small category of people who were not merely old, mentally ill or disabled, but much more so even than the typical homeless person.

Every housing lawyer has read letters from local authorities stating that one applicant for homelessness provision suffers from 'only' chronic depression or paranoid schizophrenia, and that this was not enough to make them vulnerable; or that another applicant had made repeated attempts to kill themselves but no attempts for two or three weeks and that they were no longer within the definition of vulnerability operated by that council.

For years, the judiciary co-operated with local authorities in understanding vulnerability. In 2015, however, and after many years

---

11 T Calver And D Wainwright, 'How cuts changed council spending, in seven charts', BBC News, 5 December 2018, chart 5.

12 Housing Act 1996 s189(1).

of challenges, the Supreme Court brought this practice to an end, with one of the judges describing the practice of excluding vulnerable people from homeless law as a 'reproach to a society that considers itself to be civilised'.[13]

However, even after that decision, the conflicts did not go away – they merely moved to other parts of the homelessness test, to whether the applicants were really homeless or whether they had made themselves intentionally homeless.

Most claims for possession by private landlords are brought under Housing Act 1988 s21; in them, the landlord is not asserting that they have a right to possession because the tenant is in arrears, but simply that it is the landlord's right to possession because they own the property and want it back. This is often called a 'no-fault' ground of possession. By contrast, no local authority can bring a section 21 claim. Most grounds of possession against social tenants suggest some degree of fault: the tenant loses their home because of anti-social behaviour, or because of rent arrears, or because of some other breach of their tenancy.

What that means is that if a social tenant is homeless, it is almost always open to the local authority to refuse to house them, saying that it is the tenant's fault they were evicted. When you look carefully at the cases, you can often show that assumption is wrong. For example, a tenant is evicted because of rent arrears, and they were on benefits which did not cover the rent. In those circumstances, how could the eviction be their fault? But the way intentional homelessness is used prevents that kind of patient inquiry. Local authorities stand behind it like a shield, refuse to investigate, and dare the tenants to appeal their decisions.

Between July and October 2019, 36,640 homeless families applied to be housed in England. It is sensible to assume that all of the people in this situation were homeless and believed they were eligible for accommodation (why else would they apply for it?). Yet, of that group, just 9,650 – or barely more than one in four – were accepted as eligible for homeless accommodation.[14] Three-quarters of those applying, in other words, were refused help. Some of them found lawyers and appealed the council's decision. That is when I and other housing lawyers are drawn in.

---

13 *Hotak and others v Southwark LBC and another* [2015] UKSC 30.

14 W Wilson and C Barton, 'Households in temporary accommodation (England)', Briefing Paper Number 02110, House of Commons Library, 26 November 2020; https://commonslibrary.parliament.uk/research-briefings/sn02110/.

In July 2020, by which time the courts were open again (albeit not for possession hearings), I was looking for a sign that either the local authorities or the judges were treating the lives of my clients with greater consideration. I met another client by Skype, Kayleigh, her hair grey, her skin translucent on my laptop screen.

The local authority refused to accept that Kayleigh was in priority need. She suffered from chronic obstructive pulmonary disease (COPD), which made her breathless and wheezy. She found autumns almost unbearable. If she was to become street homeless, her doctor said, she would suffer COPD attacks, her access to healthcare would be limited, and she would not be able to keep her medicine safe and dry. She was plainly vulnerable, even before we factored in the risk of the coronavirus returning in the autumn or the winter. The local housing authority offered, the day before the hearing, to quash its decision that Kayleigh was not vulnerable, to consider her case afresh and make a fresh decision within a further eight weeks.

That sounds like a victory, but it was far from a complete one. The risk in allowing the local authority a second chance was that it would reach the same decision as before. Often you read long passages of the old letter which have been copied and pasted from the old decision into the new one. Local authorities do this because of the way homelessness appeals work. As in a judicial review (on which they are modelled), homelessness appeals are a review of a decision taken by a public servant. The obligation to make a lawful decision remains with that part of government, not with the judiciary. Even if a judge overturns the original decision, they almost always give the local authority a second chance. A judge will only substitute their view for the local authority's in the most straightforward case. Reluctantly, I advised Kayleigh's solicitor to accept the council's offer.

I next represented Mrs Ortiz who had fled her home because of domestic violence and now lived in a domestic violence refuge. She had asked the local authority to pay housing benefit at her old property while she was living in the refuge, but they refused to, after which she returned home. The landlord obtained possession and evicted her. On the very day of her eviction, the local authority, appreciating that it had been wrong to refuse her benefits, paid the landlord, clearing her arrears. But it did not tell Mrs Ortiz it had done so, and a judge (not realising the debt was historic) confirmed her eviction. If the payment had a come a week earlier, she would probably have kept her home. Mrs Ortiz applied to her council for homeless housing, which was refused, with the council saying that by failing to pay her rent she had made herself intentionally homeless. We had a conference in my chambers. Mrs Ortiz apologised for taking up my time and blamed herself for her predicament. She arched a pair of drawn-on eyebrows. 'I've never been any good with money', she said.

The courts were working at reduced capacity. For all the court buildings we have sold, now the government was having to open new ones to reduce the backlog of cases. The Ministry of Justice announced that its 75 press officers had voluntarily relinquished the building in which they were housed, so that it could be turned into a new court.[15] The press treated this as a 'good news' story. But if we imagine that those 75 press officers are paid a median London salary, once we add tax, national insurance, pension and personnel, they alone must be costing the taxpayer around six million pounds in wages and other costs – or a quarter of the total sum the government spends each year on legal aid for housing.[16]

Judges deferred decisions where they could. Disputes which might not have settled did. Shortly after the appeal was issued, and without fighting it as far as a final hearing, the council reversed its decision. It agreed to rehouse Mrs Ortiz. It was a victory of sorts: Mrs Ortiz won. But she would be housed for the immediate future in a temporary accommodation, in a hotel room, not in the two-bed flat which had been her home.

I have described how in April I represented the Curlews, a family threatened with an injunction because of the behaviour of their young children. By July, the family was facing a new threat. The landlord, a housing association, had given up its claim for an injunction. Instead, it was demanding possession. It had served a section 21 notice. The Curlews, meanwhile, were refusing to leave. Their solicitor reckoned they had a robust defence: the family were being evicted mainly because of the behaviour of their son Geoff – and his behaviour had been good since the last hearing. The association was a public authority. As such it was required to make any child's interests paramount.

15 M Fouzder, 'MOJ headquarters begins new role as Nightingale court', *The Law Society Gazette*, 25 August 2020.

16 'Legal aid statistics quarterly, England and Wales: January to March 2020', Ministry of Justice, 25 June 2020; www.gov.uk/government/collections/legal-aid-statistics.

In the Curlews' case, the local authority had always been friendly. Before, it opposed the application for an injunction. Now it took the same pro-tenant approach in correspondence. A council manager wrote to the Curlews' solicitor. She described herself as 'outraged' by the suggestion that this vulnerable family should be removed from their home. 'The whole situation infuriates me', she wrote. 'If they are evicted, they will not be able to access our Housing Register.' Moreover, 'since they are reliant on benefits and rents locally being high, they would need to move out of the area'. Among the problems with moving was that it would disrupt the education of the children, two of whom were in special needs schools. The local authority asked us to tell the judge that the possession claim was motivated by the worst sorts of class snobbery among the Curlews' neighbours. 'They have paid in excess of £600,000 for their properties and are not very tolerant or understanding.'

The council's stance was an unexpected boon in fighting the landlord's claim for possession, which would resume for real as soon as the stay was lifted. But it was hard not to question the council's motives in helping us. One reason the local authority opposed the Curlews' eviction is that the family was not housed by them but by a housing association over which they had no control. If the housing association evicted the family, the tenants and their children would apply to the council for housing. Rehousing them would cost the council time and money; was that why the local authority was so determined to keep them where they were?

Another client, Ms Sykes, had been living in homeless accommodation for four years. She suffered with depression and anxiety. She was said to have made herself intentionally homeless after a dispute with the council about gas safety. In the emails between her and her landlord, what came over was the breakdown of communication between Ms Sykes and the council. She sent email after email, complaining that gas was leaking. No one ever came to investigate. The council agreed to do something only when a different tenant complained that she too could smell gas. Then, without warning Ms Sykes, housing officers went to her home, switched off the gas, and replaced her cooker while she was out. This disturbed Ms Sykes, making her angry and paranoid. The officers instructed Ms Sykes to remove her belongings from her lounge. She responded by drawing her curtains and keeping her front door locked so they could not get in. The local authority accused her of obstructing necessary repairs. She said it was their fault for not doing the works earlier or asking her before breaking into to her flat. The council evicted her, not for the dispute but for rent arrears, and then refused to rehouse her.

The local authority insisted that she was evicted only because of this dispute, when all the evidence from the possession case was that she had been made homeless because of rent arrears. The notice to quit said nothing about the gas dispute. In the possession proceedings, the only ground of possession was the rent. A solicitor asked me for my advice, and I said that the case was strong enough – just about – for legal aid.

I argued the case before His Honour Judge Pagnam, and I urged him to find that the only possible reason the local authority could have had in seeking to evict my client was her rent arrears. It was all they raised in their notice. They could have applied for possession on grounds of anti-social behaviour but they did not. Indeed, it was easy to see why they did not mention it – no landlord could ever get possession because of just a single instance of failing to allow repairing works. Even as I spoke, I knew that the judge had no sympathy for my case. He interrupted me, made me repeat the simplest of points, and cut me off as I tried to answer.

The moment my submissions had finished, Judge Pagnam signalled to the opposing counsel that he did not need her to speak. 'I've read your skeleton', he told her, 'It was excellent.' In a brisk, ten-minute judgment, he insisted that housing is a matter for the council to allocate, not the courts. He found no error in the council's decision.

Ms Sykes was ineligible for homeless support and would have to find the means to house herself. But from where? She did not have family, or any savings.

I sat at my desk at chambers unmoving, long after the hearing had ended, replaying the case in my mind. Was there anything else I could have said?

Defeat hurt. I came home. I was lying on my bed and my breathing was short. I was still, but my body was tense. I could feel my heart pounding as if I was recovering from a race. The insides of my stomach felt red and raw. I traced a finger from my neck to my waist and it felt like a knife against my skin. I bathed in self-loathing.

I have described how benefits changes cause needy families to lose their homes. The same problems can also be seen in homelessness cases, where cuts to welfare benefits prevent families from getting back into the ordinary housing system.

I attended a remote hearing in Luton to represent Mr O'Brien, whose local authority had found him intentionally homelessness after he allowed himself to get into debt on the rent account at his last home. 'Throughout your tenancy, you were in receipt of housing benefit', the council had written. 'Since signing your tenancy agreement, your rent account was only in credit in six months out of the last two years.'

Mr O'Brien and his two children were evicted from their previous accommodation because of those arrears and now lived in a room in a Premier Inn. Before the lockdown began, the children's headteacher had written a letter describing how the eviction had affected them. The youngest, who was in reception, had become unruly and the school had been obliged to allocate a teaching assistant to work full-time with him. He was not eating lunch. As for the oldest, who attended the same school, she had been heard shouting in the playground. She said she had no friends. They tried to help her by setting up a daily 'touch base', but the daughter never attended. The upheaval, the headteacher concluded, had caused the children a significant disadvantage in their education. I read the letter to the judge.

Mr O'Brien said that the eviction was not his fault. He said he was the victim of the benefit rules, and in particular the provision that a local authority need not pay more housing benefit than the 30th percentile of rents in its area. Mr O'Brien's rent was higher than the local authority was willing to pay, and after 12 months of using his other benefits to subsidise his rent, he was simply overwhelmed by debt. In principle, the case should have been straightforward. On an ordinary, unforced application of the law, the local authority was plainly wrong in refusing to rehouse my client. But in the case, I had a familiar and determined opponent: Tuck.

Everything about him was even more brilliant than before. There was a gold watch on his wrist. The colours of his Duchamp tie graced my screen – red, maroon and lilac.

Tuck had brought to the hearing three documents. Their purpose was to prove that at every stage of the past year, Mr O'Brien and his family always had more than enough money to live on. Mr O'Brien and I spent the vital last moments before the hearing started trying to decipher Tuck's schedules. 'I don't mean to be a nuisance', my client said, 'but that £1.50 a day on food – that's meant to be enough for three of us, is it?'

I told the judge that in a homelessness appeal, the court is supposed to be looking at the decision taken by a local authority housing officer at the time. We ask only whether it was rational, whether it explained its reasons, and whether it correctly understood the law. The housing officer did not have the benefit of Tuck's schedules. If he had had them at the time, who was to say what the outcome would have been – certainly, my client would have had a chance to gather evidence in response and prove it was not enough money to live on.

The judge agreed with me and quashed the decision. Mr O'Brien won. Yet, in helping to win the appeal for him, I was aware that all the local authority was required to do next was make a fresh decision. Such was the determination with which the council and Tuck had fought the case that I knew what would happen next. The council would make the same decision again. Mr O'Brien would appeal, and a judge would have to look at everything again. For another year at least, Mr Brien would remain trapped in the limbo of temporary housing.

Principled local authority housing officers are needed now more than ever. Housing is in desperately short supply. Millions of people are in poverty and they cannot afford housing except with help from their council. Local authorities are confronted with a great storm of unresolved need; and to meet it they only have a quarter of as many homes as they did 40 years ago. Any solution to the crisis of local authority housing would have to begin by building more homes. If the government was to assemble a committee of housing lawyers to advise them, the same solutions would be raised by all of us: Find a mechanism enabling the state to buy land cheaply. Use empty public land, build on brownfield sites, protect the green belt. We could encourage housebuilding by removing restrictions on councils from borrowing to build homes and by ring-fencing for councils' housing budgets the money they receive through the right to buy scheme – or ending the right to buy scheme altogether.

Under COVID-19, however, the government did none of this.

In 2016, the government had briefly acknowledged the problem and offered a retrograde answer to it. Rather than increase the supply of council housing, it chose to reduce the duration for which a new council tenancy would be granted. What the government decided was that, from that date onwards, all new local authority tenancies should no longer be for life – but now for a term of between two and ten years, or (if there was a child in the home aged under nine) until that child's 19th birthday.[17] When this new scheme was introduced,

17 Housing Act 1985 s81A.

the view of housing lawyers was that it was misconceived. It assumed that there was a large class of housing tenants who obtained housing because of some immediate crisis which would be resolved quickly, or because they were in immediate need after a child was born.

Had either of these factors been studied properly, neither would have justified a shortening of council tenancies to (potentially) just two years. For when single homeless people are housed by local authorities, or at least in London, the housing they receive is often hostel or hotel accommodation or a private sector tenancy. They only rarely obtain council tenancies. Meanwhile, it is true that the primary indicator of housing need is that a family has young children. But the need of a family with young children to be housed does not disappear after just a few years. What should happen if the family was to have a second child after the local authority granted a tenancy to them? On its face, the scheme envisaged the family's eviction, while the second child remained an infant. It is true that in those circumstances the local authority would have an option to extend the tenancy, but it would be under no obligation to do so. At the very least, the new law made temporary and unsettled what had previously been fixed and permanent. It created uncertainty – while offering no benefit to those waiting on council lists.

We worried that the scheme would oblige local authorities to employ whole new categories of housing officer whose sole duties would be to check that the local authority had accurate records of which tenancies were due to expire at the end of the fixed-term period. Or, worse still, that councils would use these automatic break periods as an excuse to evict tenants without good reason. The best that can be said for the scheme is that for all the malice with which it was planned, it has made little difference at all. Many councils have ignored it. The crisis of local authority housing has continued unabated.

In my next case over the summer of 2020, I represented Mr Anderson, who had failed to keep up with his rent after losing his part-time job when his depression, from which he had suffered for many years, became so bad that he could no longer force himself out of bed each morning. His son had been born with an enlarged heart. For months, Mr Anderson and his girlfriend had spent every waking moment at Great Ormond Street children's hospital, watching over him, hoping desperately that the condition would stabilise. After his son died, Mr Anderson was no longer capable of keeping up his benefits correspondence, still less attending court. I saw the letters from the landlord, and for every promise of understanding, a 'but' followed. Mr Anderson and his girlfriend split up; he failed to attend court and possession was ordered.

The local authority informed him that by failing to pay the rent he had made himself intentionally homeless. It refused to house him. 'I am satisfied', the local authority decision-maker wrote, 'that although you did suffer from depression, you were well aware of your rent arrears and were also aware that you had to contribute towards the rent'.

The local authority acknowledged that Mr Anderson suffered from what it characterised as 'severe' depression and was willing to treat him as a disabled person having the protection of the Equality Act 2010 against discrimination. It accepted that his depression was so bad that it caused him to lose his job. It determined, however, that 'there is no information your mental health impairment was so severe that it affected your judgment. Having considered all the evidence I must conclude that you are intentionally homeless.' Within days of Mr Anderson's appealing the decision, the local authority invited us to settle the appeal. Without admitting in any way that their decision-maker was wrong, they accepted that the decision should be quashed. It placed him in temporary accommodation while deciding what to do next.

It was a small victory, but despite having done all I could to make sure that Mr Anderson would be housed, the case left me with a bitter taste. Neither Mr Anderson nor anyone else with his history of chronic depression should have been made homeless. Yes, with the assistance of a solicitor and a barrister, Mr Anderson persuaded the council to back down. But the reality is that the large majority of unsuccessful applicants for homeless housing are not signposted to a lawyer, would not be able to draft grounds of appeal for themselves, still less stand up in court and persuade a judge that the local authority had misunderstood the law.

I saw my father in hospital, where he had been taken for tests, and we sat for hours, the sun glaring through the blinds. He tried to speak, but his words were overwhelmed by the disorder from the man in the bed opposite. From the opposite side of the ward, my father's neighbour muttered at the nurse, calling her 'Dirty, stinking.' He shouted, 'I'm being held prisoner.'

My father watched this drama. Months had passed since he'd left his home and he did not understand why he was no longer there. He told me, 'I'm homeless.'

'You're not homeless', I replied, 'you're just in hospital'.
'Hospital?'
'Yes, in hospital', I told him.

I represented Mrs Sherwood, a mother who had been living for several years with her two primary school age children in homeless accommodation supplied by the local authority. In 2016 her mother was attacked by her husband (Mrs Sherwood's father) and suffered a broken leg and hip, after which she moved in with her daughter. After months in which the council was aware there was a problem but did nothing to help, Mrs Sherwood's solicitor issued proceedings, complaining that the property was overcrowded and unsuitable. In 2018, the council agreed to move them to another two-bedroom property, and a slightly larger one, this time with a lounge and a sofa in it. The property they chose had neither a bath nor a shower on the ground floor while, because of her physical ill-health, Mrs Sherwood's mother was unable to walk up or down stairs. Mrs Sherwood obtained a GP's letter, asking for her to be moved. Her solicitor again threatened proceedings, telling the local authority the property was clearly unsuitable.

Unfortunately, the local authority refused to reconsider its decision. Its housing officers decided that the accommodation was suitable for Mrs Sherwood. They accepted that the accommodation had no bedroom for Mrs Sherwood's mother, but said the accommodation was only likely to be 'temporary' (the lease was for a year) and it was not unreasonable to expect a 76-year-old woman to sleep each night for a year on a sofa. If her mother had difficulty washing, she should not complain since there were 'facilities' on the ground floor level (in other words, a sink) and she could wash herself there.

Mrs Sherwood asked the court to decide that the accommodation was unsuitable for her and her family. She set out what she had to do to keep her mother clean. Every weekday she placed a waterproof tablecloth on the floor of her lounge and washed her mother with a flannel. She used water from a bucket. Her mother sat on a chair while Mrs Sherwood washed her. It took about an hour to clean her. Mrs Sherwood found washing her mother's hair painful. She bent her neck, triggering her arthritis, while Mrs Sherwood poured water over her. The process was demeaning to them both. She could not wash her mother at all at weekends or when the kids were home. The lockdown, she said, was unbearable.

Because of her arthritis, her mother required warm showers and baths. But now she found the process of bathing painful, even humiliating.

The local authority maintained its position. 'I appreciate this is not an ideal situation. I accept that the lack of a downstairs bathroom is not ideal. I am, however, satisfied that the accommodation is suitable.'

In a 12-page skeleton argument, the council's barrister insisted that the appeal was 'misconceived from the outset . . . entirely unencumbered by merit'. As to Mrs Sherwood and what her mother should do in this plainly unsuitable accommodation, the barrister wrote, 'The mother can wash herself in the basin.'

Yet while the local authority seemed determined to fight, behind the scenes its barrister must have advised that its case was not quite as strong as she had pretended.

The local authority wrote to Mrs Sherwood's solicitors, offering to settle the appeal, but only to the extent that it would make a fresh decision. Until then, Mrs Sherwood and her family should stay where they were. The decision for Mrs Sherwood was a tricky one. Should we allow the local authority another opportunity to stall – knowing that a judge was unlikely to do more than require a second decision from them?

The evening before the hearing, the council finally conceded our appeal – accepting that the property was unsuitable and promising to move them.

Looking back at the process from its end, it was hard to avoid the suspicion that, for all the ingenuity of the lawyers on both sides, we had been involved in merely a sham battle. The local authority must have known from the outset that its decision to house Mrs Sherwood in a home in which her mother could not wash herself was unjustifiable, and likely to be overturned. Yet by delaying for a year, its officers had saved the authority expense and passed the burden of public sector funding cuts from the council to a homeless woman and her elderly mother. The local authority had wilfully ignored the law, knowing that it would take our client months or years to obtain an effective remedy. Our legal system had given the local authority every incentive to delay in offering a vulnerable family the housing they needed.

The week after, I had a remote hearing at Mayor's and City of London Court. The judge sat with only his face showing on my screen, and I had to fill in the surrounds from memory. The high ceilings, the majestic Victorian panelling behind and above him – they belonged to another time. It was the only county court in London where it was still possible to enter the court from the street and to speak to the staff working there without having arranged a prior appointment.

My client Darius had been refused homeless accommodation because, the local authority said, he and his 15-year-old son had wrongly quit the accommodation in which they were previously housed. Darius had been diagnosed with depression and suffered panic attacks. He had long been planning to bring his wife and daughter to London, but they were still in Iran at the time that the lockdown began in March. They had been missing for months while the authorities refused to confirm what had happened to them. All this was weighing on Darius's mind, in combination with the poor quality of the home in which the council had housed him. The building which he and his son fled had been repeatedly condemned by the local authority: it was an unlicensed 'home in multiple occupation' (HMO), and plainly unsafe.

His Honour Judge Pagnam worked briskly through the grounds of the appeal. He accepted that the property was technically overcrowded – but found that in conditions of housing shortage, overcrowding was inevitable. He found that the local authority had given due regard to Darius's disability in refusing to house him elsewhere. He turned to the fire hazard, to the awkward fact that the local authority had ordered the owner to make the building safe, but the landlord had refused. 'This is a difficult case', the judge said. 'There are reasonable arguments on both sides.' His lips squeezed together, he stared at the screen, as if hoping that my opponent would give him some last excuse to dismiss the claim.

'I have asked the local authority to explain why the landlord refused to make the repairing works. They say . . . they say . . .'

I could see how hard he was trying to come up with a reason to refuse this ground too, and he tried, but he just could not think of anything.

'They say there isn't an excuse. Or, if there is, they have never been told it. I have to say that I struggle to understand how the local authority could keep this family in accommodation which they consider to be a fire-trap.'

Finally, reluctantly, he agreed to quash the review decision.

I left court, satisfaction beating in my chest.

CHAPTER 8

August: Judges, panel members

Through the summer of 2020, I represented homeless people and tenants threatened with injunctions for anti-social behaviour. The largest part of my housing practice – cases where I represent a tenant at risk of losing possession or eviction – remained on hold.

Possession hearings were due to resume on 24 August. The Mayor of London argued that without significant changes in the law, hundreds of thousands of people would be in danger of losing their home. He spoke of a 'tsunami' of possible evictions. But the metaphor was inexact. A tsunami is a force of nature, the consequence of earthquakes and landslides. You can take steps to mitigate a tsunami, you cannot prevent it entirely. With the threatened tumult of evictions, stopping them would be the easiest thing in the world. All we needed to do was to permit judges to refuse possession where the result would be unreasonable.

As the end of the eviction stay approached, the homelessness charity Crisis commissioned barristers to draw up legislation which would convert Housing Act 1988 s21 and Sch 2 ground 8 into discretionary grounds. The Welsh Government extended eviction notice periods to six months. Andy Burnham, Mayor of Greater Manchester, warned of the risk of 1930s-style homelessness in Northern England. Everyone, it seems, agreed on the necessity of legislation. But whether through ideology or inertia, the government insisted on placing as few restrictions as it could in the way of the landlords' right to evict.

A few minor tweaks were made to the Civil Procedure Rules (the code governing all hearings in the county court and High Court). After the end of the stay, a landlord would be required to file a notice at court if it wanted a possession case to be restored. The landlord would need to tell the court any information it had about the tenant's circumstances, including the effect the pandemic had had on them. But there was no sanction if the landlord failed to provide this information, or if it refused to make obvious enquiries. There was no power to stop possession if the landlord's information was wrong, or if the landlord sought possession from a tenant who was made redundant in the lockdown and they were behind with the rent through the pressure of the pandemic and no fault of their own.

By 19 August, there were just two working days before the eviction stay was due to be lifted. Housing Minister Lord Greenhalgh had insisted that it was time for COVID-19 protections to end. Allowing possession cases to resume was 'an important step towards ending the lockdown and will protect landlords' important right to regain their property'.[1]

Over the next two days, the press warned of the risks should cases resume. Housing charity Shelter estimated that a quarter of a million private renters had fallen into arrears due to the coronavirus crisis, while a YouGov poll revealed that 174,000 private tenants had already been threatened with eviction. Sixteen health bodies warned of a catastrophic wave of evictions, with all the risks that would bring for the spread of COVID-19. The position of the government remained that the stay on evictions should come to an end; yet, even as this was insisted, ministers were already briefing friendly journalists, asking them to tone down the negative coverage. As the hours ticked past, they promised that a further stay would be announced.

The measure came in a letter from the Master of the Rolls (the most senior judge in the Court of Appeal), complaining that the government had not legislated to deal with the looming crisis. Only reluctantly, and 'by a majority', did the Civil Procedure Rule Committee agree to the government's request. The stay was extended: without consultation, or any involvement from parliament. The underlying problems remained unaddressed. The government was not even malicious – that would suggest an active plan to cause harm; rather, the dominant features of its response to the housing crisis were ignorance, indifference and incompetence.

Beneath the Civil Procedure Rule Committee there was another working group, looking specifically at the question of the lifting of the eviction ban. There, two significant concessions were made. First, any possession or eviction hearing would be in person (unless both parties agreed otherwise). Second, the listing of 50 possession hearings in a morning would end. At the most, a judge would be able to hear just ten possession cases in that time.

---

1   G Demianyk, 'Government insists end of evictions ban next week is "important step" to "protect landlords"', *Huffington Post*, 19 August 2020.

Once it was accepted that possession hearings would be in person, the case for fewer hearings became overwhelming. It was obvious that cramming large numbers of people, many of them poor or disabled or ill, into a crowded court was a health risk. But the reduction of the size of possession lists would do a great deal to reduce the frequency of evictions. For by August 2020 there was already a backlog of tens of thousands of cases. The courts would barely have sufficient capacity to reduce this build-up, still less hear newer cases. The longer the process was dragged out, the less commercially attractive it would be to a landlord to evict a tenant after (say) a short period in which they had briefly defaulted on their rent.

Why did judges concede that possession and eviction hearings should be in person? A friend who attended the working group told me that there was a revolt by the judiciary outside London. District judges wrote to the Master of the Rolls' committee with stories of tenants who lacked the technology to engage with online hearings. The judges themselves refused to approve evictions without having the tenants in the courts in front of them.

During the lockdown, everyone accepted that how we saw work needed to change. On his release from hospital, Prime Minister Boris Johnson had thanked the NHS for having 'saved my life, no question'. He praised the nurses who cared for him, Jenny from New Zealand, and Luis from Portugal. He called the health service 'the beating heart of the country'. I did not trust Johnson; but I would much rather that Conservative leaders were praising health workers and acknowledging that our NHS depends on migrants. The people who kept Britain working were not the bankers, nor the politicians – but the workers who kept our pharmacies stocked, the people who delivered food from supermarkets, who cooked for a living or cleaned or cared. As the *Guardian*'s Zoe Williams wrote early in the crisis, 'all those other jobs that were previously classed as low-value . . . now turn out to be the most important in the country'.[2]

One place where you might expect to see a difference in how people were treated post-coronavirus was the employment tribunal. For employment law is shaped by what judges consider reasonable. So, if for example, a worker complains that she was unfairly dismissed, an employment judge must decide whether 'in the circumstances . . .

---

2 Z Williams, 'We say we value key workers, but their low pay is systematic, not accidental', *Guardian*, 7 April 2020.

the employer acted *reasonably*.[3] Or, in deciding whether a worker has been harassed, an employment tribunal (a judge plus two lay members of the tribunal panel) must decide whether behaviour was so bad as to constitute harassment. They do so, considering both the perception of the person complaining and 'whether it was *reasonable* for the conduct to have that effect'.[4] When deciding whether a disabled employee was entitled to a *reasonable* adjustment,[5] the focus of the tribunal is again on this same idea – how bad was the employee's need, how easily could it be accommodated – what should reasonably have been done for them?

Every time an employment judge or a tribunal decides a case, they bring to the process subjective notions of fairness. The word reasonable, in employment law, maximises judicial discretion. It means that a judge is to decide cases according to what he or she considers fair.

When barristers talk to lay clients, we often say things like – it is better to have a barrister rather than a solicitor representing you because, as barristers, we are repeatedly in court. These days it is quite usual for solicitors to represent parties in tribunal cases, but even the solicitor who is keenest on advocacy will spend a greater proportion of their time than a barrister does on the earlier stages of proceedings: taking witness statements from a client, collecting documents for them. Because barristers are almost always in court, we see judges close up and we learn to tailor our advocacy to the individual in front of us. We acknowledge the subjective element of lawmaking, its dependence on the values of the individual judge.

At its worst, the subjectivity of employment law makes it a field ripe for injustice. But, at its best, it makes the tribunal flexible. When values change, the tribunal changes with them.

I returned to Cardiff for the first time in months. My client Mr Peters was a security guard. He used to work at a broadcasting company. Before he came on shift, a member of the public had made her way into the building without a pass. By the time that she was found, Peters was on duty. He was the first person to be alerted to her presence. He was required to report the matter to his colleagues. The employer said he did not – and therefore dismissed him. Fortunately, Peters was a member of a trade union, and it was through the union that I was able to represent him. The case was an unfair dismissal

---

3 Employment Rights Act 1996 s98(4) (emphasis added).
4 Equality Act 2010 s26(4) (emphasis added).
5 Equality Act 2010 s20.

claim which meant it was heard by a single judge, and indeed one I had encountered before. Employment Judge Geisler watched me cautiously. She said, 'Your client should have reported the intrusion to his managers.'

'That's how the employer sees it', I acknowledged. 'They say that because Mr Peters didn't pass the information on to the most senior manager then on duty, they had no choice but to dismiss him.' I sipped from the cup of water on the table in front of me before continuing. 'But my client *did* report the intrusion: to his team leader. In doing so, he reported the matter properly, sufficiently, and in line with his contract.'

'What kind of contract was it?' the judge said, fishing to see if my client working on an agency contract, or was formally self-employed, or anything else so that there might be a doubt as to whether the correct employer is in court.

'A standard employment contract.'

'But what about the chain of command? Was there anything which required Mr Peters to report to the senior manager, rather than a team leader?'

'The respondent's witnesses will tell you they had a policy that complaints had to be escalated to the most senior manager in the organisation. My client will tell you that there was never any such rule. Certainly, there was nothing in writing.'

'I suppose you're saying the dismissal procedure was unfair?' The question sounded innocent but behind it there was another trap. A finding that the dismissal was badly handled might result in a victory for my client, but it would limit the scope of the judge's inquiry. My client needed her to find that he had done little if anything wrong.

'My client's claim isn't about process. It's about the outcome. He'd worked for the business 12 years, with an unblemished record. He accepts he made mistakes. But they come nowhere near justifying dismissal.'

'You can't blame his managers for sticking to the rules.'

'If that's what they were', I answered. 'One of the findings you will need to make is what exactly the rules were. My client accepts the news of the intruder needed to be passed on. He did that by reporting the incident to the manager closest to him.'

The judge turned to the employer's barrister, Mr Zhou. 'Am I right that the reason for the dismissal was gross misconduct?'

'Yes, ma'am.'

'Did the respondent have a policy which sets out the sanction appropriate for different sorts of misconduct?'

'Yes, the conduct policy', and he read from it, 'Gross misconduct includes conduct which is likely to prejudice the company's business or reputation.' He emphasised the last word. 'For my client, what mattered was its contract with the broadcaster. That agreement is worth millions to the company every year. After the broadcaster heard about the intruder, they complained. They considered cancelling the contract. The damage could have been immense.'

I was well aware that the broadcaster did indeed threaten to cancel the contract at about this time. But their letter complained about other things entirely: poor training, excessive overtime and the managers' repeated failure to recruit enough guards to staff the security desk. None of these had been my client's fault.

Zhou was still speaking. 'By failing to report the matter as fully as possible', he explained, 'the claimant jeopardised the employment of dozens of his fellow workers. That's the point the respondent's witnesses will make.'

Judge Geisler nodded at him. 'Then let's hear the evidence.'

One way in which county court and employment tribunal claims differ is that the government publishes much more detailed statistical data for the latter (as it does for all tribunals). We can say, with some degree of accuracy, which cases are more likely to succeed, and provide an educated guess why. The figures show that for many years, certain kinds of employment claim have been easier to win than others. Prior to the introduction of tribunal fees, approximately three-quarters of all claims for unlawful deduction of wages that made it to a final hearing would succeed there, as would half of all claims for unfair dismissal, and between 15 and 40 per cent of discrimination claims (with race discrimination at 15 per cent or thereabouts, and sex discrimination at 40 per cent).[6] Since that time, overall success rates have fluctuated, but always this basic pattern has remained: some kinds of case are simply easier to win than others.

There is no mystery as to why workers win more often in deduction of wages claims as opposed to discrimination claims. The former are simpler. Wages claims are often listed for an hour or a two-hour hearing, unlike unfair dismissals for which a two- or three-day hearing is usually needed. Quite often, employers fail to attend hearings. A typical contested wages claim might involve an employer arguing that a manager had purported to give a worker a pay rise but

6 D Renton, *Struck out: Why employment tribunals fail workers and what can be done*, Pluto Press, 2012, p15.

exceeded his or her authority in so doing, or a defence that a worker did not do work of a particular kind or at a particular time or at a particular pay rate. Where there is a dispute, a judge can resolve it quickly. Judges are comfortable in finding a wages case in a worker's favour. Their finding does little to challenge the normal running of a business. Where a business finds that a manager miscalculated a worker's wages, there is unlikely to be any strong demand from other workers for that manager's dismissal. It is far easier for a tribunal to find that a worker was mistakenly underpaid than it is to find that a worker was sexually harassed by a senior manager who remains in post, or unfairly dismissed for a discriminatory reason and should now be reinstated. Decisions of these sort actively curb managers' power.

In 2012/13, the average (mean) award for a successful unfair dismissal claim was £10,127. Over the next four years, the award rose each year until the average reached a peak of £16,543 in 2016/17. Then (after the abolition of employment tribunal fees, as judges' workload rose), for three years it fell and stood at £10,812 in 2019/20.[7] There appear to be distinct historical trends: times when workers are more likely to win a case before the tribunal or receive more compensation; and times when their prospects are worse.

We had reached the second day of the hearing. In an ordinary dismissal, it is the employer's witnesses who go first. The dismissing offer was a Mr Molloy. Before he joined the respondent, Molloy worked for 30 years in the Metropolitan Police force.

'You sacked my client because he didn't report a security breach?'

The question was perfectly simple, and Mr Molloy really should not have had any trouble answering. He had come to court that morning wearing a blue suit, a blue tie and a jaunty smile. Bit by bit, however, the confidence had worn off his face and after 15 minutes of questions, Molloy was sucking his cheeks in and blowing them out. He surely must have been a witness before. But giving evidence was proving harder than he had hoped.

Employment Judge Geisler looked up. For a day and a half, she had been giving small nods of encouragement to the employer's barrister, smiling at his little jokes. In Judge Geisler's view, the employer was the master in the workplace and had the right to make the rules, just as she was the master in her own court.

7 'Employment Tribunal and Employment Appeals Tribunal: Annual Tables', Ministry of Justice, 29 September 2020.

She invited the employer's barrister to pour Mr Molloy some water.

Molloy shook his head from side to side as if to say he was good without it. But the look of gratitude as he drank told a different story.

Mere weeks after dismissing my client, Mr Molloy had started working at a different security firm. He was, I assumed, dismissed by the employer; although I also suspected he received a pay-off – unlike my client. He had come into this hearing to defend the good name of an employer to whom he no longer owed any debt of loyalty. No doubt, several phone calls were needed to persuade him to be a witness. Today, it was clear that if Molloy had been given a second chance, he would not have come.

When Molloy had finished with the water, the judge nodded at me to continue.

I asked Molloy, 'It is right, isn't it, that in his dismissal letter you told Mr Peters he'd been sacked because he didn't report a security breach?'

The letter of dismissal was at page 352 in a blue folder of documents. The employer's paralegal had numbered the pages lovingly by hand, photocopied them for the judge and the parties, and there they sat on the witness table.

Molloy scanned the letter one last time.

He looked at me unhappily. 'That's what it says.'

'But Mr Peters had reported the breach, within minutes of learning about it. He'd reported it to his line manager, hadn't he?'

I waited for an answer.

And, the judge, too, was watching the witness.

'He told me he'd reported it.' The look on Molloy's face was equal parts of anger, bitterness and resentment. 'I didn't believe him.'

Mr Peters' solicitor and I spent the coffee-break teasing each other about Brexit. She was a graduate of the Bob Crow school of trade unionism and the Tony Benn academy of politics. From her perspective, the EU was a bosses' ramp, we should never have joined.

I said, 'You were on the same side as Nigel Farage.'

She answered, 'And you voted with George Osborne.'

Until his dismissal from his position as a security guard, Mr Peters had enjoyed the benefits of a steady, well-paid job in a part of the economy which was highly regulated. On his dismissal, Peters found other, less secure, and worse remunerated employment. The principal obstacles standing in the way of his return to steady work were his employer's finding that he had been guilty of gross misconduct. For months, the company had refused to give him a reference. He needed clear findings from the tribunal to have a fighting chance of returning to anything like his old job. Peters was aware that the compensation for his dismissal was unlikely to be more than a few months' wages. The real prize for him was a finding that he had been unfairly dismissed, which Peters might show to other prospective employers. (As a plan, it was by no means guaranteed of success. For, although such a finding would prove to the world that Mr Peters had been hard done by, it would also show that he knew how to litigate. There are plenty of employers who would see that knowledge as a reason not to recruit him).

As for Mr Molloy, he was sitting at the witness table. A green tinge had settled on his face as if, inside, he was travelling by ferry in a storm.

'In your witness statement', I reminded him, 'you say you sacked Mr Peters because he couldn't prove he'd reported the case to his line manager'.

'That's right.'

'What sort of proof did you need?' It was a bad question, and I tried to hide my own grimace as I asked it. The question was open, when in cross-examination every question should be closed, preventing the witness from making long speeches justifying themselves. I waited for Judge Geisler to make a sarcastic comment. But she let the moment pass. For the moment, she was giving me – and Mr Peters – the benefit of the doubt.

'If he had had an email maybe, or anything, confirming he'd spoken to his manager, I would have been lenient with him.'

'Let me get this straight', I said. 'If you could have known without doubt that Mr Peters had told his manager, you wouldn't have sacked him?'

'I wouldn't have.'

Victory was so close, but a single bad question, any relaxation of the control I had over him, and all the good work I had done would be wasted.

'Let's look at another document', I said, 'page 297. It is right, isn't it, that you spoke to Mr Peters' line manager?'

'I did.'

'And when you spoke to the team leader, he told you, didn't he, that Mr Peters had reported the security breach to him?'

A rasping sound escaped from Molloy's throat.

'Now, let's see that date. You spoke to the team leader on the 25th?'

'If you say so.'

'It's not me saying so, is it? The date's there in black and white.'

Molloy looked. Grimly, he answered, 'It is.'

'That was two days, wasn't it, before you spoke to Mr Peters and dismissed him?'

He stared at the documents, shaking his head at them.

In Employment Judge Geisler's court, a worker's path is always a harder one. That is not to say, however, that the worker always loses.

Maybe it is because I joined the bar late, maybe it is because I am white and male and middle-class, but it has long seemed to me that in many of my cases the judge was watching me and thinking, 'You're on my side, you're the same as me really.' Most judges are former barristers. Many members of my own chambers spend a day or so a week sitting as a part-time judge. When I was a pupil, I had two supervisors. One has become a full-time county court judge, while the other now sits full-time in the employment tribunal. The longer you have been a lawyer, the greater the attraction of a life deciding cases without having to prepare them, the more pleasant it becomes to think of annual leave and pensions paid by someone else.

I have seen the look of encouragement on a judge's face when I have made their decision as easy as it could be. I have also seen the disappointment when I have made arguments which the judge in front of me found less than compelling. I am thinking of the time (not so long ago) when I came to court and I fought to stop the eviction of tenant who had, admittedly, barely paid his rent in six months. The local authority's housing officer was waiting in the room when I came in and, from the judge's smiles in her direction, it was plain that she had been in his court many times before. His way of proving his gallantry was by constantly interrupting me. I just about persuaded the judge that he was on the verge of a legal error, so much so that the hearing ended in a bad-tempered draw. Afterwards, since the case was likely to come back to court, I asked the judge to recuse himself – to decide, in other words, that he would not hear any future case involving the same tenant. I said, 'In ten years at the bar, I've never had to endure such a stream of interruptions as I've faced today.' He snorted at my mere ten years and told me, 'In ten years you'll be sat where I am – then you'll understand.'

I will never be a judge. I respect that part of our profession. But I know that there are cases where the law only provides a single answer. Sometimes it will not allow you to keep a person in their home or compensate them for their dismissal. I refuse to be the person who approves an eviction or a dismissal.

I can imagine a reader asking, aren't there cases where eviction is the right answer? Where a tenant's arrears are beyond recovery? Aren't there tenants whose behaviour is just so bad, that they should be in hospital rather than living on an estate? I would be more sympathetic to the first argument if there was somewhere else for these tenants to go – if we had a stock of second-chance housing which people could use to turn their lives around.

As for the anti-social tenant – perhaps, but the reason it does not work like that is that mental health services have been run down quite as thoroughly as public housing. We have had 30 years of what a previous generation of politicians euphemistically called, 'care in the community'. A small minority of my clients would prefer the stability of psychiatric care, but it is rationed and inaccessible to them. The tenants in anti-social behaviour cases are fighting battles about access to healthcare, and demanding intervention from local authorities. The trial of possession claims becomes a front for all these different tasks. It is made to bear the weight of broader social battles which lack the same infrastructure of legal aid.

As summer 2020 wore on, I was watching the judges and the lay members of the employment tribunals for any sign of greater empathy. The judges, well, they were still judges. The law was their life, and they were just as kind or as hostile to my clients as before. The other members of the panels, though, are not lawyers. They come from business or from trade unions. They are the nearest thing we have in law to jurors: members of the public being asked to serve a public role. They serve the law, and sometimes they soften its blow.

The 2010 Conservative and Liberal Democrat Coalition Government had done its best to remove the panel members from the tribunal altogether. We used to have them in unfair dismissal claims, but not since 2012. Now, dismissals are heard by judges sitting alone. The two panel members are saved for discrimination cases, the hardest fought of all employment claims.

At the end of August, I was back in London Central Employment Tribunal. My client, Lucia, was a nurse. She showed me photograph of herself in the lockdown. She wore a blue gown, a blue medical hat, and a look on her face as if she had not slept in days.

'You were a hero', I said.

'I wasn't.'

As a practice nurse (working for a GP), for her lockdown meant a reduction in the number of patients who were allowed to visit the surgery. She helped people with ulcers, babies requiring immunisations. She met other patients by telephone or video-link. For long periods, the practice was almost silent: instead of two dozen patients a day, Lucia would see just five or six. She checked stock, she kept the rooms clean. Anything else was left to the autumn.

She joined one of the new pop-up hospitals. For a time, she felt full of purpose. Friends who had studied alongside her, sent her text messages, welcoming her decision. She was a real nurse now, serving bravely on the frontline during a pandemic. But the hospital she had joined was little more than a shell. In her first week, they had six patients. In her second week, fewer than 30 beds were occupied, and this is in a building with capacity for several thousand people. Rather than caring for the ill, she was assigned to administrative work, answering phone calls from other trusts whose own hospitals were overwhelmed. Lucia's job was to provide a medical-sounding explanation for refusing to take the dying. Patients were receiving dialysis, requiring ventilators, and her job was to keep them where they were rather than to allow into the building any patient who might die there.

Today's hearing was not about those events, but things which had happened the autumn before – when Lucia had been working for a different GPs' practice in central London. There, one of the doctors had repeatedly asked her out. Dr Jones was the co-owner of the practice. Lucia wasn't the first woman he had approached. He had previously invited two of the other nurses out for a drink, and now it was her turn. All three were more than 20 years younger than him.

The first time Dr Jones asked her out, they had gone to see the musical, *Jesus Christ Superstar*. Afterwards, they went to a nearby pub where she had a glass of red wine, but only one, while he finished the rest of the bottle. When the pub rang last orders, Lucia stood up to leave. At this point, her and the GP's account differed. She insisted that he grabbed her, and she shoved him back. Mr Jones said she had been the instigator. Lucia had attempted to kiss him, and he had pushed her away.

A week later, the doctor asked her out a second time. Lucia refused, but he was her employer, so she tried to decline politely.

He asked her out a third time. At that point, she resigned. She brought a claim of constructive dismissal and sexual harassment. To win the case, she had to persuade the tribunal that her employer's conduct had violated her dignity, or created an intimidating, hostile, degrading or humiliating environment for her.

Dr Jones seemed shocked to find himself before the tribunal. His statement sought to prove what a kind and generous employer the practice was by describing how, during the pandemic, the surgery reduced staff hours without cutting pay. The GPs wanted the nurses to be ready for when the hospitals emptied; they knew that as they did the surgery would get busier. Even Dr Jones himself caught the virus. Such an empathetic business, his statement suggested, could not possibly have discriminated against one of its nurses.

Mr Bowls was representing the employer, and on the first day, as he introduced the case, he mentioned the pandemic and his client's illness, and said, 'I am delighted to say that, after a long leave of absence, my client is almost entirely recovered.'

'Very glad to hear it', Employment Judge Featherstone answered. 'It's perfectly right and proper of you to raise his distinguished service.'

'If it pleases you, sir.'

The judge and the barrister simpered at one another, like old school friends happening upon each other in the dinner queue at Brooks's.

I looked to the panel members who sat beside Judge Featherstone in the hope that they would resist this mutual love-in. Judge Featherstone, I knew. I had been in front of him before. But with the other members of the tribunal, I had little to go on but a name.

I tried to catch the eye of Ms Dawidowicz on Judge Featherstone's left. I did not know whether she was a trade unionist or from human resources. In the old days, the workers' representative on the panel might sometimes wear a distinguishing badge – not a union badge, for that would be too obvious, but perhaps a CND pin. Ms Dawidowicz wore a lilac shirt and a blue linen jacket.

As for Ms Evans on Judge Featherstone's right, I could only see long, looping earrings; grey hair with just a hint of red at their tips, henna perhaps. She could have been a librarian. Maybe a rep in the council workers' union, but just as likely a manager.

I tried to catch the eye of Ms Dawidowicz. She turned away.

I looked at Ms Evans. She stared back glumly at me.

By close of business on the second day, the case was looking weaker than I had hoped. Bowls had wrung from my client an admission that at the time she resigned from the surgery she was suffering from anxiety and depression and was badly in need of a rest. 'There was a reason I was depressed', she insisted, 'the way he kept on pestering me'.

I was watching the judge as Lucia spoke – he had laid down his pen. He frowned. He was not taking notes.

Ever since the case began, Judge Featherstone had been interrupting me whenever I tried to speak. Any objections I made were met with a hostile stare. He gurned and he grimaced. He glowered his dissatisfaction with me.

The employment tribunal was due to close at half-past four. As we got ready to pack up our things, Judge Featherstone looked at me. 'What I'm about to tell you is just me speaking – as a panel we haven't discussed it. On the other hand, you might think when you've heard me that it's just plain common sense.'

The words struck me like a blow.

'If your client, Mr Renton, accepts that she was too unwell to work, then, even at its highest, her claim for unfair dismissal isn't going to be worth much. There might be value in her claim for sexual harassment. But at that point you're asking the Tribunal to go far beyond its remit. There are things we're good at: dismissals, redundancies. But harassment, what could we possibly know about that?'

I could hear Lucia breathing quickly.

'Obviously, we've only heard half the evidence. But Dr Jones is a public servant, who has served his country with distinction at a time of crisis. You can't imagine that any decisions we make would be insensitive to his record.'

There was no kind word for my client, no sugar on the pill.

I knew what Judge Featherstone expected to me to do. He wanted me to talk to my client and tell her to withdraw the case. But I would not make it easy for the judge. 'I'm sorry, sir', I said, playing dumb, 'I'm don't understand what you're saying.'

'I'm not saying anything.'

Featherstone removed his glasses, wiped them angrily on a piece of cloth before resuming. 'I'm reminding you of your professional duties, that's all.'

With a final glare, the judge dismissed us.

We met in the nearest café for an emergency conference. Lucia was having trouble breathing, her cheeks had quite caved in. At least her solicitor Adrian still seemed confident. While I had met Lucia for the first time only a week before the hearing, he had been her solicitor since the case began and he had not stopped believing in her.

He said, 'Don't you worry about Featherstone, he isn't as bad as he pretends.'

'He seemed to be saying I couldn't win the case.'

'Adrian's right', I answered. 'Featherstone's lazy. He's famous for it. He waits till one side's ahead and then he tells the other to withdraw. Many people do. If they do, they can't appeal. He doesn't even have to write a judgment.'

'But costs', she said. 'If I lose, will I have to pay the other side's costs?'

'Costs are almost never ordered in tribunal hearings.'

' "Almost never" – that's not very reassuring, is it?'

'We aren't at that stage yet.'

'It could be thousands, couldn't it?'

'You're insured', Adrian said. 'So long as your barrister is still of the opinion that you have sufficient prospect of success to proceed . . .?'

'I am.'

'Then, carry on', he told her.

The following morning, I was about to begin my cross-examination of Dr Jones, when Bowls reminded the employment judge that his client had recently been unwell. Judge Featherstone said that after every 30 minutes, we would take a break, to give the doctor every chance to recharge. 'And Mr Renton', he continued, 'will be as quick with his questions as possible. These sorts of allegations are never pleasant.'

'I will go no further than my client's case requires.'

'Very well', the judge said, icily.

Dr Jones affirmed that he would speak the whole truth.

I asked him if it was true that he had invited my client to go out with him.

'It was all a very long time ago', Dr Jones said, 'but I wouldn't harass anyone. That's not the sort of person I am.'

'I'm sorry, Dr Jones', Judge Featherstone said, 'could you repeat that sentence? I'm taking a note – I need to have it word for word.'

The doctor repeated his answer.

Dr Jones half-accepted asking Lucia out. 'I suggested a drink. It wasn't anything sinister. I do it with all my staff – to help them feel welcome and settle in.'

'Was that why you tried to kiss my client, to help her settle in?'

Bowls stared at the judge, ready to object, but Dr Jones held out a hand as if to say, *don't worry, I can answer this.*

He looked at me, pityingly. 'I never kissed her.'

'It's your evidence that she came on to you.'

'She did.'

'A 25-year-old woman, forcing herself on a 50-year-old man?'

'Mr Renton', Judge Featherstone said, 'at the start of this cross-examination, I told the witness that you would keep your questions within the bounds of propriety'.

He told Dr Jones, 'You don't have to answer the question.'

'But I'm happy to, sir.' Turning back to me, a look of pity on his face, Jones continued, 'I was shocked when she did. I said to myself – it isn't going to happen.'

'And after that there were no further interactions between you.'

'None.'

'You never even wrote to her?'

'Not once.'

'You never wanted to speak to her again?'

'I didn't.'

Before the questions could resume, I turned and looked for Lucia. I did not know what I was expecting, perhaps that she would look sadly away and sigh. But she was watching. Her face was red, and she stared with fury at Dr Jones.

She must have felt me watching her because she turned and looked at me. She nodded.

'Dr Jones', I said, 'would you mind please turning to page 302 in the bundle.'

'Mr Renton', the judge said, 'this had better be a legitimate question'.

'Absolutely proper', I insisted.

'I'm warning you, this hearing is going to end in its allotted three days. If I think the case is over-running, I have the power to end a cross-examination early.'

'Perhaps, sir, if you allowed me to begin my cross-examination you wouldn't have to think so hard about ending it.'

The judge glared at me.

Innocently, I smiled back at him.

'I'm not going to permit this line of questioning', the judge said.

He glared at me.

'I have to ask it.'

The person who broke the impasse was not the judge or me. It was the woman sitting on the judge's right – Ms Evans. She asked him, 'Can we have a moment?'

The judge, Ms Evans and Ms Dawidowicz left the room at 10.45am. Featherstone told us to be ready to restart by 11am.

The clock struck but they were still not ready. 'Fifteen minutes', an usher said, and 15 minutes became half an hour and then an hour.

I told Lucia that you can never know what discussions go on in private between a judge and the members of their panel.

I told her about the case I had which lasted a week. The Thursday after we had finished the evidence, I was in the same building for an unconnected case. I walked past the room where the case had been heard and there they were, all three members of the panel – in civilian clothes. One was standing at the claimant's desk, one at the respondent's, and one at the judge's table. They were re-enacting the most important parts of the evidence, repeating it all again. They were doing all they could to make sure they had understood the case correctly.

At 12.30pm, Employment Judge Featherstone invited us back in. He scrunched himself meekly on his chair – flashing a sad smile in the direction of his ally, Bowls.

'Sir', I ask, 'The parties have been wondering, is there anything–'

'Nothing', the judge said.

'I can continue with my questions?'

'You may.'

I smiled my gratitude at Ms Evans.

'Dr Jones', I said, 'page 302. You say, don't you, that after the evening watching *Jesus Christ Superstar* you never wanted to see my client again?'

'I didn't.'

'She'd tried to kiss you?' I asked, keeping my face as calm I could, while my words dripped with disbelief.

'She had.'

'And that made you feel uncomfortable?'

'It most certainly did.'

'Why, then, did you send her a text message later that evening, saying "Love your company and you are a sweet person sweeter than you know"?'

'It was a long time ago', he says, 'I can't remember why I sent it.'

'You say that my client kissed you?'

'She did.'

'You remember that clearly?'

'Yes, I do. I hated it.'

'You're sure that's how you felt?'

'I remember it as if it was yesterday. I never wanted to see her again.'

'So, afterwards, when you were composing this message to her – why did you end it with four x's?'

He looked at me and shook his head helplessly.

'Your x's – they were supposed to be kisses, weren't they?'

'I don't know what they were.'

'You typed those kisses because you still wanted to kiss her?'

'You don't need to answer the question', Judge Featherstone said.

The next document I asked the witness to read was the email in which he had asked my client out for a second time. I showed him her response – a terse 'No'.

I took him to his third email, this time insisting she go out with him.

At 1pm we broke for lunch. As I set my computer back to sleep, my phone rang: Bowls. 'Just thinking aloud here', he said, 'I mean – while Dr Jones is still on the stand. But *hypothetically*, how much would your client want to settle the case?'

'Fifteen thousand and a full apology', I told him.

The money was at the top end of what a judge could order. But Bowls nodded at my proposal. He said, 'Presumably she'd like a reference, too?'

'It would have to be a very positive reference.'

The hearing never made it to the final day.

While I was waiting for confirmation that Lucia's settlement had been paid, news reached me that the decision in Mr Peters' case had been published. Employment Judge Geisler found that Mr Peters had been unfairly dismissed. There was no requirement for every security guard to separately report an incident. If Mr Peters had done anything wrong, it was his first offence after many years' unblemished service. We were photographed in his union newspaper standing outside the tribunal ('Victory House'), with Mr Peters' thumbs pointing cheerily upwards.

I asked Mr Peters' solicitor if the respondent had paid the compensation ordered by the tribunal and she confirmed they had.

'Good', I told her, 'that means they won't appeal'.

CHAPTER 9

September: Housing conditions

In September 2020, the rain in London fell with a fury. It ricocheted upwards from the streets. Possession cases were still stayed, other housing cases continued. As I left chambers, the insides of my bicycle helmet were already damp. As I cycled to court, streams formed in the junction between my neck and my suit. I was cold and tired as I waited for the courts to open. Gee Street was a different court in the autumn compared to before the lockdown. You could only enter by pressing a buzzer and persuading an invisible member of staff to let you in. Inside, the building was empty. The metal seating had been covered with black and yellow tape. Mr Morel's case was the only in-person hearing.

Sitting at the table above me was District Judge Bose, a judge in his mid-40s, stocky, with thick black hair and dark-rimmed glasses. He was a newly appointed judge, and with new judges you never quite know. Some have spent decades of their working lives mastering the very disputes which you are now asking them to decide. Others have never had to consider the law of landlord and tenant, and you need to explain the basics to them – what a tenancy agreement is, what the different clauses mean for each party. When I saw the judge's name on the list outside court, I asked the usher what he was like and she said, 'He's a dish', before putting down her pen, pulling herself together and saying, 'he's alright – he's kind'.

The hearing began. 'I represent the tenant', I explained. 'He holds a tenancy of a first-floor flat in a two-storey building. His landlord is the local council.' At that, I had to resist the temptation to intone, in the style of the 1980s, a Labour council, a *Labour council*.

One piece of advice often given to junior barristers is to 'open low'. When you first explain a case to a judge, undersell it. Don't succumb to the temptation to make things seem worse than they were. Never call your opponent a liar or a hypocrite. If you moralise, and it turns out that the facts are less striking than you thought, the judge will have learned to disbelieve you. They will notice the gap between your point and the reality. You will ruin your own best points.

'Two years ago', I explained, 'my client first made a complaint that water was streaming into the flat from the property above. The land-lord sent contractors to inspect the leak and they saw there was a problem but did nothing to fix it.'

'What's the tenure of the flat above?' Judge Bose asked, and it was potentially an important question. For, Mr Morel lived in a five-storey house, and my client rented his home from the council while the people above him owned their own flat.

'Long leasehold.'

The judge nodded. 'But the water has damaged your client's plaster?'

'Extensively.'

The judge filled in the next sentence for me: 'So even if the leaks aren't the council's fault, now they've have happened, it's obliged to repair the ceiling?'

'Exactly.' I did not sound quite as effusive as perhaps I could. Life has taught me to beware of friendly judges. 'Thirteen months ago', I said, 'the leaks grew worse and the ceiling collapsed. The council cleared away the dust, but it hasn't fixed the beams which hold the plaster in the wall, or the plaster itself. For more than a year my client has had to live with a hole in his ceiling and mould on the walls. There are pictures of the mould in the bundle.'

Bose looked down the documents at the bundle of photographs on the desk in front of him. 'I see the ceiling . . . yes, a hole.'

'It was made by a contractor, to inspect the pipes and the leak. The date of the photograph is on the next page.'

'And through the hole, are those beams?'

'Yes, sir.' Even as I answered, I was not looking at the wooden beam but the other contents of the wall, framed pictures of my client's family and of Mr Morel himself.

'On the walls, there's some growth. They look like a fungus?'

'They are. My client says they're as large as tennis balls.'

I heard the gratifying sound of the judge swallowing. He shook his head before concluding, 'Perhaps I should hear from the defendant.'

So far, the other side's barrister had kept her head down. It was the second case this week in which I had acted for a tenant while Ms Makk was representing this council. She was not my favourite opponent. She fought hard. She seemed to have no real sense of what it meant to a tenant to lose their home, or to have to endure unpleasant housing conditions. On the other hand, she did not enjoy being embarrassed in front of a judge. We had each arrived at court an hour before the case began and she spent the time talking to her housing officer, begging him to settle.

Makk rose to her feet. The winter light shone in brightly, illuminating her dark lounge suit and the counsel's blue notepad just beyond her reach.

District Judge Bose took her through each of the standard defences in a disrepair claim, 'You accept the property is in disrepair, don't you?' the judge asked.

'We do, sir, yes.'

'And you were aware of the damp?'

'We were. But we've only known about it since the ceiling collapsed.'

'Well, that's one issue', the judge wrote on the pad in front of him as he spoke. 'The claimant says two years' notice. The defendant says 13 months.'

Her instructing solicitor had given Makk little to work with. Before the hearing started, Ms Makk had whispered bitterly to me, 'I could write the judgment now. He'll say we delayed, we had no good reason. We were just trying to save money and as for your poor client . . .'

In court, the judge was still working his way through the potential defences. 'No issues with refusals of access?'

'None', Ms Makk acknowledged.

'So why haven't you done the works? There must be some reason.'

'We can't', she said. 'The building's over a hundred years old, and it's listed. We need planning permission even to repair the walls.'

'But you're the local authority. You're the ones who give permission.'

Makk sighed, 'It isn't easy, even for us. There's a process we have to go through, and my housing officer will say we've applied for it.'

The government's English Housing Survey reported in early 2020 that one in five homes in Britain failed to meet the government's Decent Homes Standard (an informal set of rules providing for homes to be in good repair, have modern facilities, and so on), with this proportion rising to one in four in the private rental sector.[1] Among the major

---

1 'English Housing Survey: Headline Report, 2018–19', Ministry of Housing, Communities and Local Government, 23 January 2020, p30.

causes of disrepair were non-functioning boilers and water leaking through the walls. Other sources corroborate this impression of pervasive disrepair. The homelessness campaigning group Shelter carries out regular surveys of the five million tenants living in social housing in the UK. In the most recent, over half confirmed that their properties were in disrepair. Around half a million social housing tenants say each year that they have had to complain on more than ten occasions before any work was done. Of these groups of people, the ones who get access to a specialising housing lawyer are only a small minority. Their victories are small and partial, and the processes by which they are communicated are always incomplete. And yet the law serves a function in regulating the worst landlords and even obliging them to conform to certain minimum standards.

In a disrepair case, a judge needs to be persuaded of three things: first, that the structure, exterior or appliances of a property are in disrepair[2] (hence District Judge Bose's questions about the plaster in the bathroom ceiling); second (if the disrepair belongs to a part of the premises over which the tenant has exclusive control) that the defect has been notified to the landlord; and third, that the landlord has failed to remedy the disrepair within a reasonable period of knowing about it. Hence the landlord's attempts to blame planning permission. Absent those difficulties, a reasonable period to fix a ceiling might be as little as four to six weeks. The landlord needed to persuade the judge that despite the many complaints of disrepair, a significant period was always going to be spent obtaining planning permission. And the COVID-19 epidemic, the landlord argued, had only made it harder to organise works.

During the spring and summer lockdown, landlords had warned that repair works would be delayed. It was just common sense, they said. Disrepair teams were stood down during the lockdown. Or, where they kept going, the council offices were empty and there was no one to take a call or to process the request for repairing works. During the lockdown, ministers wrote to all social housing residents in England, asking them to be understanding. Tenants should not expect routine repairing works to be done: 'Many landlords have had to prioritise the repairs they provide.'

From the perspective of the courts, the reason why this advice matters is that once a tenant has notified the landlord that their home is in disrepair, the landlord is permitted a reasonable time to

2   Landlord and Tenant Act 1985 s11.

carry out works. Here the word 'reasonable' functions, as it so often does in the law, to give the maximum discretion to a judge. Reasonable can be either as long or as short as seems right and proper to them.

Most local authorities and several housing associations posted notices on their websites to the effect that they would only undertake emergency repairs: for example, if fire alarms were broken or if a home's electrical circuits collapsed, they would act. They would deal with gas leaks, or re-plaster – but only if a ceiling collapsed. Some did more work than others. In Milton Keynes, the council reported that during the lockdown it was carrying out 50 repairs a day.[3] But I saw letters from other councils refusing to do even urgent works.

An article in *Inside Housing* magazine complained that disrepair cases were being logged by claims management companies: the housing equivalent of the firms who tout for business by sending text messages to random people asking, 'Have you suffered an accident?' The author of the article complained of what he insisted were the firms' shoddy practices, for example inviting tenants to film the disrepair on their mobile phones.[4] Given the lack of surveyors willing to inspect properties during the lockdown, such filming seemed plain good sense to me.

In one case, a month into the lockdown, my client's solicitors had written asking for progress in a property where damp and cold were extensive, and the client's daughter's bedroom uninhabitable. My client used a wheelchair, suffered asthma and lung infections, and damp was pervasive through the property. The local authority responded with disdain bordering on fury: 'It seems to us that you have not given a moment's attention to present realities, staff are low in numbers across many of the Council's departments due to personnel self- isolating.' They threatened my client's solicitors with costs for simply asking when works would start.

In spring 2020 that might have been understandable – but by September, the lockdown was finished. Even then, the council's position was still that it was too soon to begin.

Landlord representatives argued that for all other works – say, a blocked gutter causing water to enter through a wall and make a home damp – the lockdown should be treated as blank time. It

3 S Murrer, 'Contractors are completing 50 repairs a day in council homes during coronavirus lockdown in Milton Keynes', *Milton Keynes Citizen*, 16 April 2020.

4 M Wilson, 'How to deal with disrepair claims during lockdown', *Inside Housing*, 30 April 2020.

wasn't practicable for works to be done during the pandemic, so the landlord should be excused financial liability for any delays.

One of the dynamics that argument missed was that, in conditions of lockdown, people were spending much greater time in their homes. That was especially true of people who had previously worked in an office or left the home to study, or who had children attending school. So if a room was cold and clammy, or if it stank of mould, tenants were now spending 24 hours a day trapped with that disrepair.

The other problem with this argument was that the tenant was still expected to pay rent. Suppose that a tenant has a four-room flat, comprising two bedrooms, a kitchen, and a lounge, and because a leak is left unrepaired the tenant has no effective use of the second bedroom (only). We might say, in ordinary circumstances, that the tenant has lost the use of some of their home, and that their compensation for the disrepair should not be less than a quarter of their rent. This reasoning does not cease to apply just because works were hard to organise. On the key issue, the tenant's use of their flat, they have still suffered a loss. Compared to landlords, tenants have less resource; why should they be the ones to suffer?

I have lived with disrepair. I know how bleak it is to be stuck with a problem that never goes away. When I was a child, I had a room in the top storey of a Georgian townhouse. In many ways it was idyllic, the room was spacious. I was allowed a life of my own. But water tumbled through the ceiling, and a hole was opened: at first the size of a 50p coin, then a brick, and for years on end, a circle, wide enough to fill the bucket below. My parents were freeholders; there was no landlord to do works. Every Friday, my father would climb onto our flat roof and daub it with a black vinyl paint. He covered every inch of the surface, many times over, but still the water came in. Looking back on what happened, I suspect the water was penetrating not through the roof but through the old, sodden, bricks at the front of the house. But they would have taken scaffolding to repair – and the works would have a cost. My father was full of ideas: plans that every supermarket should stock lactose-reduced milk, ideas to introduce computer terminals with maps and local information onto every London Underground concourse. Each of his businesses ate money and there was nothing left for our home.

The idea of disrepair is less straightforward than it sounds. It requires a defect to the structure of the property or to its gas, electricity or water systems. For years, there was an unresolved dispute as to whether mould on the walls of a building, properly counted as disrepair at all. The structure of a home was said to be 'Those elements ... which give it its essential appearance, stability and shape. The expression does not extend to the many and various ways in which the dwelling house will be fitted out, equipped, decorated and generally made to be habitable.'[5]

In one case which came before the Court of Appeal in 1985, a tenant had complained repeatedly to the local authority which housed him about damp in his home, which the court was willing to accept had been 'appalling'. Paper peeled off the walls and ceilings; woodwork rotted, inside and behind the fitted cupboards in the kitchen; fungus or mould growth appeared in places; and particularly in the two back bedrooms there was a persistent and an offensive smell of damp. There was mould on the wooden sills and surrounds of the windows, and some of these became rotten. In the bedrooms, condensation caused the nails used for fixing the ceiling plasterboard to sweat and in places the plaster fell away from the walls.

The local authority complained that if it was going to fix all its buildings which suffered from similar condensation the total bill would be £9 million. Their Lordships accepted that this was more than any council could be expected to spend. They therefore decided that the defects raised by the tenant belonged to the decorations of the property and not its structure. 'There is no evidence at all of physical damage to the walls', the judge held, 'as opposed to the decorations'.[6] That was in 1985. It took the Court of Appeal over 25 years to reverse this principle and determine that plaster was indeed part of a building's structure.[7]

Additionally, a property is only in disrepair if it has deteriorated from a previous, better, condition of repair. It has long been understood that the concept of disrepair 'connotes the idea of making good damage so as to leave the subject so far as possible as though it had not been damaged'.[8]

These practical considerations had found their way into the news, three years before in 2017. One of the many shocking pieces of information which came out after the Grenfell Tower fire in which

5 *Irvine v Moran* (1992) 24 HLR 1.
6 *Quick v Taff-Ely Borough Council* [1985] EWCA Civ 1.
7 *Grand v Gill* [2011] EWCA Civ 554.
8 *Anstruther-Gough-Calthorpe v McOscar* [1924] 1 KB 716.

72 people died was that a residents' committee, the Grenfell Action Group, had raised concerns from 2013 onwards about the risk of fire to their building. Pilgrim Tucker, a former organiser for the UNITE trade union, had worked with the Action Group. In an interview on BBC Newsnight after the fire, Tucker said, 'The standard of works was really, really, shoddy, and really, really poor. Boilers in front of front doors. Pipework sticking out inches outside of the walls ... They tried to get lawyers but, because of the legal aid cuts, they couldn't get lawyers.'[9]

It is true that the Legal Aid, Sentencing and Punishment of Offenders Act 2012 (LASPO) restricted housing legal aid. Since LASPO, it has only been possible to bring claims against landlords where the aim is 'removal or reduction of a serious risk of harm to the health or safety of the individual or a relevant member of the individual's family'.[10] In addition, disrepair claims now only extend to injunctions for repairing work and not (as they did previously) to claims for damages – even where the injunction and the damages claims raise essentially the same considerations. (Claims can still be brought, but only on 'no win, no fee' agreements, which carry risks for the tenant including that if they lose, they must pay the landlord's costs.)

These malign reforms have undoubtedly had an indirect effect on tenants seeking to protect their homes: in general, there are far fewer providers with specialist knowledge, and it is plausible to think that the ones who remain have become more cautious about taking on complex claims. But the general tenor of LASPO was to intensify the need for disrepair claims to have a safety aspect. In 2013, the Grenfell Action Group complained precisely about a threat to their lives – one area of work which survived LASPO.

In the aftermath of Grenfell, much of the public debate focussed on whether the cladding on the exterior of the building had contributed to the speed with which the fire burned through the building. The 'phase 1' report of the public inquiry into the deaths concluded that on leaving flat 16, where the fire began, it escaped directly into the cladding and it was this which caused the fire to spread.[11] Could the Grenfell tenants have brought a disrepair claim, to have their

---

9 T Connelly, ' "They tried to get lawyers": Devastating cuts to legal aid prevented Grenfell Tower residents accessing advice over safety concerns', *Legal Cheek*, 15 June 2017.

10 LASPO Sch 1 para 35(1).

11 'Phase 1 Report', Grenfell Tower Inquiry, 30 October 2019.

cladding changed? They could not, but it was wrong to blame LASPO. The real obstacle to the tenants in obtaining representation was that legal aid claims were available only for disrepair. To succeed, the tenants would have been required to show that the cladding had deteriorated since it was installed. But this was not the problem at Grenfell – the problem at Grenfell was that cladding had *always* been unsafe.

In 2018, MPs acknowledged this gap in the law by passing the Homes (Fitness for Human Habitation) Act 2018. The Act was intended to address two legal lacunae. One was the limitation of disrepair cases to deterioration. The other was the demise of what had been until the 1950s an extensive system of statutory protection for tenants. Apart from housing disrepair, the other main protection for tenants is section 8 of the Landlord and Tenant Act 1985, under which a landlord is required to keep homes fit for human habitation: that is, in line with certain minimum standard of cleanliness and safety. 'Section 8' is a very old duty, which has been on the statute book in one form or another since 1885 when a Housing of the Working Classes Act had made it a term of any housing for persons 'of the working classes' (defined, in London, as an annual rent of not more than £20 per year), that the property would be 'in all respects reasonably fit for human habitation'.

Unfortunately, for 60 years it was the unacknowledged policy of each of our two main political parties to allow this duty to disappear from the statute book, not by repealing it, but by leaving in place a cap which limited this protection to tenancies for no more than £52 per year (£80 in London). These rent limits were last increased in 1957, at which time they covered the majority of English and Welsh tenancies. By 2018, however – and despite repeated requests for the abolition of this cap – it was likely that either no tenancies anywhere in Britain, or as close to none as counted, still had the protection of this law.

The 2018 Act removed these financial limits. It also set out in clear terms those aspects of a tenancy which are required to be fit for human habitation: repair; stability; freedom from damp; internal arrangement; natural light; ventilation; water supply; drainage and sanitary conveniences; facilities for the cooking of food; and facilities for the disposal of waste water. The Act also prohibited landlords from housing people in properties with a prescribed hazard, where there is any risk of harm to the health or safety of an actual or potential occupier. The law came into force for new tenancy contracts on

20 March 2019, and for most existing tenancies one year later on 20 March 2020.

After the lockdown had ended, I found myself running claims for the first time based on a property's unfitness for habitation. I was asked to draft a defence for Joshua Yates. The landlord was a private owner, and he said the tenant was nearly £6,000 in arrears. The tenant, Mr Yates, had the large hands of someone who had worked in highways maintenance ever since he left school. He admitted falling a couple of months behind with his rent. There had been no hot water for months, and the electricity was plainly dangerous with open wires and sockets which sparked. I read the text messages between the two sides and it was easy to see who was in the wrong.

Mr Yates had written, 'Can't I talk to you about the water and the repairs?'

The landlord sent him three text messages in quick succession: 'Can't do any repairs', he wrote. Then, 'No money no repairs.' Finally, 'You need to leave.'

Under the new law, there were several claims Mr Yates could make which had not been available to him previously. He could complain about the state of the electrical installations – even though these would have been obvious at the start of the tenancy and there had been no deterioration, and hence no 'disrepair'. He was also able to complain about a bedbug infestation, which had left him with great red welts, which covered his ankles and his hands, leaving his joints red and swollen. Under the old law, we would have spent a long and fruitless time looking in the tenancy agreement to see if the landlord would accept responsibility for infestations (many do not) or we would have had to show a defect through which the insects had entered.

Normally, when a landlord complained of poverty, I left those arguments well alone. After all, the landlord's solicitor has access to their bank statements, and few solicitors would put down a direct lie without checking it first. On this occasion, however, I drafted a response to them. The landlord had been charging a rent greater than the local housing allowance, he had refused to do any repairing works. Far from being short of money, the landlord had applied for permission to convert the property into a 'home in multiple occupation' (HMO). He had paid builders to construct a second dwelling in the garden, with a view to bringing more tenants onto his land and charging more rent. Plainly, he was seeking to profit at a rate out of all proportion to his original investment in the building.

One of my solicitors, Dathi Pandania, asked me to attend a tenants' meeting in Stratford in the east end. Dathi had been on the duty desk at Gee Street, where he met a defendant Mr Varqan with a familiar complaint: water leaking into his flat from above. The housing association refused had to carry out any remedial works, so Mr Varqan put down a bucket to catch the water. The leak continued through the winter and got worse. Mr Varqan spoke to the neighbours on each side and above. It turned out that no fewer than 30 residents in the tower block had complained about leaks from old pipes. The landlord was saying that it could not do the works, as repairs on that scale would cost millions of pounds. As far as the housing association was concerned, the tenants had simply to wait in their homes, putting up with the leaks. As more complaints were made, the landlord offered to pay the affected tenants just £200 each.

Dathi thought if we could get a group of tenants to bring claims all at once, the pressure on the landlord would be irresistible. He had spoken to the local MP and she was supportive, as were the local councillors, who had written on the tenants' behalf.

It was dark as I made my way through the east end streets. There was so much traffic, the cars hurried ill-temperedly through red lights, their horns screaming.

At the heart of the estate were three concrete towers, each more than 20 storeys high. They soared into the darkness, tall, magnificent, leaving abandoned play areas far below them, a broken swing, and neglected trees.

Sylvia Pankhurst's East London Federation of Suffragettes used to have offices just a few hundred yards from here. They sold her newspaper, *The Woman's Dreadnought*, with advertisements for day nurseries, dental clinics and cost-price restaurants. A hundred years on, these services were needed as desperately as ever.

The room in which we were meeting was homely enough. There was a kitchen in the back where three of the women from the estate were chatting with Dathi's paralegal. There were biscuits, a box of Waitrose's best alongside custard creams and chocolate bourbons.

I had assumed that what Dathi wanted me for was my knowledge as a housing lawyer. But he was as well-equipped as I was to give the 40 people in the meeting his advice. 'The landlord can't keep you waiting forever', he said. The tenants wanted to know how much their individual claims for compensation might be worth. Dathi tried to keep the answer as general as possible, for fear of raising hopes which later might be dashed. 'It depends how long you've been suffering disrepair, how much rent you've been paying.'

A tenant in a striped t-shirt described how his wife, who was pregnant, had reported a leak more than 80 times. She walked to her shower and slipped on water which had pooled on her floor. They could have lost their unborn child.

A woman rose to her feet, gripped the chair in front to help her stand. She said things were better when the local authority was in charge. She called the landlord criminals. She was not interested in damages, she wanted the directors in the dock.

Mr Varqan told the tenants how he and his family had left an umbrella in their bathroom, how they could not use the toilet without it. He was a polished speaker and the other tenants clapped him from their chairs. He was one of them, their captain.

Dathi walked among the tenants, handing out letters they could return to the solicitor, asking to be considered for a joint claim against the landlord.

In the room, it felt as if maybe something shared was emerging – the distrust of the landlord was already there, but the confidence to fight was new.

As I listened to the tenants, what struck me was the variety of their complaints. One woman said that for her the problem was not so much the delays – the landlord had started fixing the walls of her flat. The problem was dust. It was everywhere, she could not breathe, and it was ruining her clothes. A man in his 40s, thin with silver hair, complained about the windows of his flat. He lived on the 14th floor, and they opened by themselves without warning. 'My daughter's three', he said, 'if she falls–'

The tenants in the block were suffering at the hands of the same antagonist – a landlord refusing to pay for works – but for each of them the issue was different. Some of the cases were ones which were capable of being taken to court, and others weren't.

On the top table, Dathi was looking increasingly anxious. Not more than one or two of the letters had come back to him, and he worried that for all the efforts his firm had put in, that moment of certainty might be lost.

When I rose to my feet, I knew not to make any promises. I told the tenants how a disrepair claim worked. I explained how compensation is calculated, how a judge begins with the date at which the landlord was put on notice and figures out how much of the value of a tenant's home has been lost to them. I made my back ramrod straight. I tried to speak simply but with conviction, not promising but showing. I want the people in the room to feel strong, to know the righteousness of their own cause.

Most of my disrepair cases settle before the final hearing. Many of my clients have the protection of legal aid. With it, the tenant is protected from costs. In an ordinary civil claim, the losing party pays for the fees of the winning party's lawyers. But this rule is disapplied when one party is on legal aid. When a tenant on legal aid loses a housing claim, costs are ordered, but enforcement is stayed. They used to be called 'football pools orders', the idea being that the unsuccessful party would only have to pay if something truly unusual happened to them afterwards: for example, if they inherited money or won the lottery.

Access to free representation gives tenants a significant protection and helps to rebalance the relationship between the parties. In other areas of the law where this shield is missing, for example employment law, I see the difference. It is normal for employers to make costs warnings against unrepresented litigants, even those with strong cases. The imbalance of resources between employers and workers enables the former to bully the latter into withdrawing cases which they would probably have won.

Another of my cases was coming to trial in the Central London County Court. The landlord, Mr Quadrado, refused to believe that he was liable to pay anything. When we spoke outside court, he grimaced, little drops of sweat form on his forehead. The evidence against him was overwhelming: a water pipe burst, the rooms of the flat were covered in mildew. The local authority served a notice requiring him to make repairs, but he refused. A surveyor confirmed the disrepair. Because the landlord was refusing to carry out works, the authority stopped the tenant's benefits, and Mr Quadrado wanted the court to accept that – without any housing benefit being paid to him – there was no money, and he was under no obligation to carry out repairs. District Judge Tanar ordered him to pay my client £8,000 in damages.

The next day I was in Croydon, south London. The tenant was a council worker who, through her employment, had been allocated a Victorian cottage with sash windows and a garden with its own ornamental pond. In the photographs, the outside looked majestic. However, the inside of the walls were damp. The main culprits were the sash windows – they sat rotten in their frame, with clear gaps around the glass and bits of paintwork fallen to the ground. In the disrepair records, it was clear that the reason for the delay was that the council was waiting for a government grant to fund the works. In the basement, the damp proof course failed, and the copper pipes carrying the gas corroded. It was by sheer good luck that my client smelled gas before something awful happened. Damages were fixed at £15,000.

I returned to court to listen as District Judge Bose handed down judgment in Mr Morel's case of the leak from above and the fungus on the walls. The judgment was brief. He did not give Mr Morel all he was asking for. The judge accepted, for example, that obtaining planning permission is a difficult task, even where the landlord is the local authority. There, he was willing to allow the landlord some benefit of the doubt. All the other areas of dispute he resolved in favour of my client. The judge said that, given all he had suffered, the way Mr Morel raised the complaints with his landlord was a model of restraint.

The judge awarded my client damages equivalent to 40 per cent of the rent (to compensate Mr Morel for the loss of amenity in his home), going as far back to when he had first warned of water leaking down the plaster. The judge ordered the landlord to do the repairing works on a tight deadline, of no more than four weeks from the trial. The local authority would also have to pay my client's legal costs, all of which they would have avoided if only they had done the repairs when asked. It was a scrupulously fair decision: not pro-tenant, not pro-landlord, but balanced, with points at which each side could claim a victory.

Mr Varqan's landlord wrote to him. For months, they had been putting off works. But, since the meeting on the estate, their position had changed. They acknowledged that there was asbestos behind by his WC, and within his bath panel, and promised to remove it and repair the damaged water pipes. They said that engineers had been appointed. The leak would be fixed; every tenant in the property would benefit. The landlord promised to redecorate afterwards. They insisted they were making a genuine attempt to seek a settlement of our client's dispute and offered him a five-figure sum as compensation.

His solicitor asked Mr Varqan whether he was willing to accept.

'It's not about me', he answered. 'We need to have another meeting for all the residents, see what they've been offered – we're all in this together.'

CHAPTER 10

October: The stay is lifted

Coming into October 2020, the question of whether hearings would take place online or in person was still a matter for decision by different judges in each court. So, on the first of the month, I was supposed to be in Croydon County Court, to represent a family who had never become tenants. They had paid a deposit and six weeks' rent in advance, and had even met the landlord, only for him to insist that he would not let them move in. The lettings agent rang them back, full of apologies. 'It's the landlord's fault', he said, 'I told him you had disabled kids.' Two years later, the question of who should pay back the deposit and the rent was still undecided. The landlord insisted that the agent had never given him the money. Yes, he and the agent had spoken but the landlord had refused to engage him, and the landlord had never given permission to advertise his home. He had only let my client into the property to see the flat because my client had felt sorry for the agent and 'embarrassed' for him.

I was confident that a judge would see through this story. The agent was, on the landlord's account, 'dodgy', and it was true that every time we found a business address for him, the estate agent closed it. When we dug up the address he had registered with Companies House, the letter came back 'recipient unknown'.

But the landlord accepted that he knew the lettings agent, and admitted that he had given the agent a key to facilitate viewings. As for whether he had taken the money, the landlord was refusing to let us see his savings account. What you could see from his current account was that every time our client made a payment to the lettings agent (which she had done twice, to cover the deposit and the rent), later the same day the landlord moved large sums from his savings to his current account – suggesting that the money had indeed been paid to him.

We asked Croydon County Court to list the matter for an in-person hearing. The building doubles up as a Crown Court and had been open through the summer, so this would have been easy enough to do. Given that neither the landlord nor the agent had solicitors, it was unclear how they would take part in an online trial. I mean the practical things: where they would keep the bundle of court papers so that I could ask them questions, or how a judge would stop them from reading a prepared script when it was their turn to give evidence.

Unfortunately, despite our request, the case was listed for an online trial. It is hard not to blame this decision on the message coming from government: that the technology was ready to go over quickly to an online court system. In order to make the technology work, as many hearings as possible needed to be listed for remote hearings.

I was therefore at home, waiting in my spare room at ten minutes past nine, when my telephone rang. I had my tablet ready to stream the hearing, a glass of water, and my blue counsel's pad. An apologetic deputy district judge introduced himself. I started thinking, 'This isn't right', for advocates are never supposed to speak to a judge without the other side there as well. But it was a simple courtesy call.

'Sorry, but I've had to adjourn it', the judge said. 'The defendant wrote to the court yesterday evening. I suppose he didn't copy you in, did he?'

'No, sir, he didn't.'

'I'll give you the gist. His email says he didn't know anything about the hearing.'

'We've rung him, we've written to him. He's had all the papers.'

'I'm sure he has. His email says that he doesn't have a working computer or even a phone – so God knows how he sent us the email. Anyway, it says that he isn't going to be able to log on to the hearing through Microsoft Teams.'

From his tone of exasperation, it seemed the judge thought the defendant was lying, but it did not matter. Fair trial principles obliged the court to believe him.

I asked, 'Can you relist it as in-person hearing?'

'I'll do my best', the judge said. But we both knew that it would be summer 2021 at the earliest before the case came back to court.

My next case was a case management hearing in the East London Employment Tribunal, conducted by telephone. We were checking that a seven-day trial, listed for November 2020, was effective to go ahead. Both sides insisted it was. The judge asked us whether it was possible for us to conduct the hearing in person. In East London, they only had two available meeting rooms. Each could fit ten people: the three members of the tribunal, two barristers, and a space reserved in case a member of the public chose to observe. There could be no more than four witnesses in the room at once. The employer's side, with their five witnesses due to give evidence, promised to stagger the witnesses to keep within the limits. The judge said that everyone he asked – represented or not – was trying to avoid online hearings. 'Everyone prefers in person', he said. 'We're all fed up with staring at banks of screens.'

At the start of October, I saw my father in hospital. He was there for a CT scan. But while the epidemic raged, nothing could ever be quite normal. The doctors talked him through the procedure. They wanted to know if he had any underlying health conditions. 'None', he said confidently, although he had had major heart surgery in the last few years. They tried to explain to him the risk that he might prove allergic to the dye used in the procedure. They told him he might feel nauseous or want to vomit. He was the one who would know first if anything had gone wrong, and it was up to him to warn them. 'Can you do that?' they asked.

He looked back uncomprehendingly at them.

'Can't you talk to him?' they asked me.

It was if I was back in court, explaining to a client what he risked, what his lawyers could do and what we needed from him.

After the scan had finished – and it went without hitch – my father sat by the window, watching the world outside. He saw a place beyond London, a world of clouds and trees. He looked at me and said, 'Do your parents live here?'

We looked through the window and his mind took us to his home in the countryside and it was Saturday and the weekend. He asked, 'Are we eating supper together?' He said, 'Everyone loves to have a place in the country.'

I told my father how happy I was to see him.

With his glassy blue eyes, he smiled back at me.

The days grew noticeably shorter; I woke in the dark. More than half a year had passed since the lockdown began. I was back in Gee Street for another disrepair trial. The building was again empty: we had a whole floor to ourselves. This case too had been listed as an in-person trial and I was glad of the chance it gave me to speak to the client, Jolene Wagoner. She was a vulnerable woman, with chronic epilepsy and a history of anxiety and post-traumatic stress disorder (PTSD). All that was left of the case was an unfinished argument about how much the client should be compensated for having lived in a house that was beset by rising damp. The timber of the client's kitchen floor had been taken up and for six months she'd had to live with a hole in the middle of her floor and water lapping beneath it, in conditions that were plainly unsafe for her.

As we prepared to go in for the hearing, Ms Wagoner was shaking her head from side to side. 'I've got nothing left. The house is ruined, my job is ruined–'

Later, as he reached the concluding passages of the judgment, District Judge Bose looked not at me but my client. 'As I listened to Ms Wagoner give her evidence', he said, 'I felt disgust, disgust for her at how she has been made to live. I don't believe that the landlord has ever properly applied its mind to her needs or her vulnerability.'

My client was asking for £20,000 damages, and the landlord was trying to cut the amount by more than half. District Judge Bose ordered £19,000.

On the other side, I had a familiar opponent – Tuck. He had been coughing all morning, although he insisted it was not the virus, only a migraine he said.

Tuck asked District Judge Bose to reconsider his decision and reduce it, simply and only because the landlord was a local authority and under conditions of coronavirus all its money was spent. 'Every year', he said, 'central government is cutting our grant, and every year it's worse. While, under COVID ... The reality is that that every penny we pay Ms Wagoner will mean another household being pushed to the back of the queue for homeless housing.'

The judge removed his glasses, cleaned them on the cloth in front of him. He twisted his lips. 'What do you say, Mr Renton?'

I replied that Tuck needed to have some evidence to support his assertions – a witness statement from a senior council manager, perhaps. But he had not brought anything to back up his points. I said that if the landlord could not afford to pay, it could file evidence, request payment by instalments rather than the full sum. The poverty of the local authority might be relevant to how quickly they would pay their debt, not to how much they owed.

I showed the judge what had happened in spring 2014, before the worst of austerity, and after Ms Wagoner's floor had been up for six months. They told her solicitors, 'The disrepair in your client's flat is purely cosmetic. We will not agree to pay her any damages.' The council should have addressed the problem then – when they had money.

The judge began, 'I agree with Mr Renton', and in the judgment that followed he commended not just my client, and her solicitor ('at the top of her trade'), but even the trainee who had prepared the bundle for the hearing and was sitting masked at the back of the court ('it was beautifully prepared, unlike most bundles I encounter, it was legible and accurate without a single duplicated page').

He said, 'Miss Wagoner has been treated shabbily, particularly when you consider she's a vulnerable woman. I know that local authority budgets have been cut but it doesn't mean that individuals should be treated without justice or equity – it's the same for all of us, the courts have been cut like everything else.' He refused to reduce the client's damages.

Bose nodded at Ms Wagoner. 'Congratulations', he said.

As preparations were made for the end of the ban on possession hearings on 20 September, the government had granted one final concession. It worked by dividing tenants into two groups. In what you could call the 'good' camp would be those tenants who were being evicted for ordinary rent arrears, most of whom would be protected by extending the period a landlord had to wait between serving a notice seeking possession and issuing court proceedings to a minimum of six months.

In the 'bad' camp, meanwhile, were those who were being threatened with eviction for high arrears (more than 26 weeks) or for anti-social behaviour. In those cases, the minimum period a landlord had to wait between serving a notice seeking possession and issuing court proceedings was going to be just four weeks.

Housing law has long passed that threshold of complexity where any ordinary tenant or landlord might keep up with it. The new changes were going to make that even worse. Suppose you were a tenant and you had been given a section 21 notice (Housing Act 1998 s21, notice of seeking possession). That notice expires if a landlord has served a notice but does not issue proceedings. Eventually the notice is too old to be relied on. Imagine that on 1 November 2020, you received a defence form from the court telling you that your landlord had issued court proceedings and asking you to respond. In that document you were asked to raise any defence you had to proceedings, including whether the notice was lawful or not. Among the things a tenant needed to check were, after the landlord served the notice, did they wait the correct minimum time before issuing proceedings, and did the landlord delay too long after sending the notice before issuing proceedings?

The correct minimum and maximum durations of a section 21 notice would be different if the notice was issued (i) before COVID-19; (ii) during the main period of the ban on possession hearings (ie between 25 March and 20 September); (iii) right at the end of the ban (on 18 or 19 September); or (iv) clearly after the 20 September deadline had passed.

Lawyers, including judges, were going to find these rules unbearably complex. But we would also be relying on tenants to point us towards possible defences.

The government was acting as if there could never be a justification for a tenant falling six months behind with their rent. But my daily workload was made up of cases where high arrears were the landlord's fault – a council tenant whose housing officer accidentally 'switched off' her rent account for two years without telling her and terminating her housing benefit claim, then switched the account back on creating an artificial debt; or a landlord who had been ordered to pay a tenant compensation for disrepair equivalent to a year's rent, but never credited the rent account and issued possession proceedings. These sorts of mistakes occur repeatedly, and bring countless families to the brink of homelessness.

The government assumed every time a person was accused of anti-social behaviour, the allegations were true, and the tenant must be evicted with the maximum speed. But many, perhaps most, anti-social behaviour defendants suffer from chronic illness, often psychiatric illness. Any fair legal system would address their cases cautiously, not speed up their eviction. Neither the reduction of possession lists, nor the extension of notice periods to six months would prevent the wave of misery rushing towards the courts, nor would they give judges any new powers to deal justly with difficult cases. But they at least meant that the crisis was heading towards us more slowly.

The Master of the Rolls published a document, 'The Overall Arrangements', which set out how possession hearings were supposed to be held in future.[1] Landlords would issue a reactivation notice and bring it to court. This would set out what information the landlord had about whether the tenant had been affected by coronavirus. Tenants would then be summoned to a new kind of

---

1 'Overall Arrangements for possession proceedings in England and Wales', The Master of the Rolls (as Head of Civil Justice) Working Group on Possession Proceedings, 17 September 2020; www.judiciary.uk/announcements/resumption-of-possession-cases/.

process, a 'review date' (or 'R date'), with anti-social behaviour cases, high rent arrears cases and subletting cases (etc) to be listed for review first.

Tenants were entitled to ask that their case should be marked 'COVID-19', but there was no clarity as to what the effect of that marking would be, and no suggestion that such a marking would prevent a judge from making a possession order.

At a first attendance, now called a 'review date', the plan was that tenants could meet solicitors, perhaps speak briefly to an adviser, and then perhaps negotiate (for example) directions orders which would list the case for trial. Landlords were expected to be contactable at the review date, perhaps by telephone, and to have provided all the documents of the case in a bundle. Judges would be allowed to dismiss claims, but only for procedural defects, for example, if the landlord failed to produce the required documents.

The legislation did not change, but the guidance did, creating an additional occasion for the parties to seek settlement. Duty advisers would be able to ask for a case to be put forward for facilitated negotiation. Judges at the review dates would be prohibited from ordering possession; while presumably the facilitated negotiations (assuming that tenants were represented) would also be likely to act, to some extent, as a buffer delaying possession or reducing the chances of the landlord obtaining quite all that it asked for.

How then did I expect landlords to react? I warned friends to await a spasm of fury on a landlord's part when they grasped that an eviction, which they thought would only take a month or two from beginning to end, would require a year to work through every stage, from initial notice to bailiff's date. I invited friends in tenants' unions to prepare for what would inevitably be an increase in the number of landlords seeking to evict unlawfully, ignoring court proceedings, and simply changing locks without an order. Housing lawyers have always had to deal with these cases, but there were going to be more of them. The options available to the tenants' union included distributing materials informing tenants of their rights, assisting those affected in applying to courts for injunctions to have tenants returned to their homes, and naming the worst of the repeat offenders. The best that could be said about the government's plans was that they deferred the crisis; they did nothing to address its causes.

My next client, Mr Barrekat, was making an application to set aside an order for outright possession. The first I knew about his case was a four-minute video which showed my client standing at the door to his flat while two policemen asked if they could come in. Mr Barrekat did not want them to; he raised his voice and gesticulated at them. Someone had told the police officers that he had had visitors and had fought with them. The officers argued their way into Mr Barrekat's flat, where they found nothing. He was cross with them and when, five minutes later, they left, one officer said to the closed door, 'And Good Night to you too, sir.' Mr Barrekat was already subject to a suspended possession order prohibiting nuisance. The video was the landlord's evidence that he had breached the order. They demanded an outright possession order, to be followed no doubt by his immediate eviction.

At first, the landlord's case seemed relatively thin – really, the landlord was asking for possession because Mr Barrekat had been cross and unco-operative, that was all. But the case became even weaker from there. For the order Mr Barrekat was said to have breached required him to avoid acts of nuisance against any person living or working near his flat 'and employed by the claimant' (in other words, the landlord).

Neither the original complaining neighbour who had rung the police, nor the two officers who had attended, were employed by the landlord. In other words, the landlord's case was hopeless. But no one had yet checked the order until now. Instead, the client was on his second possession hearing, the first of which had been adjourned because the client – who was ill with an autoimmune deficiency and had difficulty reading – had been sent papers with the details of the hearing, but failed to attend, having set off in the right direction and then got lost near Old Street and given up and gone home.

On Mr Barrekat's non-attendance, a judge had already ordered possession, and this hearing was my client's attempt to have that order set aside. The basis on which possession had been ordered was wrong, I argued – you could not evict someone for breaching a possession order when they had not breached it.

I spoke to one of the ushers, Gabriel. His hair had gone white during the lockdown. He told me that the court had been open all spring and summer. 'It's all carry-on-regardless. Telephone hearings have been smooth. Even video, they're alright – it's just a judge in court with his laptop. But when something starts to go wrong there's nothing you can do about it.' How many in-person hearings had there been? He shrugged. 'Most days, I don't see anyone.'

My client Mr Barrekat arrived at court. Given his illness, I was expecting his blue facemask to be kept fixed to his face at all times, but he could not speak through it, and now it was hooked around his chin. His cousin had driven him to court, and she stood at the back of the room, watching us both warily. Mr Barrekat told me the lifts in his flat were broken, he wanted to be moved. 'I feel helpless', he said.

I reminded him that he had not breached the injunction. I promised him I would bring the case to an end today.

On the other side, my opponent Ms Makk, was wearing a brilliantly clean white cotton mask, tied neatly behind her ears. She asked if Mr Barrekat would offer an undertaking (a promise to behave) instead of the injunction.

'I'm sorry', I said.

We hammered out a compromise – they would drop the case, so long as they did not have to pay Mr Barrekat's legal costs.

I spoke to my client and his solicitor. She agreed.

Ms Makk and I went before District Judge Tanar and she wanted to know why the landlord was withdrawing its claim.

I told her about the order. I explained this was the second hearing and neither of them would have been needed if only the judge had checked the terms of the suspended order.

The judge said, 'The application came before me, didn't it?'

'You made an outright order.' I am not sure why I told her that – it would have been easier to say nothing. After all, the parties had already reached a settlement. Nothing she could say would change that. But I was looking for something – a shudder, perhaps. Not an apology, I was sure District Judge Tanar never said sorry. But I needed something. I wanted to know if the judge was capable of grasping that she had ordered a disabled person to give up his home for ignoring an order that he had not in fact breached.

'Yes', Judge Tanar said, 'thank you. Now the order the parties are seeking today is . . .' On she went, without so much as a pause.

In my next case, Ms Alami suffered from depression, anaemia and a slipped disk. Her arrears reached their worst during the lockdown at £6,000. For three years, she told me, water had been leaking into her home, leaving the walls covered in black mould. She lived in a small tower block, and in her pictures the flat seemed pleasant enough. But the caretaker's flat was empty. There was no one in post to clear the guttering or fix the water pipes when they leaked. Even a stately home would soon be reduced to ruin if no one looked after it. The landlord had not yet disclosed the disrepair file and could not confirm whether he knew about the damp. Without that certainty, the judge was in no hurry to order possession. Once we had the documents, we would know how long Ms Alami's complaints went back.

If it was the full three years, the damages for disrepair would clear her arrears.

The landlord demanded not just rent, but payments towards the debt. 'From what?' I asked. My client nodded grimly beside me.

Ms Alami's benefits were under review. For years, she had received employment and support allowance (ESA), but that was stopped after an assessor decided that, despite Ms Alami's slipped disk, she was fit enough to work. Until her benefit was re-established, Ms Alami's only income was child benefit and child tax credit payments – money, in other words, that was meant to be spent on feeding her children and not paying the rent. Until her ESA was back in payment, she could barely afford to eat. The landlord was demanding possession, relying on ground 8 (of Housing Act 1988 Sch 2) – the rule that possession *must* be granted at a hearing where a tenant is in more than eight weeks' arrears. But the judge agreed with me that we could not decide whether that threshold was met. The answer would depend on whether the disrepair counterclaim reduced the arrears below eight weeks. If it did, the claim for possession would fail.

My next client, Mr Edie was in his 40s, with velvet-short hair and cherry-red Doc Martin shoes. He was said to be in arrears of approximately £10,000 pounds. One reason for hope was that word 'approximately': the landlord did not know how much of the rent was missing. He was a private landlord, it was the only property he owned, and his solicitor was finding it as hard as I was to explain what had gone wrong. Placing her documents beside mine and filling in the gaps, the best explanation seemed to be that just as the epidemic was starting, the landlord's estate agent applied to the local housing benefit team, asking that all payments of that benefit were made to him. The estate agent supplied a bank account, his own bank account, and for months the housing benefit was paid there. At the end of the epidemic, the estate agent vanished. The landlord insisted that the agent had never passed on any of the missing money to him. So, both parties, understandably, felt aggrieved: Mr Edie because the council had paid all his rent, and the landlord because had not received any of it. The estate agent had been refusing to answer the landlord's increasingly desperate calls and letters. I asked Mr Edie if he had seen the agent. 'It's been a year', he said. 'I told him the boiler was knackered and said when's he going to fix it. That was the last I ever heard from him.'

By the time of our hearing, the estate agent had been struck off at Companies House. The landlord solicitor shook her head at the papers. She had never been in a housing case before, her speciality was crime, and she was still struggling to accept that her client's own estate agent had stolen from him. It hardly seemed possible to her that all the papers she would need, rent statements, a disrepair file, evidence as to whether the deposit was protected, had all disappeared. The judge adjourned the case: the landlord needed to decide whether the real subject of his complaint was the missing estate agent or the innocent tenant.

My next client, Mr Emlyn, had been subject to a suspended possession order requiring him to pay off rent arrears of less than £2,000. He was laid off during the lockdown, and in three months without wages his debt increased to £11,000. Normally, an eviction would be inevitable; but he had found a job since and borrowed enough to reduce the arrears by a quarter. The local authority had known for years about cracks in his bedroom ceiling and draughty window in the kitchen and living room through which damp came in. A very fair landlord's rep agreed, outside court, that Mr Emlyn could counterclaim and to stay the eviction until we knew how much his disrepair claim was worth.

As October progressed, the numbers of people testing positive for COVID-19 were rising once more, as were the numbers being admitted to hospital, and the numbers dying from the disease. The government's Scientific Advisory Group for Emergencies (SAGE) demanded a 'circuit breaker', in other words a second lockdown to coincide with half-term in schools at the end of October. The government refused to introduce this. Instead, a 'three-tier' system of local measures was drawn up, ranging from tier 1 ('medium risk') to tier 3 ('very high risk'). The problem with the system was that while it purported to show a keenly calculated range of interventions, each tailored to the extent of the danger, none of them, not even the most serious, addressed the actions which were causing the pandemic to spread. So, even in tier 3, employers were still supposed to send their employees into work; and even at that point, universities and schools were still supposed to remain open indefinitely. Young people were capable of spreading the disease – and in just a few weeks, at Christmas, they would no doubt share it with their families.

Linked to this, the government was doing all in its power to wind down the previous furlough scheme (under which up to 80 per cent of employees' wages were supported, for all affected employees) and replace it with something less expensive. Chancellor Rishi

Sunak was photographed outside Downing Street, flanked by Frances O'Grady of the Trades Union Congress (TUC) and Carolyn Fairbairn of the Confederation of British Industry (CBI), physically showing their approval for plans to reduce the amount of support employers (and therefore employees) would be paid, while extending the scheme's duration to the following spring.

The rationale for the new system was that the government could not afford to support the entire economy. Accordingly, the Chancellor explained, we needed to distinguish between 'viable' and 'non-viable' businesses and limit our protection strictly to the former. As soon as these distinctions were applied to real life, however, they created large groups of 'winners' and 'losers' in no apparent relationship to any idea of carefully targeted assistance. So, an ordinary pub in Liverpool or Manchester (both of which were, by now, in tier 3) selling alcohol but not food was a COVID-19 risk and obliged to close (and would receive a grant) – while its next-door neighbour which also sold food as well as drink was allowed to remain open, and it received no financial assistance. Tim Martin, boss of pub chain Wetherspoons, and until then one of the loudest public advocates of Johnsonite Conservatism, could now be seen touring the television studios denouncing our Prime Minister and demanding the government change the rules. Wetherspoons served food with its drinks and was permitted to remain open – and was on the wrong side of the subsidy line.

Those treating the disease were begging for measures to stop the spread of the pandemic, while in the Conservative press a growing number of columnists were insisting that we needed to keep the economy as open as possible. The demand of the scientists for further lockdown measures, they insisted, had to be resisted: 'The cure would be worse than the disease'. The delays and equivocations of our politicians meant that we were suffering the worst of both worlds – both large numbers of cases and deaths, and a broken economy.

In many of my cases, the debts owed by my clients to their landlords were high – much higher than arrears had once been. I remember attending the annual conference of the Housing Law Practitioners Association ten years ago. Our guest speaker was a district judge from Clerkenwell and Shoreditch. Before he was a judge, he had been a solicitor representing tenants. A jazz saxophonist in his spare time, cheerful and ebullient – at the conference, he was among friends. One member of the audience asked him: 'Let's say a landlord is asking for suspended possession. Or let's say, they've got a suspended order and now they're asking for an eviction. How bad do arrears have to be before you'd move them to the next stage?'

The judge shrugged. 'It isn't like that', he said. 'It makes a difference whether the tenant is disabled, how recently the arrears arose.'

'But you must have an idea – I mean, roughly.'

'I don't know', the judge said.

'Come on.'

He said, 'In the most general terms – don't hold me to it in court – but, as a rule of thumb, I'd say a thousand pounds. If they're a thousand pounds behind, and there's no real prospect of clearing it, then I'd order possession.'

The effect of coronavirus was to change the maths. In the social housing sector, it made debt pervasive. Where tenants had disrepair counterclaims, I found that judges were increasingly willing to adjourn possession claims even on five-digit rent arrears.

On the last Monday in October, I represented a couple, Monty and Lola. They had moved into their house five years before as a favour to the landlord who they knew and had suffered a stroke and did not have the energy to maintain a large house. The rent was relatively high for a home in rural southern England at £1,625 per month. According to Monty, the proceedings were a mistake. 'We spent a lot of money doing the place up. We put in new floors and a garage. Our landlord said if we did the work, we could put it against the rent. And then, when we tried, his sons wouldn't have any of it.' At the end of 2018, the landlord had issued section 21 (Housing Act 1988) proceedings. Monty spoke to the Citizens Advice Bureau (CAB) and found out he had a defence: the landlord was not entitled to possession as the deposit had not been registered in time. The landlord came up with an answer. His solicitor wrote to the court and to Monty saying that he'd misunderstood the law, and there was a special exception which applied to their case, and the delay in registering the deposit, 'had no bearing on the validity of the section 21 notice'.

Swayed by the superior expertise of the solicitor, Monty and Lola signed a consent order agreeing to give up their home. Possession was ordered. With the ending of the eviction ban, a bailiff's date had been fixed.

I told them, 'You do understand, don't you? If you lose the case on Monday, you'll have to go. You won't have any choice. You'll have to find somewhere to put your things. Whether its storage, or wherever. You'll need to leave.'

'All our things?' asked Monty.

'All of them.'

'Surely, a judge can't just put us on the streets.'

'They can', I answered, but the words did not seem to register. Eviction, bailiffs: they were the facts of other people's lives. Not Monty and Lola's.

Lola was a professional woman – she worked, she said (somewhat airily given that they had been assessed as having an income low enough to make them eligible for legal aid), 'in the construction industry'. She told me, 'I've spoken to friends, to a police officer, and they all say the same thing. If the bailiffs come to your house, and you don't let them in, they have to go back to a judge and get a court order.'

I told her there already was a court order. The last judge to look at their case had granted possession. And he had done so because they had signed a consent order agreeing to possession.

There were defects in the consent order, I reckoned. To be effective in possession proceedings, a consent order needs to specify what the tenant was admitting. Theirs failed to do that. However, this was a speculative argument – I had to admit, there were points which could be made on both sides. They could not be certain of victory.

The hearing was supposed to start at 2.45pm. We were listed in Slough before a judge I hadn't encountered before. The hearing was meant to take place by a system called Cloud Video Platform Link. Ten minutes before the hearing was scheduled to begin, I logged into an online waiting room. I could see an icon representing me and one for my opponent, Ms Makk. At 2.45pm, everyone else was allowed in. I could see a blue dot by the names of the other people in the hearing, as the judge invited each of them to speak. Plainly, everyone else was speaking. But I could not see their faces. I could not hear them, and they could not hear me. After ten minutes, Ms Makk rang me directly in my room, and very fairly offered to fix up an alternative meeting through Microsoft Teams. The judge agreed that this would do. Actually, it would have had all sorts of problems: how for example, could we have been sure there was a proper recording of the hearing in case of an appeal? We never had to consider those issues since, when Ms Makk started a new hearing in Teams, I was once again excluded. It was not the fault of my device (an iPad) or of the software (which was working properly for every other purpose), but again the meeting was ineffective. By this point, my pulse was beating at 200 beats a minute. I shudder to think what it must have been like for my clients.

The judge tried a third time: arranging a telephone hearing through BT Teams. Forty minutes after the hearing had been meant to start, I finally heard the calming words, 'Hello, this is Sam, the court usher . . .'

If I was grateful to be admitted at last to the hearing, I was immediately put on the defensive. The judge let me know that she had taken a phone call from the court bailiffs. Apparently, Monty had rung them, asking 'Hypothetically speaking, if we had to move on Wednesday, then how much time will you give us?' Monty had not consulted his solicitor before making the call. According to the bailiff, he had told them that he would be fine to move on Wednesday, he had another place lined up, he just needed to know how long he would be given to pack. 'Your client has lined up alternative accommodation?' the judge asked.

I wanted to say, this was the first I had heard of it. I settled for the diplomatic. 'Let me take instructions, madam. I'm sure there's been some confusion.'

With that, we began. Friendly as Ms Makk had been until now, she had been instructed to fight – and did so, as hard as the rules allowed. I pointed out that under section 21 a judge can only order possession if certain minimum requirements had been met (including that a deposit was registered in the first 30 days). No, Ms Makk said, that was true in general, but not in this case, since at the moment the parties had consented the order, they had in fact agreed to have the case determined on quite other grounds to the original section 21 claim. 'Plainly the tenants had surrendered the tenancy. That's why my client signed the order.' They hadn't surrendered, I replied – rent was still being taken, they still lived in the house. The tenancy was ongoing.

For Ms Makk, the tenants had signed an order, and that was the end of it. A consent order, I pointed out, which nowhere addressed the actual statutory tests. 'So what?' Ms Makk answered. 'This was a claim for possession. If they signed a consent order, they must be deemed to have authorised the judge to find that the property was surrendered; there's no other construction which can be put on the order.'

Just as I had cited cases asserting that the law provided a clear answer in my client's favour; so, Ms Makk had dug up cases of her own.

As for the letter from her solicitor, the way he had misrepresented the law, and the effect his letter had had on my clients – this was not the solicitor's fault. '*If* it was a misrepresentation', Ms Makk said, 'it can't possibly have had any effect on proceedings. It's not my client's fault if the tenants were stupid enough to believe him.'

Someone once told me that if you want to sound charming down the telephone, you have to make yourself smile. Bitterly and resentfully, I tried to do just that.

The judge had promised us a decision that day, but the clock wore on: past 4pm, 4.30pm ... We stopped at 5pm precisely, with no decision but the promise of a judgment the next day. As I cycled home, all I could think about was my clients. The bailiff's appointment was coming closer. By the time of the relisted hearing, they would have less than 24 hours to get out of their home, if that was what the judge decided.

In pre COVID-19 conditions, when a tenant applied for a hearing to consider staying a warrant of eviction, they could expect to have that meeting with a clear week before the eviction. That extra time made a difference. It gave tenants who lost a chance to appeal. A more senior judge would not grant permission to appeal just because a tenant had asked for it, but most would at least delay enforcement until the appeal was heard.

We would not have a week. The way the case was looking, we would have around two working hours to do the following: perfect my notes of the judgment into a typed document; type up the grounds of the appeal (ie a short document, setting out how the judgment was at fault); get permission from the Legal Aid Agency (LAA) to appeal; send the appeal to court; chase the court officers to ensure that the papers arrived to the desk of a circuit judge who could decide whether to stay the eviction or not while permission was sought; and (assuming the judge agreed to a stay enforcement pending the appeal hearing), get the news of the circuit judge's decision to the bailiffs to prevent the eviction. The odds of getting all that done in time would be around the same as Leicester City FC winning the Premiership League (which they did in 2015–16, at odds of 500:1) not just once but this season, and next season, and the four seasons after that.

Tuesday morning was dark and grey. I asked my clients how they felt. 'Terrible', said Monty. 'We couldn't sleep', added Lola. Monty was thinking of their son in year 12. He suffered from dyslexia and had a statement of educational needs. They had been expecting to take him out of school after his GCSE exams, with a view to him attending a sixth form college in the nearby town. However, his mock grades had been so poor (and, because of COVID-19, they had become his final results) that he had been forced to stay at school another year while he resat his exams. That was why they were staying in a home which they had always hoped to leave.

'The idea that we might have to move in less than 24 hours – it's making the poor boy desperate', Monty told me.

Lola was focussing on the practicalities: they would not be able to find a moving company. They had never had more than a few days' warning of the bailiff's date. She and her husband had already taken 20 trips to storage; they had already moved all they could. What they had left was heavy furniture, things they could not move without someone else's help. They had asked the local authority for assistance, but it had refused to help. The council was saying it would not even consider their case until their bailiffs were at their door.

'We can't do it', Lola said, 'I'm sorry – but we can't.'

COVID-19 was making everything harder than it would have been in the past. Their son would have done better in his exams without the pandemic, and my clients would have moved in the summer as they had been planning. It was the disease which made everything rushed, which meant they had no proper of warning of the bailiff's appointment, and not enough time for the hearing. It was the fact of the pandemic which also made it so difficult to think of getting the case – if we lost – before a second judge.

I was in my room in chambers, the telephone on speakerphone as the judge gave us her decision. She thanked both sides' counsel for our submissions. She spoke gently and softly, but also quickly – I was struggling to keep up with her as I typed. The judge said that the background facts were largely agreed, which was true. She described the efforts she had taken to check them for herself. She had read the landlord's original claim form (it was not in the papers for the case, as the clients had not kept their copy). She pointed out something I did not know, that with the claim form the landlord had supplied a document supposedly from the tenancy deposit service, claiming that the deposit had been properly registered. Although the judge did not use emotive words or speak of forgeries, she made it clear that there was a document on the court file and that the facts contained in it could not be true.

The judge did not accept my argument that there had been a misrepresentation. She had read – and re-read – the solicitor's letter to my clients. She was plainly unhappy with the thought of a lawyer writing in this way to an unrepresented opponent. But, 'I'd need more than that', she said.

The judge took rather longer over the order, and my argument that a consent order could not resolve a case in a possession matter without recording what the tenants had agreed. She set out the cases I had quoted at her. She noted the cases Ms Makk had cited.

'I did double-check that these were the latest Court of Appeal authorities', the judge said, raising the awful possibility that there were other cases that I had missed.

I stopped typing, I squeezed my hands into fists.

She said that the other cases she had found also 'set out the law just as Mr Renton says. In order for the court to have jurisdiction following a consent order, the admission must be clearly shown. That's the dividing line.'

She accepted my submission that there was nothing in the order which said directly whether the deposit had been registered on not; nothing which said clearly if section 21 had ever been properly complied with.

Accordingly, she set aside the possession order, and dismissed the warrant. Court officers would call the bailiffs and tell them the appointment was cancelled.

When I rang Monty later, he sounded drunk with relief. 'It's David!' he told his wife, 'David!', as she laughed in delight beside him.

CHAPTER 11

November: Legal aid

I went to see my father in hospital again. I packed water and grapes. Even with my face covered by a mask, he recognised me. But all that time apart from his family had taken a toll on him. I showed him a photograph of me with my partner and friends. He thought the picture was of me at school. Ten minutes later, he told me that he was proud of the work I do. But what was my career? He tried his hardest to remember, pinching his face thin with the effort. Looking at me with love and pride in his face, he congratulated me on my choice of career. 'If you're a socialist', he tells me, 'then I reckon being a doctor is the best job you could do'. I smiled, I held his hand. What would have been the point in correcting him?

He was too ill to walk. This was my father – he'd rowed in the Boat Race and won the Ladies' Challenge Plate at Henley – and now he was too weak to stand.

The results of the CT scan came back negative. He left the hospital and returned to his care home. Days passed, and they maintained their rule against visitors from another household.

I rang him – he hardly knew it was me.

On 5 November 2020, England went into a second lockdown for four weeks. The news was heavily trailed in the papers beforehand, accompanied more often than not with photographs of the Prime Minister's adviser Dominic Cummings. My sister refused to call him by name, rechristening, 'Him – you know – nasty weaselly toady.' Not for the first time, the government was giving lawyers two incompatible pieces of advice at once. Insofar as we were workers, we were instructed to stay at home and work from there. On the other hand, the eviction ban had now ended, and courts were – along with schools and universities – supposed to be working normally even as the rest of the country closed.

Lawyers were not the only people to question the terms of the second lockdown. The National Education Union (NEU) – the trade union representing school teachers, further education lecturers, education support staff and teaching assistants – launched a campaign saying that schools and colleges should be included in the lockdown. At the start of November, compared to the prevalence of the disease within society as a whole, primary pupils were nine times more likely to be infected with COVID-19, and secondary pupils 50 times more likely to have it. Within two days of launching its campaign, 150,000 teachers and support staff had signed up.

The government sought to cushion the impact of the second lockdown on tenants by writing to the High Court Enforcement Officers Association asking them to hold back from evicting tenants. Landlords complained, rightly, that this move was almost certainly unlawful. Bailiffs are not decision-makers, but servants of the law. They did not have the power to decline to enforce warrants, even if the Lord Chancellor had asked them.

Faced with the threat of judicial review, the government changed tack. On 16 November, a statutory instrument was laid before parliament prohibiting bailiffs from delivering writs of possession or notices of eviction. Such notices could be issued however, in exceptional cases, for example if an order for possession had been made against trespassers or on grounds of anti-social behaviour, or where the tenant had by 23 March 2020 been in arrears by nine months' rent or more.[1] Again, last-minute decisions made bad law. Why should *anyone* be evicted for rent arrears, midway through a lockdown? If the point was to protect public health, that purpose did not cease to apply merely because a tenant was in severe debt.

The thing which struck me was the imbalance between employment and housing law. In housing law, over a period of eight months, we had seen three stays on possession proceedings; mooted alterations to the pre-action protocol; changes to the duration of notices seeking possession; new procedures for reactivating possession proceedings; letters to the bailiffs; and now a statutory instrument. All of these changes had protected tenants, and tenants only. Indeed, of all the measures which the governments could have introduced, the one they had resisted most determinedly was the scheme which would have helped landlords most, in other words, some sort of fund to compensate for rent arrears caused by COVID-19.

---

1 Public Health (Coronavirus) (Protection from Eviction and Taking Control of Goods) (England) Regulations 2020 SI No 1290.

In employment law, the government addressed the crisis with one main measure: the furlough. This did not assist only workers. Rather, it protected employers by subsidising wages.

In housing law, tenants were being protected by slowing down the pace of litigation, in order to give people who had lost their jobs a fair chance of finding new employment and clearing their arrears. From the point of view of the social wage, what workers needed was the opposite: a speeding up of litigation in order to ensure that workers' rights were respected in what would otherwise be a situation of fast rising unemployment. To be consistent, the government should have funded the employment tribunal, encouraged the recruitment of judges and formulated additional penalties when employers broke the law.

There was nothing like that. The nearest we came was a single modest change to procedure, and one unnoticed by the press. Since 2013, there has been an obligation on employees, prior to issuing a tribunal claim, that they inform the Advisory, Conciliation and Arbitration Service (ACAS) that they intend to bring a claim. The employee was then required to wait one month before issuing a claim, in the hope that employers would make proposals to settle the claim. If the month passed, as it usually did, without settlement, then the employee could issue their claim,

From 1 December, the government announced, the ACAS settlement period would be extended from one month to six weeks. It was a modest change, but a malign one, putting off a bit further the prospect of a hearing, which for a recalcitrant employer was the only thing which would pressure them to settle.

I spent much of November advising friends, on whether or not to accept settlement packages offered to compensate them for what would otherwise inevitably be unfair dismissals. The story was the same whenever anyone contacted me. An employer had decided to make large numbers of redundancies. The ordinary requirements of a fair redundancy procedure were ignored. Rather than rationally selecting certain parts of the business to target, everyone in a business was at risk. Rather than drawing up fair, objective criteria to distinguish those whose work was still needed from those whose posts could be cut, decisions were made on a whim and without reasons. Finally, no attempt was made to find alternative positions for those being dismissed; how could that be done if half the workplace was leaving?

Workers approached me, and I drew up letters on their behalf, promising them every prospect of success should they turn down their employers' offers and fight their case as far as the tribunal. I told a junior IT worker that she had a 60 per cent chance of success. Other workers, I told 70 per cent, or 80 per cent. My constant refrain to all of them was to hold out for more money, and a proper reference. But the companies had lawyers too. And the advice they were giving was straightforward – offer as little as you can. If the workers put in a tribunal claim, it wouldn't be heard until 2022 at the earliest. What was the protection against unfair dismissal worth, if it could not be enforced on any meaningful timescale?

In some workplaces, unions were having a positive impact. The NEU was campaigning not merely for the inclusion of schools and colleges within the lockdown, but for greater school safety, hiring more staff, better use of IT equipment and the release of vulnerable teachers from face-to-face duties. Members of the lecturers' union University and College Union (UCU) could be seen speaking at events alongside their rent-striking students.

Workers contacted me: Software designers asking for advice on whether their collectively agreed pay-scales would remain enforceable if the employer derecognised their union. Bus drivers sought to frustrate employer arguments that competitive tendering could be used to relocate workers, and reduce the proportion of the workforce on older, better-paid contracts. Protest, I told them – there was no way that a garage would dismiss dozens of its most experienced drivers, not when it was simultaneously recruiting.

There needed to be some institution capable of sharing these experiences of campaigning and using them to promote a different vision of how the economy should work. The Treasury was saying that its assistance needed to be targeted at viable companies, meaning those capable of making a profit in current market conditions. But all across Europe and the US, demands were being raised to reorient business, in favour of a 'Green New Deal' which would encourage high-paid jobs in sustainable sectors, reducing our dependence on fossil fuels and polluting technologies. Why should companies be assessed on their short-term viability, when COVID-19 had given us a chance to plan a more sustainable economy?

The changes which had been made to housing law were criticised by landlords. For some time, the sense had been growing among landlords' bodies that tenants were being unduly protected from eviction by overly prescriptive housing laws and by a group of lawyers who were raising technical defences gratuitously. There were moments when practising in housing law felt akin to what it was like in employment law in 2013, in the days immediately before employment tribunal fees were introduced when newspapers ran stories demanding the reduction of the tribunal system and government was signalling its intention to make those changes. A demand was made for the abolition of legal aid for housing, and the replacement of the county courts with something worse.

Two years before, in 2018, the government had already consulted on moving some or all housing cases into a new housing court, which would be a new and separate chamber of our existing First-tier Tribunal.[2] There, landlords would be able to pay for their lawyers, but as legal aid does not extend to tribunals, all tenants would go unrepresented except for the tiny number who could afford their own lawyers. Under the government's proposal, there would still be judges specialising in housing law. All the formal content of housing law would, in theory, remain the same. The only two meaningful differences is that all housing cases would be heard in a single, and different, court; and that legal aid would be ended.

The consultation was neutrally posed. 'We want to explore ways of reducing delays', its author wrote, 'and improving the service for all users who bring housing cases to the courts and tribunal services'. The idea of reducing delays sounds like an unambiguous good: if the relationship between landlord and tenant has irretrievably broken down, then surely neither party should be forced to put up with the other. However, we live in a society characterised by housing shortage. I have, once in my ten years as a barrister, represented a tenant who wanted to leave a tenancy early, when the landlord was refusing their permission. But this was a once in a career exception. Almost always, it is the landlord who thinks that by replacing their present tenant their situation will be improved, and the tenant who wants to remain.

The authors of the proposals for a new housing court acknowledged that the demand for quicker outcomes came from property owners: 'Landlord groups argue that a barrier to longer tenancies in the private rented sector is the belief that it is difficult for landlords to repossess their properties quickly and smoothly if the tenant defaults on their tenancy agreement and forces the landlord to apply to the court for possession.' At the heart of the suggestion, in other words, was the goal of making it easier for landlords to obtain possession.

2 'Considering the case for a housing court: call for evidence', Ministry of Housing, Communities and Local Government, 13 November 2018; www.gov. uk/government/consultations/considering-the-case-for-a-housing-court-call -for-evidence.

The consultation document stated that the average time it took a private sector landlord to obtain possession, from issuing a claim to obtaining a bailiff's date, was 16.1 weeks – slightly less than half of this period (seven weeks) was taken up by court proceedings, over half by delays in obtaining bailiff's dates. If the government was willing to leave the balance between landlord and tenant alone, and was solely concerned with speed, in other words, they could significantly improve the situation for landlords by better funding the bailiff system. That, relatively modest, expenditure would have also the significant advantage that where tenants had a defence to possession, they could still use it. The gain to landlords would be relatively large; the loss to tenants would be more modest.

Instead, the government was proposing to move landlord and tenant law into a new housing court, with all the consequences that would follow.

In the county court, there are two routes to legal aid representation. One is where a tenant, having received warning through the post of a court hearing, contacts a local solicitor in advance of the hearing. This is always the preferable route. On the other hand, given the long hours worked by many of my clients, their precarious lifestyles and dependence on benefits, it cannot catch everyone. A second safety net also applies: when tenants arrive at court, they are entitled to speak to a 'duty' representative under the Housing Possession Court Duty Scheme (HPCDS), a solicitor funded by legal aid, who can help them through a contested first hearing. Often, that solicitor will then represent the tenant at any further hearings. Both the initial advice on the duty scheme and the subsequent representation depend on the availability of legal aid for county court hearings.

The government's seeming hostility to housing lawyers was giving me awkward memories of the introduction of employment tribunal fees in 2013. When they were introduced, they did not alter the content of discrimination law – it was still wrong to dismiss a worker unfairly. But, overnight, the number of claims brought to the tribunal dropped by two-thirds. All the old statutes were still the same, but workers could no longer enforce them. A law without a means to enforce it was useless. (After the decision of the High Court, twice, and the Court of Appeal upholding tribunal fees, the Supreme Court finally struck the fees down as unlawful in 2017.)

For the people I represent, the abolition of legal aid would be no less dramatic. There might be all sorts of defences available to them – but without someone to guide them through the system, explain what those defences are and gather the evidence to corroborate them, they would lose all the benefit of those protections.

My next client, Veronique Schultz, was already sitting in the first-floor waiting area at Gee Street. She was a mother in her late 20s. She wore a smart black leather jacket. She had the thickest eyelashes I have ever seen, as if she attached the mascara not with a wand but with glue. Ms Schutz's daughter was clutched to her side, in a new anorak.

When the claim was issued Ms Schutz was already in arrears of £4,000 and they had risen by the time I met her. Her landlord, a housing association, was seeking possession relying on ground 8 (two months' rent arrears), ground 10 (rent lawfully due) and ground 11 (persistently delayed paying rent) of Housing Act 1988 Sch 2. The one which worried me was ground 8, since it is a mandatory ground of possession. If the landlord could prove that the tenant was in two months' arrears at the time that they served a notice seeking possession and was still in that arrears by the date of the hearing, the judge would be obliged to order possession.

Time was short, we could get called on at any point, but I asked Ms Schultz how she had fallen so far behind with her rent. She worked as a cashier, and life as a single mother was a daily struggle. She told me that she had been diagnosed with depression and anxiety. She had been trying to prioritise the rent, but it was not easy with two children. There was never anything for them. The month before she had gone to the shops and her daughter was asking for new trainers, those same bubble-gum-pink trainers she was wearing now. Ms Schultz skipped a week's rent to buy the shoes.

Ms Schultz had two defences to possession. The first was that the housing association sent her the notice seeking possession two days *before* the rent became due. When they sent it, she was only one month in arrears. It was the sort of mistake that happens all the time and is fatal to a ground 8 claim for possession.

The other defence was disrepair. For four years, there had been water leaking into her flat from the windows. When to I told District Judge Tanar this, she glowered. 'Your client is £8,000 in arrears. How on earth did she let that happen?'

I explained that the rent was high. In the five years since she sent her first email complaining about disrepair, my client had paid more than £90,000 in rent. If the court accepted that the housing association had delayed unreasonably and found that even a small proportion of that sum was owed to the tenant, then it would more than extinguish her arrears.

The judge turned to the barrister representing the housing association. It was my old acquaintance, the no-longer-raw Tuck, with a confident smile on his face, and a tan which could only mean he had been on a break somewhere warmer than London.

'Did you know about the disrepair?'

'The defence was the first we'd heard about it. I've checked the landlord's records and in the past five years there hasn't been even a single complaint about damaged windows or water getting in through them.'

Ms Schultz said that she had complained often and in detail to the housing association about disrepair. Every call she made was ignored. I told District Judge Tanar, and she looked at my opponent and shook her head in solidarity with him. I showed the judge an email from four years before in which Ms Schultz had asked the housing association to fix her broken windows and her child's damp bedroom.

Reluctantly, District Judge Tanar agreed to adjourn the case. She ordered my client to pay the rent in the meantime, plus £250 per month towards the arrears. But Ms Schultz was on benefits, I pointed out. 'There's no way she can–'

District Judge Tanar cut me short. 'It's your client's fault. She shouldn't have allowed her account to fall into arrears. I'm not going to change my mind.'

Outside court, Tuck seemed to think he had won a great victory. And, maybe he was right, for the hearing had ended as well for the landlord as any other battle we'd been in. 'Bad luck', he told me, 'I really thought she'd agree with you.'

I held back the unkind words running through my head. He and I were going to spend the next ten years of our lives on opposite sides of a courtroom. For the sake of those cases to come, I said something neutral back to him.

Tuck smiled. 'I don't know how you do it', he says.

'Do what?'

'Tenants.' And he spoke the words not with cruelty or contempt, but something else – with confusion, even disappointment in me.

Over the days that followed, the landlord maintained that it owed Ms Schultz nothing. Their solicitor wrote to the Legal Aid Agency (LAA), asking them to make their own finding that the defence was hopeless, and therefore that it should not be funded. No doubt this last kick at my client was another of Tuck's schemes. To Ms Schultz's good fortune, the landlord's correspondence went unanswered.

The demand for the abolition of legal aid had received surprising backing from voices within the reforming wing of the legal system. One of the country's best-known housing lawyers had acquired the ear of the human rights campaigning group JUSTICE, and that group had proposed a scheme in line with the government's intended housing court, albeit with a modest tweak. In JUSTICE's version of what they termed a 'housing dispute service', tenants should still receive legal aid, though it would be restricted to giving advice at the outset of the case. Each side, they proposed, should leave their lawyers at the door of the court.

The author of JUSTICE's document conceded that there might be a small group of cases where there was a need to 'recognise an ongoing relationship between the parties in certain circumstances' or, in plain English, where a tenant might be allowed to remain in their home. If more people were evicted in future, the author suggested, the system could make up for that by increasing the availability of council housing for the now-homeless former tenants.[3]

Yet a new legal system which worked harder to house a tenant post-eviction within the limits of the law, while also making it easier for landlords to evict, could only harm the likes of Ms Schultz. Having lost her home, and on applying to her local authority, she and her children would be placed in temporary accommodation, possibly a single room in a hostel. After a couple of months, the local authority would decide whether to not to accommodate them afterwards. Assuming that she was unable to challenge the finding of intentional homelessness, the local authority would be under no obligation to offer her housing thereafter. Its options would include housing her children and not her, by taking the children into care.

Even if the local authority agreed, for the children's sake, to keep the family together in hostel accommodation – such a result would still be a significant loss for Ms Schultz compared to her present housing association flat. Unless and until the court ordered otherwise, her flat was her home. She had the same right to live there as anyone in their home, as much right as any millionaire, any politician, any judge.

'We want to explore', the government had written, 'whether housing cases could be resolved in a different forum more cheaply'. Between 2009/10 and 2018/19, total civil legal aid funding fell from £1.1

---

3 'JUSTICE launches "Solving Housing Disputes" report', JUSTICE, 5 March 2020.

billion to £710 million. Plainly, the government had every incentive, post-coronavirus, to cut the legal aid budget further. Under the government's spending plans, total spending at the Ministry of Justice was intended to be around one-fifth lower in 2020/21 than it had been a decade earlier.[4] And this was the spending plan drawn up in late 2019, prior to a great wave of public expenditure which would no doubt bring cuts in its aftermath.

If it was possible to make real savings to the Ministry of Justice by cutting civil legal aid, then this would be a priority for the government. The replacement of the present county court with a new specialist housing court would undoubtedly have a cost – simply relocating staff, providing new headed notepaper, obtaining a new centralised building or group of buildings – and these upfront costs could be as much in a single year as the abolition of housing civil legal aid would save in a decade.

Part of the reason why legal aid is so cheap is that the amounts paid by the state for legal aid work are modest. The fee for advocacy in the county court, for example, is £59.40 per hour (in complex cases, this can be increased by up to 50 per cent, however this level of enhancement is rarely granted). Until 2010, barristers' hourly rates were determined by the Legal Services Commission, and based on what was set to be 'an unpublished set of "benchmark" or "reasonable" rates' which 'var[ied] according to level of barrister, the role they play and the level of court', but starting at £120 per hour for junior counsel in the county court.[5] This was double what we are paid now: and the fall since then has been an absolute cut; the reduction in advocates' earnings would be even sharper if inflation was factored in.

Not all barristers are paid the same: where chambers predominantly act for businesses, it is not unusual for them to pay the pupils, the most junior members of chambers, a guaranteed income of £60,000 or even £70,000 a year. I presume that the more senior members of those chambers earn much more. But it is different when you represent workers or tenants. I remember when I was a junior barrister and I was representing a librarian, who was threatened with the loss of her home. She had a salary of £30,000 a year, on top of which the council paid a pension contribution of ten per cent of her wage.

4 G Sturge et al, 'The spending of the Ministry of Justice', House of Commons Library, Debate Pack Number CDP-2019-0217, 1 October 2019; https://commonslibrary.parliament.uk/research-briefings/cdp-2019-0217/.

5 'Proposals for the reform of legal aid in England and Wales', Consultation Paper CP12/10, Ministry of Justice, November 2010, paras 7.10–7.11.

'It's a good job', the librarian told me, trying not to look too proud, before frowning, 'but it must seem such a pittance to you'.

I explained to her that on paper, it looked as if I was better paid than she was. But once I had factored in delays in payment, the cost of the books I needed for court, the proportion of my income I paid to my chambers (a little over a fifth of my earnings) and VAT, I received an income which was much the same as hers – only that on mine there was no sickness or holiday pay, no maternity or paternal leave and no pension.

'You're lying', she said.

Any legal aid lawyer could tell you a version of this story. The total amount that the state spends on legal aid in housing is trivial, at just £20 million a year.[6]

This is the reality which stays the government's hand, despite the demands of the landlords' representatives for the end of legal aid. The system is so cheap that the costs of its abolition would be greater than costs of keeping it going.

Legal aid improves any client's chances of success – but it does not guarantee them victory. In November, I walked to Islington Law Centre. A dozen years ago, I used to work there in the evenings and on my holidays, and I assisted claimants with tribunal claims through the Free Representation Unit. In those days, the Law Centre was located round the back of the Nag's Head pub in Holloway. We relied on a shifting mix of legal aid and local authority funding. We were always short of money: the computers broke, the telephones died, the photocopier was always on the blink. One painful morning, the drains beneath the office collapsed and after that the caseworkers could stay in the building only by hiding in the uppermost floors.

I was nervous as I walked in. A previous chapter described how the Legal Aid, Sentencing and Punishment of Offenders Act 2012 (LASPO) made life harder for tenants bringing disrepair claims. This was just one of dozens of changes introduced by LASPO, all of which tended to undermine law centres and those working in legal advice. One of the worst changes in the Act was to take welfare benefits advice out of legal aid. In consequence, even when housing lawyers are defending possession proceedings, we cannot give clients advice on benefits or write letters for them; we cannot be paid for that work. This change helped to devastate the sector: half

6 'Legal aid statistics quarterly, England and Wales', Ministry of Justice, 25 June 2020.

of all legal advice centres in England and Wales closed between 2013 and 2019.[7]

Yet when I visited the Islington Law Centre in 2020, I was delighted by how much better everything seemed. The ceilings were high, the conference rooms well-lit. Former colleagues rushed to greet me, showing off the new and clean desks at which they worked. They told me that their situation had begun to improve around a decade ago. After the global banking crisis, the freshly elected Labour council realised that demand for legal services would rise and decided to increase the Centre's funding. That help had made up for government's cuts.

I was due to meet Jim Murtagh, a man in his late 30s whose mother had recently died, potentially entitling him to succeed to her council tenancy. To do so, he needed to show that he had lived with her as her carer during the last year of her life. His difficulty was that the council did not believe that he had lived with her. During her final year, Mr Murtagh had also been the tenant of another property, rented jointly with his girlfriend. For Mr Murtagh to be entitled to legal aid, he needed to establish that his case had a certain minimum threshold for success – and on what I had read, I was doubtful.

Cases like Mr Murtagh's pose in an intense way certain conflicts of interest which are structured into the legal aid lawyer's role. In a civil legal aid case, the bills are paid for by the government. The government insists that they must have a minimum likelihood of success. They must be at least 'marginal', or 'borderline' – in other words, have at least a 45 per cent prospect of winning. Less than that, and a client cannot be represented on legal aid, not even if the case has a public interest or is of overwhelming importance to the client. Those are the rules.

Every lawyer will be familiar with the question, 'How could you represent someone you know is guilty?' To which the stock answer is, we never know. No criminal defendant ever tells their lawyer, 'I pleaded not guilty but, yes, I did it.' If they did, we could not tell a judge something we knew to be untrue. The difficult cases are the one where your client insists on what happened, but their account is vague. We might have an opinion, but that is all. That is why courts exist – because the people who serve in them have the repeated experience of fighting a case which at one time seemed weak, only for a key detail to emerge or for a witness to tell a judge something unexpected. For that reason, lawyers do not make decisions

7   O Bowcott, 'Legal advice centres in England and Wales halved since 2013–14', *Guardian*, 15 July 2019.

prematurely, we wait and leave it to for the judge or jury to decide what happened.

The decision to refuse legal aid offends – it rubs against some of the deepest-held values of the professions. We do not judge our client's innocence or guilt: that is for the court, not us. We do not turn down cases just because they would be hard to win. And yet our client (the government) requires us to make an objective assessment of each case's prospects. If legal aid lawyers were to ignore the rules and repeatedly run defences which were doomed to lose, we would be lying to our funder, and legal aid would be in even greater danger than it is already.

To win his case, Mr Murtagh needed to prove that he had lived with his mother for the whole last year of her life. To persuade me that his case was strong enough to proceed to trial, I needed to believe that its chance of winning was 45 per cent or more.

On the face of it, this task should have been easy. Mr Murtagh said that he had lived with his mother continuously, not for one year but for ten. The biggest single problem with his case was that he had very few documents to corroborate that he had lived there during the final year. She was the tenant, so the rent was in her name and not his. Because it was a council flat, all the utility bills were paid for her. Normally, any adult child living with their parents would generate a treasure trove of documents, bank accounts, mobile phone bills, GP's records, entries on the electoral register – but Mr Murtagh had been able to find almost nothing to corroborate his case. For example, Mr Murtagh had been registered at his mother's home to vote, but two years before she died, he registered himself at his girlfriend's flat. 'Did I really?' he asked, and he was not bitter or ironic, but genuinely surprised by the news.

There were letters from his dentist in the bundle.

'The letters are good', I told him. 'The problem is when they end. You see, they stopped writing to you there a year-and-a-half before your mum died.'

Unfortunately, that was all the positive evidence he had.

We turned then to the paperwork which the landlord had disclosed. The first was a letter from his mother four years before she died. In it, she asked the landlord to award her council tax on the basis that she was living as a single person.

Mr Murtagh insisted that his mother had lied. At this point, he said, he had been living with his mum, caring for her every day. He could not explain why she wrote the letter. He told me she had suffered a haemorrhage a couple of years before and did not know what she was saying. He said that maybe she wrote it to get a council tax rebate. 'She's done everything from a selfish point of view', Mr Murtagh said.

The next document was a statement from the mother's social worker. She also disclosed diary notes saying she had seen Mr Murtagh's mother repeatedly in the last year. The social worker said she hadn't seen Mr Murtagh once.

'But she did', he insisted. 'I am sure I remember her.' We went through the diary notes, and Mr Murtagh explained that he had been working from 9am to 5pm during the last year. The social worker only came during office hours, no wonder she hadn't seen him.

'Mother's world was mother's world', he told me, 'I let her get on with it.'

The next set of papers concerned a tenancy agreement which Mr Murtagh's girlfriend had signed just over a year before his mother died. Mr Murtagh's name was also on the tenancy agreement. I said, 'You can see, can't you – this doesn't help?'

'The landlord said if I didn't put myself down, my girlfriend couldn't move in. I had more money coming in than she did, and he wanted me to guarantee the rent.'

'You could have added yourself – not as a tenant, but a guarantor.'

'I didn't know you could do that.' Mr Murtagh motioned around him, 'That's what I'm up against', and for a moment I could not say whether he meant the case, the large pile of landlord's evidence – or me, his lawyer.

Mr Murtagh told his employers to send his payslips not to his mother's home, but to his girlfriend's flat. His bank accounts went there, as did his online purchases.

The girlfriend's landlord had written a statement. He insisted that Mr Murtagh had slept every night at the girlfriend's flat. Whenever the property was in disrepair, it was Mr Murtagh who phoned in. The landlord said the rent was paid by bank transfer, and not from the girlfriend's bank account but from Mr Murtagh's.

'She's a female', Mr Murtagh said. 'Of course, I dealt with the repairs.'

'Ok', I said, 'but what about the rent?'

'She's no good with numbers.'

'She's a chartered accountant', I said.

I explained to Mr Murtagh that I had read his witness statement and I had seen the passages describing living with his mother, watching her decline. I believed him, but I wasn't the one he needed to persuade. The only way he could win his case was by persuading a judge that in that the crucial year, he had lived with his mother and not with his girlfriend. We were not talking about what happened, but the decision the judge had to make and evaluating evidence that would be before him.

I told Mr Murtagh what my duties were. I explained that we were past the information-gathering stage of proceedings. All the documents that were going to be before the judge had already been disclosed. If you looked at the papers, the pieces of evidence connecting him to the girlfriend's flat outnumbered those linking him to his mother's flat by ten to one.

'I don't believe it', said Mr Murtagh, clenching his hand into a fist.

I told Mr Murtagh that he could wait before deciding. That, if he wanted to, he should sleep on it overnight. He could talk to his girlfriend.

'Go through it all again', Mr Murtagh asked me. 'One last time.'

I did.

As I spoke, he sank into his chair.

A look of determination settled on Mr Murtagh face. 'I'm in the wrong for trying to be with my partner. But I can see how it looks. I've had enough with fighting.'

In the end, he conceded to the inevitable. He told the solicitor to write to the other side and withdraw his defence.

I have told you already; I will never be a judge.

There was an old copy of *Legal Action* on my desk. It is a monthly magazine written by and for legal aid lawyers and the law centre movement. The magazine is glossy and well presented, with images of the House of Commons, of our clients and of their solicitors. One article showed a table with the number of applications for legal aid for disrepair cases. Since LASPO, legal aid has only been available to tenants, in bringing a claim of their own, to remove or reduce a serious risk of harm to the client or their family. It is no longer possible to bring such a claim to seek damages.

The changes to the funding of disrepair cases, contained within LASPO, were relatively modest. In principle, they only affected a minority of claims. But the disrepair provision in the 2012 Act was part of a much larger series of changes to the funding of legal aid, including the removal of access to free representation for most family and immigration cases, and the removal of welfare benefits work from legal aid (preventing solicitors from chasing up the benefits providers in a possession case where the tenant is in rent arrears). The net effect of these changes had been to cause many solicitors to withdraw from legal aid work entirely.

The magazine told me that in 2010–11 (that is, before LASPO) there were 2,063 applications for legal aid in disrepair claims. But in 2018–19 (five years after LASPO came fully into effect) the number of applications had shrunk to 168, or a fall of 90 per cent.[8]

I bring about as many disrepair cases now as I did before LASPO. The grim thought struck me that I had probably represented tenants in around one in ten of all disrepair cases brought on legal aid in 2018–19. Just me, alone. I knew from my day-to-day experience that almost every disrepair client I represented had a home somewhere in south-east England. So, what had been happening in other parts of the country – in Sheffield, or in Sunderland? What about Truro?

An article in *Inside Housing* reported that over half of the district and unitary authorities in England and Wales do not have a single legal aid provider.[9] That is why even groups like JUSTICE with a radical past were making the case for something like the abolition of housing legal aid. They did so in despair, telling themselves that it was too late to save legal aid.

Ms Schultz's solicitor received a letter listing the case for a final hearing. To prevent unnecessary expense, the housing association told us that if Ms Schultz agreed to a possession order, they would agree to give her counterclaim a nominal value of £500. She would still have to leave, but the debt would be reduced. She declined their offer.

Ms Schultz's health was suffering under the pressure of the case. A psychiatrist assessed her, found that on a scale of 1–28, her anxiety was 28, or as bad as could be. Her depression, at 27 on the same scale, was little better.

Her children had been diagnosed with asthma and with eczema.

The housing association disclosed Ms Schultz's housing file. They included records of calls between Ms Schultz and her housing officers. They showed that Ms Schultz had complained about the windows as long ago as 2013, and that the housing association's

8   S Mullings, 'Homes and (dis)contents: getting full value out of the Homes (Fitness for Human Habitation) Act', January 2020 *Legal Action*.

9   L Heath, 'Behind the numbers: what impacts have legal aid cuts had on housing?', *Inside Housing*, 7 February 2020.

in-house surveyor inspected and found that water was getting in through the windows and damaged the plaster in the flat. That was six years ago – after which the windows were repaired. All we had were those records and Ms Schultz's email to the landlord, and no proof that the landlord received it.

I found myself checking the email address on Google – hoping beyond hope that my client had not mistyped the address. She had written it accurately.

Ms Schultz's solicitor applied to the court for more documents. The housing association told the judge that all possible checks had been made. No further orders were given. Everything was to be ready for the final hearing of the case.

The case reached its nadir. Ms Schultz's arrears were now above £10,000. The judge had ordered her to pay both her rent and towards the arrears. She had breached that order, making her liable not merely to losing her home, but also in theory to committal proceedings – potentially jail for breach of a court order.

Ms Schultz's solicitor Michael, who is the calmest and kindest lawyer you will ever meet, told me there was a perfectly good explanation. The client had stopped working and her rent was being paid by universal credit. Each month, a deduction was taken from her benefits, and paid to the rent. The money had got lost between the benefits authorities and the housing association. Dozens of phone calls were required to be made. The landlord denied responsibility. The Department for Work and Pensions, unlike the old housing benefits agency, could not be contacted.

The landlord finally agreed to credit Ms Schultz for the money which had been sitting in their bank account since the summer.

That decision, alone, reduced her arrears back down to £8,000.

My mother rang with news of my father. He'd suffered another fall. The home was allowing her to visit, but she was the only one permitted. Even she was required to argue her case. 'I want to see him. I told the nurses – it's the only thing he wants. He wants it more than anything.'

The pandemic was putting ever greater numbers of people at risk of losing their homes. On 16 November 2020, the Joseph Rowntree Foundation published its summary of the housing crisis. On what it termed a 'conservative' estimate, Rowntree calculated that across the UK rent arrears had reached £400 million. Some 600,000 households were in rent arrears. A third of all renters had seen their household's income fall. Of this group, 60 per cent of private renters and 56 per cent of social renters had reduced their spending to pay their rent. More than 350,000 families had been served with an eviction notice or had their landlord threaten to evict them.[10]

Yet the effect of the multiple changes to county court procedure had been to dissuade landlords from issuing possession proceedings. This reality could be seen from the statistics of the housing courts, which were also published in mid-November. They covered the period from July to September 2020 (two-thirds of which was inside the stay on evictions). Between July and September 2020, possession claims (3,954) and orders for possession (131) decreased by 86 and 99 per cent respectively, compared to the same quarter in the year before. Warrants of possession (911) also decreased (by 94 per cent). Between June and September 2020, according to the county court bailiffs, not a single eviction had taken place anywhere in the UK.[11]

The best part of a million households were at risk. Landlord were relying on the hope that all these tenants would leave voluntarily without anyone needing to take their tenants to court; but why should they leave? They had nowhere else to go.

Ms Schultz finished her witness statement for the hearing. As she did, it felt at last as if the case was going in her favour. Her arrears had come down, and the landlord tentatively increased its offer. They accepted now that Ms Schultz should not lose her home. Rather, the parties should agree a suspended possession order. Their offer for disrepair was still low at £3,000 – but it would significantly reduce Ms Schultz's debt. I estimated that if we refused and went before District Judge Tanar (after what she'd said last time), there was still a risk that possession would be ordered. Ms Schultz's solicitor Michael insisted on rejecting the landlord's offer. He pointed out that Ms Schultz suffered depression and anxiety; and had had repeated problems with benefits payments. Once the case was over, she would come off legal aid, and he would not be able to assist her. All it would need would be one month's default, and the landlord could apply to the court for a bailiff's appointment.

In preparing her witness statement, Ms Schultz had gathered compelling evidence that the landlord's records of disrepair were inadequate. She had held on to several months of her own telephone records. These showed that over a three-month period in 2018 she rang her landlord's number ten times and spoke to housing officers for between 15 and 20 minutes per call. Only one of the calls was recorded in the landlord's disrepair logs. We were starting to gather compelling evidence that the tenant had repeatedly phoned the landlord to complain of disrepair, and the landlord had not even bothered take a note of her calls.

For the first time, I could envisage persuading a judge that Ms Schultz had been telling the truth when she said she had complained to her landlord about disrepair and told them about her depression – and that the reason the landlord had no record of these calls was because of its poor administration rather than any failure by her.

The Housing Law Practitioners Association (HLPA) had published a dissenting report to JUSTICE's scheme.[12] Under a 'housing dispute service', they wrote, or under a 'housing tribunal', there would be no legal aid, and there would be no means for poorer tenants to be represented. JUSTICE's proposals, they noted, were 'not supported by a single tenant/homeless persons solicitors' firm, organisation, charity, or law centre'.

Any fairer system, HLPA wrote, should begin from the understanding that in possession proceedings the tenant is at a disadvantage. 'The landlord is likely to be more financially secure than the tenant, even if just because in most cases they will own a property, and the tenant will not; the landlord generally has less at stake than the tenant, even though the case may well be financially very important to them, because the tenant is facing the loss of their home, which the landlord is not'.[13] Many housing clients lead chaotic lives or suffer substance abuse. It was naïve to think that a panel in a 'housing tribunal' or a non-lawyer in a 'housing dispute service' could substitute itself for a tenant's solicitor and take instructions and gather evidence to the same standard as is done now. In practice, they would not – and cases would be decided with less evidence than they have now.

12 'Solving housing disputes: A report by JUSTICE', Chair of the Committee: Andrew Arden QC, 2020, 'Annexure B: Dissenting report of the Housing Law Practitioners Association members of the Working Party', p126. See also 'JUSTICE publishes report setting out proposed model for housing dispute resolution', March 2020 *Legal Action*.

13 'Solving housing disputes', p131.

JUSTICE responded by maintaining its commitment to a future without legal representation for tenants. It accused tenant lawyers of taking an 'aggressive approach' when representing our clients. There is a 'conflict of interest', its document maintained, 'between legal aid solicitors and their clients, who rarely want to find themselves in court'.[14]

I hope anyone who reads this book will have seen how hollow that claim is. Like every tenant lawyer I know, I do not take points unnecessarily. I try to take the heat out of my cases. Even on the landlord's side, the lawyers who fight for the sake of the pleasure of battle are a minority. Almost every experienced landlords' representative I know will seek to resolve a matter amicably wherever such a possibility is open to them.

In Ms Schultz's case, a second surveyor employed by the landlord found damaged plaster in every room of Ms Schultz's home. He checked the wooden structure beneath the bathroom and found that the floorboards had rotted. The defect in the windows was having the same effect, in other words, as in 2013 when she had first complained. Water had been entering the rooms of Ms Schultz's flat, damaging the plaster in the walls and the structure of the property. Any works done by the landlord had not addressed this long-term problem.

The landlord offered £5,000 for the disrepair. This, we were told, was their last and final offer. Ms Schultz refused it.

The landlord's next offer included the dismissal of its own possession claim in its entirety, as well as the payment of all Ms Schultz's £8,000 arrears.

The parties agreed a consent order.

Ms Schultz and I met at court. She remembered the previous hearing, how Judge Tanar had looked at her, 'The expression she had on her face, when she saw what the arrears were. She looked at me, at my clothes, and made a judgment on the sort of person I was.'

When the order had been approved, even the landlord's barrister smiled.

As I left the court, I reflected that if the system had relied on the merits assessment of the case made by the landlord's solicitors, or on the judge's informal opinion at the first hearing, Ms Schultz would have lost her home long ago.

If legal aid was removed, what would replace it? In a different and fairer system, the creation of an increased stock of genuinely

14 'Solving housing disputes', 'Chair's response to dissent', p147.

affordable public housing would significantly reduce the need for anyone to do the work I do. Living in a time when that sort of mass housebuilding seems remote, I return to the situation of Ms Schultz. Legal aid saved her home. Any alternative to legal aid could only be justified if it gave other tenants whose homes were threatened the same fighting chance of staying.

CHAPTER 12

December: Online courts

The news of my father's death came in a phone call. I spoke to my sisters, and we made ourselves a pact – to think of him not as he had been in the last year, but before: as a younger man, as the rowdy, gregarious participant in our Christmas dinners. As the man who in his mid-50s had taken up Buddhism, who had made himself a calm and gentle and supportive presence in our lives. Friends rang. They said, 'If there's anything I can do to help . . .'

For a time, I couldn't work. There were pains all over my upper body, beneath and behind my shoulders. My head felt as if it had been replaced with a cabbage, a block of wood, or stuffed with cotton wool. I could work on documents; I could write short pieces for the newspapers. But when I wanted to concentrate for more than an hour at a time, I couldn't. All evening, I would sit on the sofa at the back of our kitchen, staring wordlessly at my phone.

Three friends of mine noticed: one who lives just a mile from my home; one who lives 100 miles away; and one 3,000 miles away. Every day they would write, ask how I was. Even when I didn't answer, still they wrote. They rang. Our and their families shared meals across Skype – they brought me back to life.

Ten days after my father's cremation, I returned to work. At first, my clerks took pity on me, restricting me to paperwork and advices.

The mornings were grey and blue and cold, but the days were mild, warmer than they should have been. I returned to work after the second lockdown ended which it did on 2 December. In the first week of December, the official count of COVID-19 deaths in Britain passed 60,000, the same figure as the total number of British citizens killed by air attack during the whole of the Second World War.

One client, who lived in a house in multiple occupation, was in the middle of possession hearings when a fellow tenant broke into his room. The tenant had a boiling kettle in his hand and flung its contents into my client's face. The solicitor wanted to know if he could apply for legal aid in order to obtain an injunction to stop the harassment, and how that could work if the client's flat was in danger. We can, I told her. Up until the morning he's evicted, he's entitled to live there in peace. The same as anyone else.

The Curlews were back in court. We were before His Honour Judge Pagnam once again, and it was his responsibility to decide what evidence would be allowed at the trial of the possession proceedings. Before I could start, Judge Pagnam cleared his throat. He told us that our hearing would have to be delayed. The landlord had emailed a bundle of papers for our hearing, but the file was too large for the court's IT systems to read. No one in court had thought to ask the landlord to send a new version, and now it was too late. The hearing would have to be adjourned, to give the landlord another chance to get its documents ready.

'We'll relist for after Christmas', Judge Pagnam said, his words pinched. Then, speaking directly to the landlord's barrister, he continued, 'I'm sorry – but we can't go ahead.'

More than two years had passed since the landlord had begun its first claim for an injunction. In nine months, the court had considered the case at two remote hearings, and the case was no closer to a substantive hearing that it had ever been.

I felt the cold on my face. I saw it reflected in frozen stalks, in unmoving leaves studded with frozen drops of dew, diamonds of winter stillness.

At work, life was racing onwards. One client had lived in the UK for more than 20 years without ever regularising his immigration status. When his partner died, he was in principle entitled to succeed to his deceased partner's tenancy. The housing association had no discretion to refuse it. But the housing association would not grant succession. When my client repeated his request, the officer working on a rule of his own imagination that people without immigration status may not succeed to a tenancy, decided that the claim was not only unlawful, but it was also fraudulent, and opened a criminal file. This caused my client understandable distress, while it also gave the officer an excuse to refuse to answer his or his solicitor's letters, or to reveal what documents the housing association held on him.

Another client was asking to be housed by his local authority and it too was refusing. It had made a finding of intentional homeless, based on the last year of my client's accommodation at his previous address, during which his arrears had risen from £1,000 to £12,000 before the landlord had evicted him. Rent arrears on that scale surely had to be his fault – didn't they? The client said they weren't – he'd been suffering from depression. 'There is no evidence that you were experiencing an aberration of mind that would have prevented you from managing your own affairs', the landlord wrote. 'There is no evidence to confirm that you experienced a temporary aberration or aberrations caused by mental illness or frailty.'

But there was evidence to support his condition: the client had written to the landlord and told them he was exhausted. He had been to the local authority and completed a housing form, which referred to his depression and anxiety. With that form were his GP records, in which he was recorded saying, 'I am at the end of my tether. I wish I was dead, but I don't think it would do anything.' His GP was so concerned that he prescribed antidepressants, and then increased the dose two weeks later. If that wasn't an aberration of mind, what was?

I met clients by telephone; my diary began to fill with court hearings. I studied my face in the mirror and saw my reflection smile cautiously back at me.

During the first and second lockdowns of 2020, the pressure for the replacement of physical with online hearings was acute. After the first lockdown had passed, that desire did not abate but intensified. The opinion of the senior judiciary was that the technology existed – accordingly, we were obliged to do as much as we could with it. In speaking of online courts, the enthusiasts tend to merge together what are in reality several different packages of reform, some of which are necessary, others which are well-intentioned but poorly conceived, and a third group of changes which would reform nothing but could only reduce access to justice for anyone caught by them.

In the first week of December, I found myself talking again to Gabriel, the usher at Gee Street. What mattered to him was the kit: the tape which had to be switched on and left running at the start of the hearing, the forms for the judge to complete if possession was ordered or if an eviction was stayed. It was his job to keep the cupboards stocked.

The most important thing he did was to make sure that each district judge had on their desk a series of cardboard files holding the cases that the judge was due to hear that morning, each of them marked with the parties' names and the case number. In the guts of the building, there was a physical archive of all the court's live cases, and Gabriel was in awe of all that was held within it. 'You can get lost down there', he told me.

The first and most basic idea common to all proposals for online courts was that this paper archive should be replaced with an electronic one. And that the way to do this was to require all parties, in all civil cases, to issue their cases online, in the same way as people carry out their online shopping or replace their passport remotely.

Gabriel would be glad of the change. All the time, vital bits of paper were getting lost. Parties might issue two claims at once, in slightly different ways, and the courts would proceed with one and not the other. A landlord applied for a possession order ('judgment') and then for an eviction ('enforcement'). The two cases became separated, although a challenge to the second was really a challenge to the first. If a fully computerised archive of all online cases would mean that judges stopped shouting at Gabriel, then he would be delighted. As would I. My only request was that the government bought that online database at a reasonable price.

This is the point, however, at which the clear good of an online as opposed to a paper system ends. As we continue to think about online courts, every further step combines modest reforms with other malign consequences. An online court enables cases to be determined with the parties and the judge in a separate location. Hearings might be done by telephone or via an online screen, or some combination of the two – but either way, the defining act is the physical separation of the parties from the decision-maker.

The first serious proposal for an online court was made in reports written in 2015 and 2016 by one of the most senior civil judges in Britain, Lord Justice (now Lord) Briggs.[1] What he proposed was that by 2020 all civil disputes where the dispute had a value below a ceiling of £25,000 would be heard by what he called an 'Online Court'.

For Briggs, this reform could only be a positive; it had the potential of making court proceedings easier and more accessible for all:

[Litigants] will be able to view court files about their cases online, and to be automatically prompted on their smart-phones about hearing

---

1   Briggs LJ, 'Civil courts structure review: Interim report', Judiciary of England and Wales, December 2015; and Briggs LJ, 'Civil courts structure review: Final report', Judiciary of England and Wales, July 2016.

dates and time limits for compliance with directions. There need no longer be a default assumption that every interaction between the litigant and the judge need take place in a physical court room.[2]

Lord Briggs acknowledged that perhaps an online court was not in all respects preferable to a properly resourced justice system. But after a decade of austerity, he wrote, the government was committed to closing as many courts as possible. '36 County Court hearing centres are planned to close', Briggs wrote, and 'this round of closures is unlikely to be the last'.[3] In terms of the middle ranks of the judiciary (deputy circuit judges, those capable of hearings cases lasting longer than a day), there was by 2015 barely any judge in post to hear more complex cases in Devon and Cornwall, or in Hampshire, Dorset or Wiltshire, or in East Anglia, or in Northumbria or North Durham.[4] And these were not small parts of the country: the population of each ranged between a million and a half, to four million people.

Structured into the rationale for an online court, from the outset, was precisely the sort of Faustian pact-making that we saw in the last chapter when discussing the possibility of a 'housing court' without legal aid. In ruling out the possibility of restoring the court system to an adequate amount of funding, it was just inevitable, Briggs insisted, that all of us would have to accept a future in which the link between justice and physical presence was broken.

One advantage of an online court, Lord Briggs maintained, was that it would convert into automatic processes much of the present routine labour on which the courts depend: the thankless, petty tasks of identifying a case and gathering the documents to support it. All of these could be done in future by litigants themselves, equipped only with automated help. As Briggs put it, 'Advances in the sophistication of online services and the large increase in the proportion of court users for whom online communication is both easy and normal make an Online Court designed for litigants in person a practicable proposition for the first time.'[5]

In the first stage of future litigation, 'triage', the person initiating the complaint would complete a form which was intended to be as wide-open as possible, so as to encompass any possible claim. The example Briggs gave was of a householder ('A') who had asked a

2 Briggs LJ, 'Interim report', p69.
3 Briggs LJ, 'Final report', p10.
4 Briggs LJ, 'Final report', p11.
5 Briggs LJ, 'Interim report', p8.

builder to do works for her, and was dissatisfied with the quality of work done:

> [A]fter providing her name and contact details, A would be asked to identify the object of her grievance by reference to a series of tick boxes which might include her bank, her holiday company, her next door neighbour and her builder. Having ticked 'Builder' the software would present new questions designed to elicit the essential nature of the dispute, for example whether it was about the quality of the work, the amount charged or delays in completion.[6]

Having established the nature of the dispute, the computer would then gather short detail of the defendant, and obtain the key documents in the case:

> Ticking (or clicking) the appropriate box would reveal further successive pages, including a page requiring A to identify B and provide his (or if a company, its) contact details, to state whether the building works were covered by an agreement and, if in writing, requiring A to attach any electronic copy, or scan or photograph with her smart phone any paper copy, so that the central document required by the court for determination of the dispute would be lodged electronically from the outset.[7]

The computer system would signal to the litigant the basic legal principles of her dispute. It would research and analyse and instruct. As far as Lord Briggs was concerned, this interactive box was the main feature of his reforms. The parties would then be urged to mediate and if it proved impossible to resolve their dispute; cases would then be allocated to a judge with a presumption that most cases could be determined on the papers, some by remote hearing, and only a vestigial tiny residue left for resolution in a physical court.

Sophisticated software of this sort did not exist already, and the cost of its development would be likely to run into the several hundreds of millions of pounds. But, of course, the government was already generating money on this scale through its programme of court closure. So, to understand the rationale for online courts we need to grasp the unspoken logic on which they are based: because so many courts have closed and people are already distanced from justice, the solution is to distance them further. Beneath the façade of utopian vision was a pragmatic determination to save as much of the present as could be kept.

---

6 Briggs LJ, 'Interim report', p76.
7 Briggs LJ, 'Interim report', pp76–77.

From the outset, the online courts have been intended to centralise the court system in a very small number of the largest cities, with hearings taking place in these cities, and the function of any other legal premises being limited to the provision of basic assistance in how to administer an online form to the very large number of people who do not find it easy to write or count or use online forms. But, historically, law and legal advice have always been concentrated near courts. This is not particularly obvious if you live in a city of half a million people or more, but everywhere else in Britain county courts have operated as hubs around which firms of family and civil solicitors gather. Lord Briggs assumed that in cities the size of Preston, Derby, even Coventry, courts would close. But every time a court was shut, this reduced the local legal infrastructure, until much of Britain became an 'advice desert' with access to neither legal aid nor any legal representation.

The triage process was intended to displace tasks presently done by solicitors or law centre workers. The algorithm would do the equivalent of meeting the client, taking the papers from them, working out the issues in the case and applying to the appropriate court for a hearing. Insofar as Lord Briggs envisioned a role for solicitors in future, this would be polarised. A small number of solicitors would still exist, guiding companies and the rich (ie those whose disputes were worth more than £25,000) through the stages of prestigious litigation. Most work now done by solicitors and advisers could be done in future by volunteers, assisting people not with the law but simply explaining to the 15 million or so people in the UK who do not use the internet how to fill in the boxes on the all-knowing computer screen.

The online court, Lord Briggs wrote, 'would be the first court ever to be designed in this country, from start to finish, for use by litigants without lawyers'.[8]

An online court would achieve cost savings. It could be accessed through a much smaller network of physical courts. It was a vision of the law in which most disputes would be resolved without representation of any sort.

The destruction of courts would mean the loss of jobs. One group of workers who disappeared in the Lord Briggs model were ushers, security guards and court administrators: a document published by the National Audit Office (NAO) estimated that court closures would result in the 'physical reduction' of 5,000 court employees by spring

---

8   Briggs LJ, 'Interim report', p75.

2023.[9] The same report quoted figures from the Court Service to the effect that a shift to online courts was meant to save the public purse some £265 million pounds a year by the same date. What was not set out, however, was how much the scheme would cost. The government is an inept purchaser of large database projects, which come in delayed and massively over-budget (for example, the digitisation of the NHS and GP records, and of universal credit, each cost billions more than originally announced). Like its predecessors, the Lord Briggs triage system was repeatedly delayed: first to 2018, then to 2020.

In the previous chapter, I described how proposals for a hearing would result in the abolition of legal aid, deprive tenants of representation, and make it vastly harder to enforce the many rights which are contained in our housing law. Compared to the modest trench that would be the abolition of legal aid, the online courts would dig a mine of wilful devastation. Such courts are intended to displace not merely barristers and the solicitors – but the entire infrastructure of public legal advice on which the lawyers rest. For this is the way the law works now, with a very large group of paid advisers working in Citizens Advice Bureau and other charities passing on cases to law centres and solicitors firms, inside which they ascend, from paralegals to senior fee earners and then – only in the most complex and unusual cases – barristers. Lord Briggs' vision of the future is one where all these component parts will have given way to the greater knowledge and efficiency of the algorithm.

The idea of a world without lawyers is one with deep roots. In Shakespeare's *Henry VI, Part 2*, the line 'Let's kill all the lawyers' is delivered by Dick the Butcher, a brave fellow and a conspirator in alliance with Jack Cade whose envisaged future is almost comically small ('All shall eat and drink on my score; and I will apparel them all in one livery, that they may . . . worship me their lord'), so that the line is both absolutely serious and bleakly comic. But Dick the Butcher was no lawyer, still less a judge, and he can be excused the pettiness of his and his comrade's visions. When senior judges start promising a legal system without lawyers, you know something has gone badly wrong.

The model of an all-seeing algorithm effortlessly allocating cases to the right jurisdiction is a fantasy because none of the computerised processes which structure our lives are that successful at what they do; and because few litigants know in advance what their best legal case is, or which documents are most likely to prove it. Often

---

9 'Transforming courts and tribunals: A progress update', National Audit Office, 13 September 2019.

lawyers represent a client and develop a 'case theory', only to find mid-way through that the real issue in a case is something quite different from what we thought it would be. What happens to lawyers is still more common among litigants in person.

That Monday in December I had three cases in the County Court at Clerkenwell and Shoreditch in central London, all of them before District Judge Bose.

In my first case, an adjourned possession hearing, I was representing Mr Hernandez, a disabled man in his 50s, who suffered from chronic depression as well as a brain injury, for which he had been repeatedly hospitalised. He had been subsidising his rent from his other benefits, relying on food banks to eat. He had somehow kept his rent arrears below £2,000, despite hospital visits, lack of money, and a friend who promised to pay his rent money to the landlord before disappearing with it.

His solicitor was a trainee, who had been at her firm for more than a year. She was clever and focussed. You could see her efficiency in her grey cardigan, the wire rim of her glasses. She wanted me to run a defence that possession should not be ordered because of the client's vulnerability. I wanted our case to emphasise rather the disrepair in Mr Hernandez's home. Its bathroom and walls had been affected for many years by water leaking in from the outside. In the pictures, the flat was crowded. Board games wrestled with cooking books on the shelves. But it was clean. The cleanliness made the black spots of mould stand out.

I tried to explain to the solicitor why I saw the case differently from her. Part of it was that the landlord was applying for possession on grounds of rent arrears, meaning that possession could only be granted if reasonable. Without needing to structure this as a disability defence, we could say already that Mr Hernandez was vulnerable and that his illness should count against possession. I was also worried that if we hooked everything on disability, the landlord would argue that the arrears were not caused by disability. They were caused by the gap between Mr Hernandez's benefits and his rent. Even the dishonest friend did not sound as strong an argument to me as he did to the trainee. I would understand if the friend had taken many months of rent, but what the client seemed to be telling us was that the friend had taken just a couple of hundred pounds. That might explain a part of his arrears, but only a small part of it.

I stood before District Judge Bose, with Mr Hernandez grey and sweating beside me.

'What's the defence?' asked Bose.

'Disrepair and the Equality Act', I said, while taking much more care in explaining the former than the latter.

District Judge Bose granted Mr Hernandez an adjournment.

Representing Mr Hernandez required a constant exercise of judgment. It involved working out which of his possible defences was the strongest and doing enough to keep different arguments in play in case we had to change our case theory later. There is no algorithm which could explain these choices to him, nor will there be one at any time soon.

In 2020, we saw the costs of the online courts, the closure of county courts, and the loss of solicitors' jobs in town after town. But the benefits of the system, if they ever arrived, belonged to the distant future.

In Lord Briggs' model of the online court system, the purpose of the triage was to act as a sorting device to allocate cases into different levels of complexity. Where a case was simple enough, he proposed, it should be determined without a hearing. So that in place of the present assumption that all cases would go before a judge for a physical hearing, in future, most would be decided by a judge without hearing from the parties; a second group would be decided at a remote hearing (in other words, by telephone or online); and only a third group would be determined as they are presently, by a judge in the same room as the parties.

When Lord Briggs' critics responded to his vision, their arguments were ones of pragmatism and of principle. In terms of making the courts work better: we have held case management hearings by telephone for years and any practitioner could tell you that they are unwieldy and waste judges' and the parties' time. Hearings are blocked in fixed units of 30 minutes, and it is almost impossible to move cases between slots, even if it becomes clear that a case is much more complex or simpler than expected. Opportunities are lost for the parties to speak informally and agree, while judges are rushed to work in a narrow and compressed timetable.

Lord Briggs did not mean that only listings hearings should be done remotely, but so too should final hearings. When you think of a person being asked to prove their innocence on a murder charge, the idea of remote justice appals. Everyone grasps that the significance of asking a jury to decide whether or not to believe an accused, based on their demeanour, their body language, and the tone of their voice, is diminished when the accused appears to them not in the flesh, but as a blurred image over an uneven internet connection.

The same problems apply in a civil case. If your home was at stake, and you were promising a judge that you would pay the rent or be kinder to your neighbours, you would want the judge to see the whites of your eyes.

This expectation is rational. Studies have shown that when a court system moves online, judges make different decisions. For example, one report on bail applications in immigration cases heard by video link in 2011 and 2013, found that a mere 32 per cent of remote applications were granted bail, a significant reduction from the 50 per cent success rate when bail applications were made in person.[10]

An even sharper disparity was noted when 1.7 million social security appeals determined between 2000 and 2015 were studied. Nearly half (48 per cent) succeeded where litigants appeared before the tribunal and were seen in the flesh. This proportion fell to just 15 per cent when appeals were conducted on the paper.[11] It is one thing reading a file and deciding that an applicant's disability has no effect on their life; it is quite another thing to have to explain that decision to a disabled person in court with you.

Bad as the vision is of a future of remote hearings, a world where most cases are determined on the papers would be even worse. 'eBay', Lord Briggs wrote, 'resolves more disputes than do the English civil courts'.[12] That might be true, but it misses the character of these disputes. They arise in a contest where it is already agreed that both parties made a contract, and its terms are not in doubt: 'You promise to pay £10 and I promise to send you the goods.' To think that tenancies and employment contracts can be limited to disputes of equal simplicity is to ignore the reality I have described in this book, that even arguments over relatively small sums of money – the unfair dismissal of a low-paid worker, a request that a landlord do long-delayed repairing works – are complex and high-stakes for those involved. They count for more than whether a cup was broken on arrival. They involve the filtering of objective facts through a subjective filter (a judge's assessment of how high rent arrears need to get

---

10   'Still a travesty: Justice in immigration bail hearings', Bail Observation Project, 2013.

11   M Doyle, 'Oral and paper tribunal appeals, and the online future', UK Administrative Justice Institute, 31 January 2017; https://ukaji.org/2017/01/31/oral-and-paper-tribunal-appeals-and-the-online-future/.

12   Briggs LJ, 'Final report', p44.

before they are 'too much'). In the absence of a chance to persuade a judge face to face, all that remains is people with power finding excuses to ignore the demands of those without.

In my next case, I represented Mrs Dahan, a woman in her late 60s whose children had left the family home long ago. She was £4,000 in rent arrears, which was a significant sum, but half the arrears had arisen in the last three months while (she told her solicitor) she'd been keeping the rent to force her local authority landlord to carry out works. The boiler had been broken for six months. There was a hole in an air conditioning vent in one of the bedrooms, through which water leaked into the bedroom. Mrs Dahan was a fighter. She had kicked her husband out when he drank. She was fighting for herself, for her children.

Before we came in, I asked Mrs Dahan the one question which had been troubling me. 'If you've been withholding rent, and you've got the £2,000 in your bank account, could you pay it to the landlord – today, maybe?'

She squirmed. 'It's all gone.'

The landlord – a housing association – demanded immediate possession. In response to which, District Judge Bose invited me to make an estimate of the value of the various disrepair claims set out in her counterclaim.

'Two thousand for the boiler', I said, 'there or thereabouts'.

'That's all?'

'Add a thousand for the damp', I told him, 'and there's been a rat infestation which the landlord has done nothing about'.

'So, £4,000 altogether?'

'Give or take', I said.

'You've seen the repairs history?'

'I have.'

Judge Bose turned to the landlord's barrister and said he was not going to order possession, not while the disrepair counterclaim remained to be investigated.

'It's up to you', he told them, 'but I reckon if I was to calculate the value of the rent arrears and the value of the disrepair they'd match. Mr Renton is a very experienced tenant representative and when he says a claim is worth £4,000, my experience is that he's not one to exaggerate. We can make directions for trial, if you like, but wouldn't it be the most sensible thing if the two parties "dropped hands" – with the tenant staying in their home, while you do repair works, and the rent account is set to zero. I mean, wouldn't it just save an awful lot of time, when there's public money funding both sides?'

I and the landlord's barrister went outside to talk. We returned to court, half an hour later, with an order in exactly those terms.

I do not want to exaggerate my praise of the judge's handling of Mrs Dahan's case. It was a practical and sensible thing for him to have said. I can think of other judges at Gee Street who might well have expressed themselves in similar terms.

District Judge Bose is not a lazy judge; there are other judges who almost always invite the parties to settle. He is not one of them. He was not dismissive of the landlord's claim; he heard and acknowledged the complaint that it was unfair for them to be expected to put up in silence while a tenant refused to pay her rent. But the effect of his intervention was to help the tenant most of all. He brought the landlord to admit something it perhaps already knew – that the claim was not worth fighting now that we had a counterclaim. With the time the case would take, and the cost of fighting it to a final hearing, it was better to negotiate a settlement.

The idea of online courts ignores any possibility for a case to find an outcome beyond the one that is legally obvious on an initial reading of an electronic file. In the rationale of Lord Briggs, and others who justify these courts, low-value cases are always simple. They are immune to complexity and nuance. The party which wins is the party that was always inevitably going to win. There is no space for good or bad luck, no opportunity for regret. There was no chance for a case to have had an outcome other than the one it did.

But something which any advocate could tell you is that the law is constantly surprising. On a first reading of the case, we have been time and again presented with charges to which no possible answer could be given, except that an answer was found. Disputes which were meant to be locked tight, turned out to open. Behaviour which seemed impossible and inexplicable was a moment later explained. A judge who you were certain would dismiss a case, paused, shrugged uncertainly – and gave you what you asked.

My final case that day took up all of District Judge Bose's afternoon. My client Mr Spark had worked at a private college teaching English as a Foreign Language. But his school closed at the start of the lockdown and had not reopened. Money was short, and after years without being in rent arrears, he was now £2,000 behind. The housing association was determined to evict him, while Mr Spark was fighting to remain.

His was another section 21 (Housing Act 1988) case, and the landlord was entitled to possession so long as the correct process had been followed. As the use of section 21 has grown, parliament has provided an increasing number of defences to this procedure. A landlord cannot rely on a section 21 notice where the tenant paid a deposit and the deposit has not been registered, or where the landlord failed to give the tenant a gas safety certificate before the tenancy began (in a home in multiple occupation (HMO), it can be publicly displayed).

The existence or non-existence of that certificate was the only issue in the case. For Mr Spark to stay in his home, he needed to persuade District Judge Bose that no safety certificate was given or shown to him when the tenancy began. If the landlord was going to evict him, the burden was on them to persuade the judge that a certificate had been shown.

Mr Spark's solicitor had asked me to advise on merits and I told her that our client's prospects were only borderline. Because there was much at stake for him, the loss of his home, the Legal Aid Agency (LAA) permitted me to fight the case even if his prospects were as low as 45 per cent. And, if any case was 45 per cent, it was his.

My reasons for that assessment were as follows. Long after Mr Spark had moved in, the landlord began displaying the safety certificates on a main noticeboard in the kitchen. Mr Spark took photographs of them, which showed that over the last six months before the section 21 notice was served, the landlord had consistently displayed a certificate – but the wrong certificate. When Mr Spark pointed out that the wrong certificate was up, the landlord changed it, but only for another wrong one. So, while the landlord was saying, in effect, 'Trust us, we always get this right', there was a clear pattern of them having made mistakes before.

The case was not really about what had happened in the last year, but what happened five years before, when the tenancy began. Then, a different housing officer had been employed. She had since retired, but the landlord had asked her to come to court anyway and, to my surprise, she had agreed. Ms Hessian had written a statement saying that she remembered putting the certificate up. There was no suggestion that she was biased against my client or indeed that, apart from briefly meeting him at the introduction of the tenancy, she had any contact with him at all. I struggled to think of anything difficult I could ask her.

We went before District Judge Bose. Ms Hessian had a green scarf knotted under her chin. She said, 'Yes, I gave Mr Spark the certificate. I remember it like yesterday.' And she rolled the words in her mouth, slowly and scornfully.

'It wasn't yesterday, though was it? His tenancy began five years ago.'

'I gather so.'

'You were a housing officer in one of London's largest housing association. You must have opened what, half a dozen tenancy files every week.'

'It was more than that', she told me, 'three or four most days'.

'And you worked there more than 20 years.'

'I did.'

'Twenty files opened a week, 50 weeks a year – and you were there 20 years altogether. That's 20,000 files. There's no way you could remember Mr Spark.'

'I remember him', Ms Hessian answered, the slightest tremble in her voice.

'You *think* you handed out the form, but there's a checklist, isn't there. You were meant to tick it when you showed him the certificate – and you didn't.'

'I remember Mr Spark', the witness said. 'He was a very particular gentleman. He was quite put out when I told him that smoking was prohibited in his room.'

'That's as may be', I answered. 'But it was your job to give him a gas safety certificate and if you had, you would have ticked for it, wouldn't you?'

'I gave him the certificate.'

I sat back beside my client. I'd done all I could – and it wasn't much.

Mr Spark rose. He stood at the witness table, he promised to tell the truth, the whole truth and nothing but the truth.

Tuck asked, 'When you moved in, you weren't expecting this would end up in court?'

'I've never been in court before.' There was a look on Mr Spark's face as he addressed Tuck, a look of suffering. I thought of all the students he must have taught. Their missing homework, their implausible excuses.

'I am sure you haven't. I'm sure that when you started your tenancy, you were watching the documents no more closely than anyone else ever does.'

'I can't speak for anyone else. I can only say that what I was given, I kept.'

'Come now, Mr Spark. It's five years ago. You don't know, do you, whether you were given the certificate or not.'

Mr Spark stuck out his chest. 'I kept every piece of paper I was given. The tenancy agreement, the deposit protection certificate. There was even a pamphlet, "How to Rent". I can tell you now that if the landlord had given me a copy of the gas certificate, I'd have kept it – and I haven't. That's how I know they never gave it to me.'

Tuck shrank a little. 'Let's take that in parts', he said.

For half an hour they fought. Tuck challenged my client, he found a dozen different ways of asking the same question.

But Mr Spark's voice was iron-clad in its certainty.

In his judgment, Judge Bose said he did not believe the certificate was ever given. 'Ms Hessian in no way sought to mislead the court. I have every sympathy for her. But I have to go by the documents. She was a very impressive woman, I don't believe that if she had in fact given Mr Spark the certificate, she would have forgotten to complete the form. On the balance of probability, I find there was a breach in the compliance.'

We sat on the chairs outside the court afterwards, shaking our heads in mutual delight. I asked Mr Spark, 'What would you have done if you'd lost?'

He shrugged, 'Then I'd have moved out.'

'How would you have paid the deposit?'

'There's always somewhere else', he insisted. But his blazer was old. There was a tear in his corduroy trousers – ripped, then sewn, then ripped again.

The corridor was empty, the security guard signalling to us to leave.

Mr Spark said, 'Do you think they'll try again for possession?'

I tried to make my voice reassuring. 'Maybe – plenty of landlords do. But they've lost this case, and they won't be able to run section 21 next time. Keep your solicitor's number. If I'm free, it would be a pleasure to represent you again. People think it's about lawyers – but it's not. It's about you. The best you can do is reduce your arrears and keep them low. If you can get them down further, eventually, your landlord will know it's not worth fighting.'

What would have happened if Mr Spark had given his evidence by video link? Maybe if both Mr Spark and the housing officers had been two small boxes of moving images, perhaps the housing officer would have come over worse. Perhaps the claim would have dismissed with fierce words, criticising the landlord and warning them against any bringing any such frivolous claim again. Maybe it would have gone the other way and Mr Spark would have lost his home. I would love to tell you that the more times I replay the hearing in my head, the more certain I am of my client's victory. But it was always too close to call.

The case could so easily have gone a different way – with a different judge, or if my client had not found the strength to stand tall. It is because it was so evenly balanced that I would take the risk of a physical hearing over an online one, every time.

CHAPTER 13

Closing submissions

My father was cremated. When I saw the coffin, I could hardly breathe.

We played the same hymn which had accompanied his own mother's funeral. Afterwards, in the cold of winter, we toasted my father with Barbados rum. We ate squares of dark chocolate in his memory.

At the end of this book, I want to pause, and answer a question on which I have been mulling ever since the first coronavirus lockdown in spring 2020. Is our legal system becoming fairer, with judges more sympathetic to the victims of the pandemic? I have described how our black letter law gives judges and tribunals a very considerable power to intervene on behalf of vulnerable tenants and employees. As the pandemic began, opinion columnists predicted that it would legitimise state intervention, ushering in a new epoch of reforms. Have we seen that shift in opinion that would mean we are better protecting people's jobs and homes?

The first thing to acknowledge is that with or without coronavirus, our political parties had already accepted the case for reform. I have described how the legislation had already been passed, long before the first lockdown began, prohibiting landlords from letting properties which are below a certain minimum threshold of fitness for human habitation: the Homes (Fitness for Human Habitation) Act 2018. There were no prominent press stories welcoming the news. It was the great scandal of the Grenfell Tower fire in June 2017 which forced the government to act, reversing the previous roll-back of tenants' rights which both main political parties had tolerated over many years. New tenancy contracts were covered by the Act on 20 March 2019; one year later, on the day that all existing tenancies became covered by this protection – 20 March 2020 – the worldwide death toll from coronavirus passed 10,000.[1] Not even our usually publicity-hungry government sought any credit for the reform.

Before the pandemic, the Conservatives had also accepted the case for a second significant reform, the abolition of section 21 of the Housing Act 1988 – which is, at present, the main way in which private landlords obtain possession from the courts.

If all political parties in the House of Commons contain an excess of private landlords among their MPs, no party has more landlords than the Conservatives. Among the largest donors to Boris Johnson's party in the 2019 general election were several property businesses, with just one of them – Countrywide Developments – giving half a million pounds. (Several other Conservative donors gave the same, or more.) The only Labour donor to match this sum was the trade union UNITE.[2]

Among the campaigners who have been calling loudest for the abolition of section 21 were groups of renters and young voters – notably Generation Rent, the London Renters Union, Tenant Union UK and ACORN. It is hard to resist the suspicion that the Conservatives wanted to be seen to be offering 'something' to a demographic of younger renters in order to pre-empt criticism that the majority of its policies favoured landowners and the rich.

Assuming that the government does indeed stick to its word, the abolition of section 21 will give tenants much greater security than they have now. Landlords would need a reason for possession. And if the reason was arrears, possession could only be granted if it was reasonable.

For the National Landlords Association (NLA) (now the National Residential Landlords Association (NRLA)), 'Section 21 is not a cause of homelessness, rather a symptom of a much larger problem. Low wages, insecure jobs, the frozen LHA [local housing allowance] rate, and problems with universal credit cause tenants to get into rent arrears, which in turn is the leading reason for landlords to use Section 21 as they are unable to sustain tenancies.'[3]

1   See www.worldometers.info/coronavirus/.
2   M D'Arcy, 'General election 2019: Who is paying for the election?', BBC News, 7 December 2019; P Geoghegan and J Corderoy, 'Exclusive: Property tycoons gave Tories more than £11m in less than a year', *Open Democracy*, 26 June 2020.
3   'Save section 21 postcard campaign', National Landlord Association, 3 May 2019.

What is left unsaid in this account is the presumption that low wages, government reforms to cap housing benefit and the reduction in benefits levels associated with the introduction of universal credit are all the responsibility of the tenant. And that when a tenant falls into rent arrears, the right outcome is a court order requiring them to leave and to pay back their debt to the landlord, with the threat of bailiffs should the tenant fail to leave. To the landlords' representatives, it just seems obvious that if a change to welfare benefits makes life unpleasant for tenants, then tenants only (and not landlords) should be the ones suffering the consequences.

What the landlords could not acknowledge is how well served they had been by the 'much larger problem', whose causes they refuse to analyse. It was not a work of nature, but the inevitable outcome of a series of decisions from the 1980s onwards: of the 'right to buy' scheme, the repeal of the Rent Acts, the decisions taken after the 2008 economic crash to make benefit claimants pay an ever-higher share of their benefits on rent – etc. The solution has to be a different housing law framework, one which limits the power of landlords to increase rent or evict.

In abolishing section 21, the Conservatives would, however partially, share the burden of a decade of austerity between landlords and tenants. That reform would make the situation of tenants vastly more secure. Housing lawyers, tenants and their campaigns face, in other words, a very considerable task in simply making sure that the government acts on its manifesto commitment and changes the law in the way it has promised.

The figures from employment tribunals suggest that there have been times when, without anyone planning it, judges have been more generous. Yet should this happen once more, there are still many subtle ways in which employment law is loaded in favour of employers: in the presumption against re-engagement; in the maintenance of the reasonable responses test; and in rules on compensation whose effect is that where a worker is found to have been unfairly is dismissed, their award is never more than a fraction of their loss.

In previous chapters, I have given instances of both employment and district judges choosing a justice approach over other possible results which the representatives of landlords and employers urged on them. I like to think that perhaps there is more give in the system, more empathy, than there was. But the real challenge will come later this year, when the claims backed up in the system start to be heard in any significant number.

The measures taken by the government, the ban on possession hearings and then the stay on evictions, have done nothing to address the problem caused by COVID-19, that hundreds of thousands of tenants are in arrears and their homes are vulnerable. Staying evictions has meant that moments of personal catastrophe were deferred but not addressed. Our housing law maximises landlords' powers to evict and deprives judges of the opportunity to find a balanced way through – by permitting tenants to remain, for example, where they have credible plans to reduce their debts. As previous chapters have shown, we need more than a temporary ban on evictions, we need mechanisms by which both sides can recoup the debts incurred in conditions of economic turmoil which were beyond either landlords' or tenants' control.

Housing and employment law remain vulnerable to other processes which will squeeze away at these modest gains. Court buildings have been sold off, initially as part of the government's general programme of savings ('austerity') and then later to fund the introduction of online courts. The closures are scheduled to continue. Each one increases the physical distance between a court user and justice. Every time a court is shut, solicitors reconsider whether they can sustain a presence in that town. It is no real loss to the larger firms should they be required to consolidate their operations in the nearest city. The smaller, local firms simply fold.

Previous chapters have described how Britain suffers an increasing number of 'legal aid deserts'. The areas without adequate legal provision are growing larger – and the oases of adequate protection are ever smaller.

It is not enough to say that vulnerable people will find it easier to engage in court proceedings if these can be heard online. Listening to a judge on your screen is not the same as being there in court. The substance of the proceedings will still be that tenants could lose their home. To say, as the advocates of court reform do, that these are low value cases is to actively prioritise the desires of the rich (to maintain a properly funded court system for them as little changed as possible from the one of ten or 20 years ago) and to choose their interest over the many.

But online courts are The Future, in the same way that the demand was being made (with greater urgency as the year continued) for Britain to pay back the debts incurred during the lockdown. The cutters and the privatisers are still waiting for their chance.

We have seen through this book how the government has distinguished between housing law, where it has legislated repeatedly, and employment law which it has left alone. But these were simply two different ways of addressing what is at heart the same problem. People's homes were in danger because their jobs were at risk, because of redundancies and reduced hours, and the universal insistence that there was no money for wages. To save people's homes, we needed more secure jobs and stronger unions as much as we needed better legal protection against eviction.

I know there is something artificial, wrong even, about our present system. If we had a properly resourced social housing system, with rents at genuinely affordable levels, more generous social security levels, and a higher proportion of secure jobs, then fewer tenants would be at risk of eviction. A different kind of social housing would also be a net saving to the taxpayer. It is grotesque that a housing association providing accommodation to low-paid workers should charge – as this association charged Ms Schultz – a rent so high that the average worker would be paying more than half their salary on rent.

A programme of building social housing and reducing the waiting lists would reduce the cost of legal aid and the costs to the housing association, each of which is paid for out of taxation. I am well aware that the decision to establish legal aid was the product of a different time in British history, and a different balance of power between those who owned and those who worked. If our governing party could start over and truly remake the state, there would be no place for people doing the work I do. And that party has not stopped winning elections.

The thought occurs to me that maybe I have been asking the wrong question. I have tried to consider whether a small but definite change in our shared values might have the long-term consequence of making Britain a better place.

I have attempted to consider the question from the perspective of court hearings, yet there are many forms of representation and advocacy, and representation in court is only a small part of this whole. The most important laws were made to appease, sometimes to tame, great social movements. Rent protests in Glasgow in 1915 led to the introduction of the Rent Acts; the drafters of the Industrial

Relations Act 1971, which gave birth to the employment tribunal, had, as their main ambition, the ending of the unofficial strikes in the 1960s. And this process continues: our new laws requiring homes to be fit for human habitation were passed in recognition of the great injustice of the Grenfell Tower fire. The law is merely the echo of these larger processes. Only an active public, distrustful of our leaders and conscious of how much is at stake, can ensure that we maintain even the limited protections that we have now.

During the pandemic, something like a million people made fresh claims for universal credit in the space of two weeks. It came as a great wave of human need rushing towards the beach. But, prior to coronavirus, the employment tribunal was processing just 40,000 cases a year. That small vessel was always going to be overwhelmed by demand on that scale.

When they find themselves in trouble, most workers do not take advice from a barrister, or a solicitor, or even a caseworker at a law centre or Citizens Advice Bureau. They take advice from their union, where there is one. They ask their friends.

Faced with a society where the law threatens to be overwhelmed, the best single step any reader of this book can take is to join a union – either one of the old unions or their newer counterparts who have fought for the rights of precarious workers. In joining a union, you link yourself to networks of specialist advice, participate in them, and you increase the collective potential for unions to campaign in workplaces for a shift away from managerial power in the direction of greater safety, more secure employment contracts and equal pay.

The same is true when you think of housing. A decade ago, almost the only representative groups were tenants' associations where council housing was still pervasive. There was nothing for tenants in the private sector. But in the past decade, we have seen increasing numbers of tenants' unions, sharing knowledge, and defending their members whether through court proceedings or outside.[4]

The virtue of these organisations is that they seek, however incompletely, to make workers and tenants the masters of their own destiny. They take back social grievances from judges and the courts and require managers and landlords to address them.

The law is something that each of us shapes, by demanding changes to Acts of parliament where they get the balance wrong and by enforcing the rules that limit, to however modest an extent, the power of those with the greatest wealth.

4   N Bano, 'Critical support for renters unions', *New Socialist*, 31 August 2020.

The politicians are already planning alternatives which would be much worse than the law we have now – a new round of employment tribunal fees perhaps at a lower level than before; housing courts without legal aid; online courts informed by an all-wise algorithm. Every unfair dismissal which goes unremedied, every unchallenged eviction, makes it easier for cynical voices to say 'This is what we have now. And you'd protect *that*?' It is true that our present employment and housing laws have their faults – but the only system worth fighting for is one that offers *greater* justice, not less of it.

Index